# Having Maddie

## JASON MANDEL

# DEDICATION

To Our Three Angels.

# CONTENTS

# ACKNOWLEDGMENTS

To Carrie, my beautiful wife. Writing this book has in some ways been cathartic and in others a reminder. Reliving the incredible events leading to the birth of our daughter refreshes one particular time in our lives when we tackled challenges together, growing as a couple and ultimately as parents. Thank you for surviving and somehow thriving through countless needle sticks, medical tests, activity restrictions, and surgeries. Thank you for braving difficult decisions and frightening times, all the while relying on me for strength and similarly allowing me to lean on you for the same. I'm proud of us.

To Madelyn, my beautiful daughter. You were a fighter before you even knew it. You've overcome so many obstacles and by your own hard work developed into an incredible dancer, student, and deeply good person. Sometimes you teach us more than we teach you. We love you.

To Carter, my awesome son. You've had to listen to talk of "the book about Madelyn" for years now. Well, here's a little secret: it's a book about Mom and Dad, not Madelyn. Sorry, Madelyn. Carter, you have always been so much fun to watch in your athletics, your adventurousness, your creativity, and more now in your academics. Keep up your natural energy and humor. We love you.

To my family and Carrie's family. Guiding our teenagers toward what we think will be better decisions for them is hard, it turns out. So, when I reflect back on the moral dilemmas we brought to you for advice while having Maddie, I realize the extent of thanks I owe. Thank you for listening, guiding, and backing off. The balance is an enormous feat.

Thank you to the doctors who cared to get it right. We learned through Madelyn's pregnancy that doctors are just humans with medical training. To those who cared enough to put forth their greatest efforts to find the right diagnosis and treatment while remembering that patients are just humans needing help, thank you.

Edited by:  Carrie Mandel, Christine LePorte, Dawn Klemish
Cover by:  Mirjana Krasojevic

# PREFACE

Fortunate. That may be the best word to encapsulate this true story. My wife, Carrie, and I are fortunate for the life we have, for our children, for the support system that is our parents, siblings, and cousins, and for our country. We are fortunate in spite of the obstacles, surprises, and moral challenges we faced along the way. We were forced to make tough decisions with imperfect information, and we live with our choices in our minds and in reality every day.

We are fortunate for the advanced medical care available in this country, but also for the ability to seek qualified second, third, and fourth opinions. We gained a new level of appreciation for the reality that much of medicine is based on opinions. They are extremely well researched and educated opinions, but still they are opinions.

We are fortunate that we live in a free country. Fortunate that we live in a country where we are free to seek professional advice, but then to internalize our learnings, evaluate the risks, prioritize the issues by importance to us, and ultimately make decisions. We are fortunate that we live someplace where we are permitted to make our own decisions.

The two biggest lessons Carrie and I took from our experiences in the early 2000s were the following:

Advocate for yourself. Doctors and other experts may provide their best advice, but we all must live with how we use that information. It is our responsibility to seek other views, do our own research, and use our support systems. It is our responsibility to trust our instincts to chase down alternative possibilities and not let them be quashed without fully vetting them. We each have to live with the decisions we make, while those giving the advice do not.

1

Appreciate and advocate for freedom. Many complicated situations have too many possibilities to capture in a simple rule or law. Even well thought-out and carefully worded rules can fail to capture a new permutation, unintentionally stymieing reasoned decision-making. Overly broad rules risk treating our incredibly brilliant individual human minds as incapable of reasoned decision-making.

Our family thanks you for joining along in the journey we have chosen to share. Looking back at our experiences, Carrie and I often shake our heads over the twists and turns we faced and the incredible regularity with which we had to make major life-altering and morally challenging decisions. Remember when you read this, Carrie and I were just two kids in our twenties trying to figure out life.

We still are.

Figuring out life.

(Not in our twenties.)

*Many of the names and places have been changed for the writing of this book. All of the events are real.*

# 1. SEEING THE FUTURE

On a beautiful late summer afternoon, under the cool dome of overhanging trees, we planned our lives. Carrie held an anxious smile as she stared at me, asking without words if I meant what I said. Her wavy blonde hair sat on her shoulders as she leaned sideways, holding her weight on her left palm. She reached her other hand toward my crossed legs as I sat upright. I smiled back at her without reservation. Fears left me. "We shouldn't wait anymore."

I had always wanted to have a baby, but Carrie's plan was always ahead of mine. I think it's at least partly a cultural difference, but people tend to get married and have children younger in the Midwest—and Carrie is a country girl who had wanted to be a mom for as long as she could remember.

Carrie grew up in Swartz Creek, Michigan, a small town near Flint where it seemed everyone's family had someone working for General Motors. Things move slower, people are nicer, and open fields abound.

I grew up in Syosset, New York, a relatively well-to-do town on Long Island where the schools are good, the homes are nice, and people tend to have a bit less patience. Until I graduated from high school and left for the University of Michigan, I don't believe I quite realized that my hometown was considered wealthy and that New Yorkers had a real reputation for being mean and spoiled.

I thought back to that night we met, back in Ann Arbor, Michigan.

A smattering of pop, rap, alternative, and '70s was blasting out of the three-foot speakers as the DJ bounced along with the beat and colored dance lights jumped around the room. There were a handful of ladies on the dance floor, a room that spent daytimes as the dining room, grooving to the sounds and smiling at each other. The men were more sparse, with most out of sight and packed into a couple of rooms watching the Yankees close out the '96

World Series. The Delta Sigma Phi fraternity at the University of Michigan in Ann Arbor certainly had its share of New Yorkers, who clearly could not be pulled away from the game for the sorority not considered to be the hottest. This was a bit pompous for members of a fraternity far from being considered hunks and dreamboats. Their loss.

One of my fraternity brothers and I were the only ones smart enough to get out on the dance floor, where we enjoyed a generous guy-girl ratio.

The party was just getting underway. Certainly not a formal gathering, the common dress was jeans and a plain white t-shirt. Markers were strewn about tables and countertops to accommodate the "Graffiti Party" theme. The dancers drew pictures and comments on each other's shirts between gulps of Labatt, mystery punch, or Long Island Iced Tea.

One guy had the letter "W" drawn three times, one stacked on top of the other on the belly of his shirt, creating a false six-pack. Another had boobs and yet another listed "penis" in the center, with an arrow pointing down. Again, formal, this was not.

A gorgeous blonde with a trim figure and taller than most in the circle traded glances and smiles with me. I was trim, just under six feet tall. I sported short but coarse brown hair and considered myself reasonably good-looking. As such, I tried to play it cool, returning with crooked smiles that were likely smoother in my mind than on my face.

It was not long until the beauty crossed the circle and continued her effortless dancing at my side.

Another minute or two passed.

"Hi," said the hot blonde, making the first move.

"Hi."

"I wanted to dance next to you."

Smiles.

"What's your name?"

"Carrie. Yours?"

"J."

"J, as in J-A-Y? Jay. Jason?"

"Just J, as in the letter."

Then I turned to the typical fraternity-guy query. "Can I get you something to drink?"

"I'm driving home after this. How about water?"

Water? I thought to myself I can get her a beer, a Jack and Coke, a tequila shot, and probably even a whiskey. But water? I thought further: Can I borrow a cup from someone? Should I run all the way up to my room to get her a cup? Does anyone have a bottle of water?

Eventually, this otherwise intelligent college student was able to figure out how to come up with this seemingly simplest of drinks.

We chatted and danced some more that night, until the time neared for

Carrie to head back home. I asked for her phone number. This time unable to come up with something as simple as a pen and paper, I offered a marker and my shirt. This was all before everyone had cell phones, I remind you. To be certain that I would be the only caller, she asked kindly to write on a piece of my shirt that was tucked in. She wrote her name and number and I retucked. She turned her back and I left a note on her shoulder for later, "U of M kicked MSU's ass," referencing the hockey game earlier that evening. Not smooth.

With absolutely no good reason to wait, I called the very next day.

Our first date was Japanese and a movie on a Tuesday night.

From that night on, we've been together.

In a flash we graduated from college and moved into a small, quirky studio apartment in Manhattan. If I were to write an honest real estate ad for the place, it would read something like this:

"Quaint studio apartment, southern exposure, views of gardens with a sleeping homeless regular. Converts to one-bedroom with built-in homemade sliding Asian-themed pink divider. Wall-to-wall pink bathroom tile. Compact toilet and toilet seat. Grime-covered two-person balcony. Please call eccentric public-access TV star for appointment. $1,650/mo."

I make fun, but we had a ball living in the city. Spanish food late nights. Darting up, down, and across town to meet up with friends at bars with strikingly different vibes, from the cheeky Hawaiian-themed bar to the $15-a-glass Champagne room, to the thumping club packed with dancers grinding and waving light sticks. Pizza to top off the evening at 2 a.m. All the kinds of things a typical responsible working couple would do. We lived in three different apartments in five years. From just above Gramercy Park to Union Square, then Columbus Circle. In the middle of all of this, our love grew further and we celebrated it with a gorgeous wedding at the Bethpage State Golf Course Clubhouse in August of 2000.

By the time we were searching for our third and final apartment, our wants were beginning to shift. We looked all over the city and settled on the Upper West Side, largely because it was a bit quieter, closer to Central Park and more family oriented.

After looking at an apartment out of our price range on the thirtieth floor of a building in Columbus Circle, we sat in Central Park on a beautiful day and plotted.

"It's a two-year lease minimum. So, we wouldn't be moving out until earliest June of '03," Carrie said. We had decided long ago that we would want to raise a child in a house with a lawn and neighbors that don't share our walls. Moving out of the city before having a child was a priority.

"I know. But we weren't thinking of moving out until then at the earliest. So, we could take this apartment, and then add another year when it expires, if we want. Let's get it."

    We signed the two-year agreement in June of '01.

# 2. 9/11

It was a magnificent September day. Blue skies and warmth. I was hard at work in my cube at a major brokerage firm in downtown New York across the street from the World Trade Center, putting the finishing touches on a publication intended to be a primer for investors in the major airlines.

There was a deep and low rumble. John, a senior analyst in an office in view of my cube, calmly peeked his head up at the same time as me. We looked at each other. I squinted my eyes for a moment and then raised my right eyebrow, indicating *oh well.*

He did the same. He likely thought the same as me—the irregular pounding of ongoing construction in the area.

I heard a muffled voice over the "box" in John's office. The box was an internal broadcast speaker system for traders and salespeople to communicate offerings, trades, and often other nonsense.

John called out to me calmly and confused, "Someone just said a plane hit the World Trade Center."

I returned a quizzical look, trying to determine if this was the nonsense that so often spewed from the box, or something real.

We both stood up, not sure what to do. I called Carrie.

"Car," I said. "Do me a favor and turn on the TV. I think something is going on."

"OK. What do you mean?"

"I don't know. Let me call you back in a minute," and I hung up.

John and I considered our directions. "Which way is east?" Our offices were on the west side of the building, looking out at the Hudson River and to New Jersey.

We headed to the east side of the floor, facing the World Trade Center complex. There was not too much action on the floor, though as we got closer to a corner office with a view of the Towers, we noticed a few people gathered, looking out the window.

As we walked into the office, we could clearly see the Twin Towers, which looked as normal and beautiful as they did on the day I brought Carrie to see them for the first time years earlier. I remember how proud I was to show them off on Carrie's first trip to New York, as though I built them or had something to do with their enormity.

I took a few more steps into the office, toward the window, then had to bend down and look nearly straight up.

Thick black smoke poured out of a massive slanted gash in the side of the Tower. I could see flames raging from inside and dancing up along the outside of the building. A ticker-tape parade of documents, files, resumes, and business cards fluttered around the smoke.

It was eerie. I attempted to process the scene. One of my first thoughts was that it would take a very long time to repair the building, and that you can't get scaffolding up that high.

I looked down for a moment to the street. Blue-tinted glass covered the street and entryway. Two fire engines, which I am certain later were crushed, sat at the base of the building.

Looking back up, I watched as a very small, dark piece of the building fell.

As it dropped toward the ground, I recognized the reality. A life had just plunged nearly a hundred stories to the street below. The reality of the grave situation began to set in.

Not entirely certain what to do, and somehow not feeling much danger, I headed back to my desk. I picked up to call Carrie, dialed, and then the line died. I tried again, but the lines were coming and going. I ran into Brian, another colleague of mine.

"A plane just hit one of the Twin Towers," I said.

"Shut the fuck up," he replied, laughing. We joked around quite often, so his response was not surprising nor as inhumane as it may seem in retrospect.

"No. It's true. It's on fire, and there are people jumping out."

"Are you fucking serious?" he asked as his cheeks dropped and expression changed dramatically.

I led him over to the east side of the building and was nearing the office when another deep, muffled thunder rolled with a sudden brightness in the office. The people staring through the window a moment ago were now running toward us in terror. "Run! It's falling!"

I turned, enveloped for the first time that day with fear of death, and ran for the hallway. I had a vision in my head of the Tower tipping over on top of our building and destroying it.

We ran first for the elevators until someone had the sense to yell for the stairs. Like a flock of birds turning with the wind, we shifted toward the fire stairs. The person in front of me tried the door, which was locked. He turned and ran another direction. I tried the door as well, pushing instead of pulling.

It opened and I yelled back for others to follow.

I ran into the stairway, followed by the others, and lunged forward to grab the handrails. I swung my legs underneath me and ahead, bounding from landing to landing and skipping all of the stairs. I even ducked slightly for fear the roof could be coming in at any second. It wasn't until the seventh floor that I saw a single other person in the stairwell. The seventh floor was our trading floor and I saw a couple of our traders calmly opening the door to come into the stairwell. I was perplexed by their calm attitude and quickly felt embarrassed about appearing so frightened. This only lasted a second as I continued down, landing to landing. After twenty-one floors, I reached the ground floor and pushed through the exit onto the street, flooding the bottom of the stairs with sunshine.

I jogged away from the building and around the end, allowing the Towers to present themselves to me, over our office building.

There stood two burning candles, sending a long trail of black smoke into the crisp blue sky.

The second explosion, I would learn later, was the second plane hitting the second tower.

I dropped onto a curb and stared upward.

I have no idea how long I stared. It felt like an hour, but later figuring on the timing, it could only have been a few minutes. I watched body after body drop. I looked away several times, each time turning back to a scene that I already realized would never be properly captured by words, photos, or videos. For those who did not see it in person, there is no way to fully capture the sight, sounds, and confusion.

I gradually caught my breath and my senses began to return. I reached into my pocket to call Carrie on my cell phone. No signal. No signal. No signal.

I wondered for some time if I should be going back to work. The idea must appear crazy to anyone reading this and to me in retrospect, but in the moment it was difficult to understand what had happened, and without knowing what was still to happen. After all, there was nothing wrong with our building. I finally decided to leave.

I headed briskly uptown toward Union Square, where Carrie was working in an apartment as a nanny for a family with a little boy. People stood on the streets staring back in the direction from which I was walking. Radios played on the streets. Queues twenty people long attached themselves to any pay phone. Cell signals were few and very far between.

As I walked, I tried Carrie over and over, getting *beep beep beep* each time. As luck would have it, I finally got through. Our conversation was hurried, as I feared losing the signal.

"J! Where are you? Come to me now!"

"I am walking uptown to you right now. I am okay."

"Another plane just hit the Pentagon, and there are reports of other planes in the area. Please hurry!"

"Fuck. Assholes. I'm coming. I'll be there in fifteen or twenty minutes. Let me go so I can walk faster. I love you."

With that, a woman ran up to me, asking to borrow my cell phone. I explained that it was just lucky that I got through, having dialed about fifty times. I let her try—to no avail. She thanked me anyway and hurried onward.

As I got closer, I heard talking. "The building fell," I heard someone say. *Idiots*, I thought. *It's on fire, but it didn't fall.*

I arrived at Carrie's building and the doorman waved me past and right into the elevator. I pressed for Carrie's floor and the car rose slowly until finally stopping for the door to open. At the same time, the apartment door opened, revealing my bride—with a look of panic. She gasped and we embraced tightly.

"One of the buildings just fell, and I didn't know which way it fell—if it fell on you!" she cried.

# 3. REASSESSING THE FUTURE

The events of the day continued to unfold, as we got in touch with, then lost contact with, family members several times. That was the only time someone ever tried to kill me. Like so many others, that day led us to reassess our lives. We were lucky to have the opportunity—too many did not.

Over the next few days, we talked about what we wanted to do from here. Carrie had lost her interest in the city immediately. I felt the desire to have the great things in life soon—before someone else took it from me. We both agreed it was time to venture out to the suburbs and start a family.

Unfortunately, our landlord didn't see it the same way. They saw a New York City rental market that could crash with people fleeing the newly discovered danger. We tried to cut out of our lease early, but were summarily denied, especially since we were such fresh meat—tenants with nearly all of a two-year lease remaining, which had clearly become well above market.

A year had passed since 9/11 when we sat in the park under that dome of trees and felt a moment of clarity—it was time to go for it—to have a family. With another year left on our lease, we realized the possibility that quick success would leave us with a baby in the city for a couple of months. Not exactly our plan, but nothing was going to stop us at this point. We leaned in and kissed, knowing at that moment that we had embarked on a new journey.

Carrie stopped taking her birth control pills, which had safely guided our way through college without child. We still used physical protection largely for three reasons.

First, we feared that with all the years of birth control pills, hormones would require at the very least a month's cycle to cleanse from the body. We later found this idea to be horribly false.

Second, Carrie was a "Fertile Myrtle." We figured she had to be, given her

11

family's history. Nearly all of the mothers in her family got pregnant on the first shot. So, we thought even using condoms left the door open to pregnancy.

The last issue stemmed from my brother. He and his wife had used IVF (in vitro fertilization) to conceive a child. They ultimately gave birth to their daughter at twenty-five weeks' gestation (that's more than three months early and right on the precipice of viability). She weighed in at just one pound, thirteen ounces. Hanna, their daughter and our niece, struggled through three months in the NICU (neonatal intensive care unit) before emerging as a miracle baby and heading home. Why was this a problem for us?

We felt oddly guilty about our assumed ability to get pregnant so easily, and carry a healthy baby to full term, so soon after my brother and his wife had wiped the sweat off their brows from awful brushes with death and permanent disability for Hanna. We felt that using condoms for a few months would likely leave more time for emotional healing, before announcing our news.

So, we were off to the races, having sex without the pill and only with the protection of a condom. After living in fear for so many years of accidentally getting knocked up, it was a strange feeling to be carefree about such a life-changing event. If it happened—wonderful.

We started looking for houses. Open house to open house and broker to broker, we went every weekend. We saw more than fifty houses over several towns. We grew comfortable with valuations and could immediately spot overpriced and underpriced homes. Our list of needs was long, and probably the most restrictive requirement was a long lead time to closing.

One weekend at the real estate office, after seeing a few duds, the clouds parted. The sun shined. The birds whistled. One of the brokers stormed in with a brand-new exclusive listing and we were off to see it within minutes.

The house was located well inside of a development, away from major traffic, and sat on a corner lot. The brown split-level home was dominated in front by bay windows and a beautiful white flowering tree. To the right of the bay windows, a garage door stood guard at the tip of a circular brickwork pattern blended into clean blacktop. Above the garage peeked two more windows and smack in the center was the front door, topped by a frosted main window and two tall, narrow sidekick windows.

We entered the house with the broker to find a couple in their late fifties seeking to abandon their home of more than thirty years for greener pastures, literally. They told us they were moving to a new condominium complex called "The Greens."

Walking in gave two choices; up the stairs in front of you, or to the den at your right.

We followed the broker up the stairs, revealing a pleasant living room that blended into the dining alcove. The decorations and furniture were classy and top-notch, raising the aura of the home. Farther ahead we entered the kitchen, which presented tastefully, though it hadn't been remodeled in years. The vaulted ceilings and oversized glass door looking out on a large deck expanded the feel of the room. Outside, we found a spacious deck with stairs angling down to the side, presenting a peaceful, park-like mixture of varied shrubs, plants, and some more exquisite brickwork similar to the driveway.

In all, the home had everything on our "must" list, though certainly missing a few items from our "want" list. Most importantly, the feel was there, the price was there, and the owners were also seeking an extended move timetable to allow for their condo to be completed.

The deal was done quickly. We signed the initial papers, went to contract, and planned an extended close date.

One less extremely important item to worry about.

When the two of us cleared the gestational math—fewer than nine months to our move date—we left the condoms in the drawer. For the first time, we were flying an open cockpit plane without our seatbelts and loving the air rushing past our faces. The first few times, we both wondered in amazement if we had just created a life.

Carrie and Jason Mandel were clearly on the way to becoming Mom and Dad.

Little did we know, hidden obstacles sought to lay ruins to our best-laid plans.

# 4. USING THE BOOK

With no worries about protection or missing a pill, we started into "deep practice." We both thought without question, the pregnancy test would shine positive in very short order. However, we also lacked patience. Even from the beginning, it was never a purely simple process with us. Carrie is an incessant planner, and what's not done right is not worth doing at all. Timing, temperatures, the Donna—the process sometimes seemed more of a science experiment than caveman and cavewoman mating.

Carrie had already read a number of books and articles to best equip her to raise our odds of success.

First, we would have sex every other night, especially during the heat of her cycle when chances are best. If we tried every day, that would dilute my sperm count—and we wouldn't want to do that.

Second, temperatures. First thing every morning, Carrie reached into her drawer for her basal body thermometer and dropped it in her mouth, under her tongue. After a couple of soft beeps, she read the digital display and marked a dot on a grid. Every morning, a new dot and a line to connect to yesterday's. Using the example of a normal cycle in the book, a sudden spike in temperature meant she'd ovulated. Unfortunately, that is much like letting a third strike pass just to be sure it was hittable and in the strike zone. Once the temp spikes—you better have already had sex the prior night.

Third, the Donna. Following the recommendation of our OB/GYN, Dr. Nadler, we purchased the Donna. Now, we are talking about some serious science—Bunsen burners and beakers and meniscuses. The Donna is a small device that looks much like a keychain flashlight. It is in fact, a mini microscope. You twist and open the keychain, exposing a small layer of glass. Carrie would spit on the glass and then close the Donna, wait a few moments, and look through the lens of the device into the light. The idea was that when Carrie was most fertile, and ready to ovulate, her saliva would form fern-like or crystallized patterns. Simple, yes? No. Perhaps because Carrie never in fact ovulated, the saliva always looked a little bit different from day to day, but mostly just looked like spit on glass. We would take turns looking up into the lens toward the light.

"I think I see a fern, over on the right side. Here, take it."

"Where? I don't see anything on the right, but I see something near the top."

"Maybe you twisted it a little when you took it from me."

Pathetic losers.

It was absolutely fun to have sex every other day, but after the first few weeks, even that started to wear thin. We wouldn't skip a night for working late, being tired, or anything at all.

"Don't masturbate at all—we need all the swimmers you've got."

"Wasn't even a consideration. We've done it fifteen times this month already."

"Do we have to do it tonight?"

"No, I think we did it last night."

"Nice! Turn on *Law & Order*."

"We have to do it tonight."

"OK."

"We can just do *it*."

The month drew on, and Carrie's body temperature chart was not matching the samples in the book.

"I think I should have ovulated here," she said, pointing at a spot on the graph paper, "but my temperature didn't do anything when it's supposed to be up a half to one degree, I think. I guess I must have ovulated on the twenty-third, which is good, because we had sex that day."

"When do we test?" I asked her.

"Well, the test is supposed to be done about ten days after ovulation with the testers I bought at the store." She showed me a box of pharmacy-style home pregnancy tests. Back in college, this was the kind of thing you would hide, pay for at the register as quickly as possible, get it into the bag, and get out of the store. This time, Carrie was proud to plunk down the box on the counter in front of other patrons.

She continued on, grinning like she had found a ten-dollar bill on the ground, "But I found these other ones online that are better. We can test as little as five days after!"

She showed me a handful of nondescript white plastic packages that each looked as though they contained something about the size of a pen. The ten or so boring packs sat inside of a blank brown box. I was always skeptical that marketing could convince me of quality, but I asked doubtfully, "These are the better ones? They look like the cheap version we'd get at the discount store at five bucks for a hundred."

She assured me that she'd done her research, and that the bland testers could detect way fewer parts per million of HCG hormone than the name-brand versions. As an aside, the female body begins producing HCG after a fertilized egg implants in the uterine lining, so presence of this hormone in elevated concentrations is a clear indicator of pregnancy.

"Does that mean the store-bought versions won't detect pregnancy in some people?"

"No. It will just take another day or two for the hormone to build up enough for those tests to detect it."

Fair enough, I figured. She'd done the work.

We decided that on the fourth day after the date we thought Carrie had ovulated, we would test using the super-secret special spy pregnancy testers. This was a day earlier than even the super-duper decoder tester said it could detect HCG, but we wanted to try.

"Domo arigato—Mister Roboto…" my radio blared at four fifty a.m. *That's going to be in my head all day now*, I thought to myself.

Carrie woke with me and we both walked to the bathroom. Carrie pulled the tester from the cup, where she had laid it out in preparation the night before—she's always prepared. I ripped open the wrapper and passed along the directions, which were fairly simple. Urinate on the stick, or dip the stick in a cup of urine up to the red line for five seconds. Replace cap. Wait two minutes. Check indicator. If there is one line, the test is negative. If there are two lines the test is positive. Check again after another two minutes, but do not recheck after five minutes, as a second line may appear, but the test is no longer accurate. Best if first morning urine used.

Here goes. Carrie peed into the cup and then placed it on the counter. I dipped the stick into the fresh urine, then removed it and replaced the cap.

"You didn't put it in past the line, right?"

I looked at her with my right eyebrow raised and paused before responding, "Right."

"Was it five seconds?"

I tilted my head to the side and crumpled my lips.

"Okay, just checking," she said.

"Let's just leave it," I suggested. So, we walked back into the bedroom and sat quietly, staring back and forth at each other, the floor, and the walls until two minutes had passed.

I walked back in to check and turned the light on to see better. I looked very closely, tilting it up toward my eyes at different angles.

"I don't see anything. I think it's negative."

"Let me see," Carrie immediately responded.

I handed the stick to her and she studied it. She then stepped on the pedal to the garbage can, dropped the stick, and released the pedal.

"I'm sorry, sweetie. We tested early. We'll try again tomorrow."

The next day, we tried again with the same result. Then again the next day. One more day. We hugged after each test. A few days later, Carrie called me at work to share what we now expected. "I got my period."

Each month there would be a weeklong series of tests and each month ended in disappointment.

As the months drew on, our anxiety grew. While we had only been trying actively for a few months, we were quickly growing more pessimistic for several reasons. First, our expectations were too high—Fertile Myrtle. But also, the other aids never seemed to line up properly. We never saw a clear fern-like pattern in the Donna. Carrie never drew a temperature spike when connecting the dots with the basal body thermometer and graph paper. There were no long, stretchy egg whites.

Wondering what that is? This one makes for an interesting visual. One of the many body cycle books that Carrie read indicated that early in the cycle, a woman's vagina would be fairly dry. However, as the body neared ovulation, mirage turns to oasis. An ovulating woman experiences significantly more wetness. In fact, if one were to reach down for a sample, the result should be an egg-white consistency and stretchiness of the fluids between your fingers. Got the picture? Carrie had noticed some, but nothing quite like what the book described, even after following the book's advice to take Robitussin to enhance the egg-white consistency.

All evidence taken together, something did not seem quite right.

# 5. IT'S JUST A CHECKUP

We continued this way for close to a year. Then one night, we met my brother and his wife for dinner at a nice Italian restaurant in downtown Manhattan. Gorgeous little baby Hanna joined us, though she was out cold for the duration of our meal.

Carrie has always been a very open person, and thus the dinner conversation was nearly instantly on the topic of conception.

"We've been trying, but it doesn't seem to be working, and nothing is happening like it says it should in the books."

"You should go see Dr. Matz."

Dr. Matz was the reproductive endocrinologist (we'll call them fertility doctors for ease) who helped Adam and Alyse get pregnant with Hanna.

"But we've only really been trying for a few months," I said.

"And they say you're supposed to try for a year before you go to a doctor," Carrie finished.

"Oh, that's a bunch of crap," Alyse responded, waving her hand sideways and tilting her head back. "You don't have to do anything. They can just check you guys out to see if there is an obvious problem. There's no good reason to wait—it's just a checkup, really."

"I guess so," Carrie replied.

I think this was really what we were hoping to hear. We were both already discussing the idea of seeing a doctor, but this was what we needed to get up the confidence and not feel crazy for going so soon. "Just a checkup" seemed to make a lot of sense.

In hindsight, this is where one would hear the noisy clicks of the roller coaster climbing the hill.

We promptly called for an appointment and landed an exploratory meeting with Dr. Blum. Dr. Matz was going to be out of town for a while, so we booked with his partner.

After work on one cold February evening, Carrie and I met at the corner of 59th and Broadway, which was littered with scaffolding, building materials, and construction workers as the Time Warner Building in Columbus Circle was just beginning to grow. We walked together down the street to a set of open black metal gates. We entered toward the main doors of the building, set back from the others on the block. There, we signed a security logbook, continued to the elevator, and punched three. The doors opened, and straight ahead were the frosted glass doors of "Dr. Michael D. Blum and Dr. David L. Matz, Reproductive Endocrinology."

We opened the double doors, exposing a cozy waiting room with the typical couches lining the walls, small tables with magazines and brochure displays—and carpeting with what appeared to be patterns of little sperm cells. The dark wood reception desk was straight ahead, with a lady hard at work. We approached and introduced ourselves as she hung up the phone.

"Fill out these forms. Do you have your insurance card with you?"

We took the clipboard and pen, handed over our card, and headed for a couch. The list of questions was fairly extensive, from basic personal information and contact details to our reason for visiting the office, to previous experiences with attempting or succeeding at conception and giving birth. I handed back the completed clipboard and sat back down next to Carrie.

Calmer now, we scanned the room. A couple not much older than us sat patiently to our left along the adjacent wall, sharing a brochure taken from the side-table display. They read bits to each other quietly, whispered comments, and pointed to sections. Another couple seemed in their late thirties, the man dressed in an expensive suit with the tie loosened and top button unhooked. The woman was still wearing her coat, though her dark stockings and high heels expressed that she was otherwise dressed formally as well. There was a Hispanic couple hurriedly filling out forms and whispering in Spanish. A woman in her mid-thirties sat alone, off in the corner, reading a novel.

I couldn't help but wonder what stories were held behind each set of eyes in this fertility office waiting room. Some may have wondered the same about us.

I assumed: The older well-dressed couple had been so busy with careers that they only recently married and had encountered difficulties conceiving because of age. They were in the office to talk about moving forward with IVF.

I assumed: The woman in the corner had been here before—many times. She was in the office for yet another checkup, after another month of disappointment. Her husband worked late and could only make it to the appointments for which his presence was required.

I assumed further for the others in the room but was cut off by the receptionist. "Mandel."

She emerged from behind the reception desk and led us into and down a hallway. She stopped, pointed to an office, and smiled. We walked in and sat down.

It was a small but sufficient office. Enough room for the doctor to sit at his desk, and two seats for the happy couples. There was a bookshelf filled with spines showing the words "endocrinology," "anatomy," "reproduction," "non-invasive," "pregnancy," "in vitro," "pharmacology," and "medication," all in random order.

The window was mostly covered by aluminum blinds I would expect to see in a school classroom. Across the way, the windows of another building watched back at us. The desk was mostly covered with papers, files, and a few books that had been removed from the shelf.

A short, balding man with an invitingly pleasant smile entered the office. "Hello. I'm Dr. Blum, it's nice to meet you." His voice was modestly high, but matched his build, and his words blended together into a drawl. It certainly was not a Southern drawl; rather, an open-mouthed hum drew together his words and sentences into a single, unbroken sound.

He began by asking why we came to him and what he could do for us.

"My brother and his wife used Dr. Matz to get pregnant with IVF," I started. "We've only been trying for a few months now, but when we talked to them, they suggested that we at least come to you for a consultation. No harm done." At first, I felt the need to defend our presence since we figured most of the people he helped were forty years old and had been trying unsuccessfully for ten years.

He eliminated our concern right off the bat. "Yes, I remember. Adam and Alyse Mandel, right?" I nodded. "Well, I'm glad you came in to see us. There's every reason in the world to just let us evaluate you both. We may very well never need to move forward with any therapies at all. I think what we should start out by doing is have you explain your situation and your goals, and then I can explain what we will do to evaluate you, and then we can just move forward from there."

We smiled at him in agreement. I nodded at Carrie to let her explain. "Well, as Jason said, we've only been trying for a few months now, but I can tell something does not seem quite right—I don't think I am ovulating. "

"Why do you say that?"

"I've been taking my basal body temperature every day, we've used the Donna, and I also haven't noticed certain other things that I think I am supposed to when I ovulate," Carrie said. She continued onward, "And I had my Synthroid prescription for my hypothyroidism changed because my thyroid results showed a three, which is within the normal range of one to four, but supposed to be lower if I want to get pregnant."

"All right, all right, all right. I can see you've done some research," he said, clearly impressed that she was not a pure novice. Carrie smiled at his acknowledgment.

"The first thing you need to do," Dr. Blum started, "is to stop taking your temperature and worrying about signs and the Donna. By the way—what signs, and what is the Donna?"

"Well, I mean that I read my fluids are supposed to be stretchy and egg-white consistency when I am ovulating. And the Donna is this little thing that you put your saliva on, and look at up close to see if there is a fern-like pattern."

He squinted and tilted his head. There was a silence for a brief moment and then we all chuckled as he began, "I don't know what the Donna is, but I don't think you need to use it anymore."

"Okay," said Carrie, laughing. She continued, "And our goal is to get pregnant. I don't want to say that we are in a huge rush, but we also don't want to wait for no good reason, so we came here just to make sure nothing is wrong."

"Very good." The doc smiled. "Well, I can see that you've certainly done some homework on the subject. Let me tell you a little bit about what we do. I am going to take a quick look at Carrie to see if there is anything at all readily apparent that we need to consider. And I think Jason, we should get your sperm checked.

"But before we get into all that, let me tell you, you both look healthy and you are young, which is a huge mark in your favor. I have to tell you that while nothing ever is for sure, I think you are going to be successful. Whether it is with no therapy at all, some medication to just balance out something, or more involved therapies, I think you are going to have a baby."

We smiled and looked at each other, grabbing each other's hand.

He continued, "I have to knock on wood, but our office has had some really great success lately. We have a woman who was trying for ten years to get pregnant—we put her through an IVF regimen and she just found out yesterday that she's pregnant. We have another couple that had a lot of difficulty on their own, and they both looked fine, so we just tweaked a little bit by putting her on Clomid, and they just found out they are going to have a baby. We have just had a huge success rate. It's really wonderful."

We looked at each other and couldn't calm our smiles.

"I should tell you that I also have personal experience with this. My wife and I used several methods that did not work. We then went to IVF, and we had a great little boy." His story and comforting comments appealed directly to our worries and desires.

For the next fifteen minutes, Dr. Blum described therapies he could offer to help us along, should we need them. They ranged from simply testing for and correcting hormone imbalances that could make Carrie's body inhospitable to a fetus, all the way up to IVF. He explained to us the importance of hormonal balance. "The trick to getting pregnant is creating an environment where the *right* hormones, in the *right* amounts, are present at the *right* times. A successful pregnancy is inextricably tied to a well-balanced endocrine system." We took turns nodding back and forth around the circle.

He broke the silence. "So, let's go take a look. I just want to do a quick exam." He rose from his chair and we copied. He walked out of the office and down the hall with us in tow and then pointed to an exam room. "Go ahead and get undressed from the waist down and cover up with this." He handed Carrie a blue paper sheet.

We walked into the exam room to find an orange examining table with metal stirrups and plastic footholds. As this was my first time seeing an arrangement like this, my eyes bulged and I hesitated for just a moment. Carrie had seen stirrups numerous times before and turned to me, chuckling, saying, "Come on," and waving me on in. Fast forward, and I've seen enough that I would no longer hiccup if I came upon a pair in our living room.

Next to the table sat a monitor with a black background and green lettering. In front of it sat a keyboard with dozens of buttons over and above the alphanumeric keys. The classroom aluminum blinds were drawn, and the room was a little cool. Carrie complied with the instructions and sat on the table.

"Come in," we replied to two knocks at the door.

"Hi there," chimed a pleasant nurse with brown hair resting on the shoulders of her blue scrubs. "I'm just going to get everything set up."

We greeted her as well, as she quickly typed "Mandel," then reached to the shelf below the keyboard and came back up with a condom. She pulled out a white instrument connected to the computer by a long thick cord. The wand looked like Bob Barker's *The Price Is Right* microphone, only thicker. In fact, it looked more like a vibrator. She tore open the condom wrapper, pulled out the condom, placed it at the tip of the vibrator, and rolled it down to the base.

A knock, and then Dr. Blum opened the door. "Okay, let's just take a look."

He grabbed the "vibrator" and tapped the stirrups with his hand, signaling Carrie to put her legs up. He reached under the cloth she used to cover up, peeked in to help his aim, and inserted the device into Carrie.

The dark monitor suddenly jumped to life. Dots and shaded areas on the screen slid from side to side as the doc moved his hand.

"All right, everything looks good here. This is your uterus. Nice and clean."

He switched the angle of his hand and a series of green dots showed up near the center of the screen.

"All right, it looks like you have some cysts here in your left ovary," he said, calmly. Then he moved over to the right ovary and repeated his comment.

"Is that normal?" Carrie asked. To both of us, the comment sounded like a problem, but his demeanor said otherwise.

"No. That is not normal," he said, still in a calm, unalarmed voice.

We looked at each other. I raised my eyebrows and shrugged my shoulders.

He pulled out the device, rolled the condom off with one hand, then used the other to grab the wrist of his rubber glove and pull that off, trapping the condom inside. He removed the other glove and threw them all in the trash.

"OK. You have what is called polycystic ovary syndrome, or PCOS. This is often seen in women with thyroid problems, like you, so I am not very surprised to see it. "

"So, what does that mean?" asked Carrie.

"Each of the cysts that we saw on the screen is really an immature egg. With PCOS, your hormones are not perfectly balanced and what's happening is that your eggs begin to mature, but don't get enough of the right signal to fully mature and then release. So, the eggs become cysts in your ovaries. There's nothing that needs to be done in terms of the cysts, we just need to trick your eggs into fully maturing and ovulating. So, you were right, you probably have not been ovulating. In fact, you may have never ovulated."

I caught an exonerated nod from Carrie. While she was not happy to get news that there was an identifiable problem, she was glad to have her suspicions confirmed.

"My guess is," Dr. Blum continued, "that this is the reason you guys are having trouble conceiving on your own. That's good news, because we can do something about this. Go ahead and get dressed, then you can come back to my office so we can discuss this further."

He turned and walked out. As Carrie got up to get dressed, I noticed her eyes well up. I spoke just over a whisper. "It's OK. He said we can do something about this."

"But there's something wrong with me," she whimpered.

I wrapped my arms around her body and told her not to worry, I knew we would get pregnant. After all, we had found the problem already, in just one visit.

We gathered up and returned down the hall to Dr. Blum's office for the rest of the meeting. Almost as soon as we sat, he began to explain Clomid. "It's a drug, a pill, that you take orally, once a day. It helps to trick your body into ovulating." He continued describing the treatment as a simple form of therapy that for many people is just enough to help them.

"But before we get to that," he continued, "we need to do a few other things."

We nodded.

"Carrie," he turned to her, "I want you to get a test called a hysterosalpingogram, or HSG. It's a test that shows us for sure that your fallopian tubes are intact and unobstructed, so that the egg, when released, can travel down to your uterus. The test involves a small amount of dye being injected into your vagina and then taking an X-ray to make your fallopian tubes stand out."

I jumped in. "This hystero-papagiorgio test, will that hurt Carrie?"

"It's certainly not comfortable, and there may very well be some pain. There is also a very small risk of infection, which is why they'll have you sign papers first. So someone should be there with her, if possible."

"And you," he now turned his attention to me, "need to have your sperm checked." Like a six-year-old, I giggled.

Of course, I knew at some point this was coming, so to speak. I was not excited for the idea of jerking off into a cup while staring at a *Juggs* magazine in the bathroom of a doctor's office. Considering the alternative of having dye injected into your vagina and getting an X-ray, I did not complain!

He finished up with a few other instructions, such as telling Carrie to stop taking her temperature and telling me to get genetic testing for diseases that are common in Eastern European Jews.

We left the office with mixed emotions. We had discovered what the likely problem was and it appeared we could do something about it. However, we had found out there truly was a problem. We also found out that it would be at least another two cycles until we could get rolling with the Clomid since Carrie would have to wait six weeks after the HSG test before starting the drug.

# 6. LET THE TESTING BEGIN

Early March brought Carrie's HSG appointment. I left work midday to meet up for the test and help her home afterward. This would be the first of many hours of missed work in our quest.

I sat on a chair made of a single piece of curved plastic attached to two U-shaped metal bars that formed the four legs. Each chair's plastic was a different color in an apparent effort to add life to this oversized, high-ceilinged waiting room supported by speckled cold dark synthetic tile flooring with some mismatched squares that had been replaced over time. The last time I sat on chairs like these I was back in Berry Hill Elementary School in Syosset. The layout was open, with a dozen chairs dropped near the window and several closed examining rooms visible from our seats.

We were called into a spacious examining room with a large, cushioned medical table abutting a huge X-ray machine. The X-ray's large lens was attached to a massive arm reaching over the table and peering down.

"Hello. Can you tell me why you are here?" a less than inviting voice droned from a white-coated technician.

"Ah, yes," Carrie stumbled, surprised at her coarse demeanor. "I was sent here by Dr. Michael Blum to get an HSG."

"I mean, why did he send you here?" Our opinion of Dr. Curmudgeon did not improve.

"I am having trouble getting pregnant and he wanted me to get my fallopian tubes checked. He diagnosed me with PCOS."

"OK." She cocked her head and furrowed her lips disapprovingly. "What is PCOS?"

We both snapped our heads back, widened our eyes, and glanced at each other. By the second, our already low opinion was dropping. Carrie began slowly, not sure how much knowledge of an apparently common fertility problem to offer up to the fallopian tube technician. "It's polycystic ovarian syndrome."

Doc Lovely dropped a short "Hmm," furrowed her lip again, turned, and walked to the other side of the room. Carrie and I turned to meet eyes and had a brief conversation with only our facial expressions. Not a word was spoken, but our minds chatted:

"What the heck is that?"

"I have no idea. How does she not know what PCOS is?"

"No clue. It sounded like a standard test for a common problem."

"Why is she such a bitch?"

Dr. Happy began typing into a computer and broke the silence in the room by explaining the procedure. She never looked up from the screen as she orated. Following her directions, Carrie removed her pants, wrapped herself in a paper cover-up, and scooted onto the table.

"OK, just wait outside." Dr. Wonderful motioned to me.

"Can't he stay?" Carrie asked.

This was apparently an odd request given Dr. Playful's quick glances back and forth at our waiting faces. "Uh. Sure. Just stand behind there." She pointed to a glass partition.

The doctor covered Carrie's chest with a lead blanket and then bowed down at Carrie's feet. She lifted up a syringe that had a snaking tube in place of a needle and told Carrie to "just relax" as she began inserting the long tube into Carrie.

Carrie cringed.

I cringed.

"You have to relax," commanded Dr. Smiles.

Carrie struggled to lie still on the table.

The doctor squeezed the syringe, releasing the dye inside Carrie, forcing her to cringe again.

I cringed again.

"Be still, please," said the doctor just before finishing. She removed the tube, stood and quickly positioned the arm over Carrie, then walked around the partition next to me. She stood at the controls of the computer and offered the demand again: "Please hold still for this."

"I'm trying, but it's burning," said Carrie.

I cringed.

No reaction from Dr. Sympathy, who clicked the mouse a few times. Finally, she said, "OK, we're done."

Carrie slowly rolled to her side and curled. "It's really kind of burning a lot. Is that normal?"

"Yes, that's fine. You can take some more Advil later in the day if you still feel discomfort." Carrie, under instructions from Dr. Blum, had taken Advil a half hour in advance of the HSG test.

Carrie slowly rotated to a sitting position, and I offered her pants back.

"You may see a small amount of bleeding today. That is totally normal," said the doc.

"Oh great," Carrie said, holding up and emphasizing her white pants. Apparently not the best fashion choice for this day.

The doctor walked out from behind the partition a few moments later. "Everything looks normal to me." She was dropping the X-ray into the oversized envelope as she handed it to us. "You have no blockages."

Our pleasure at hearing the news was at the moment overshadowed by Carrie's pain. With the doctor's discomforting bedside manner and a test result in line with our expectations, we could only each manage a very small smile and a quiet "Thank you."

A few days later, we returned to Dr. Blum's office to discuss the results. He reviewed the film and agreed with the diagnosis that Carrie's tubes were clear. He started Carrie on Metformin to hopefully balance her hormones and allow for ovulation. Metformin should help with Carrie's PCOS, though it would still be another cycle until we could start on Clomid, our first real therapy.

# 7. MY TURN

Just days after Carrie's HSG, it was my turn to be tested. I headed to a clinic to give a sperm sample for a proper count to be performed. Even though we had determined PCOS was to blame as the likely cause of our delay in conceiving, there could always be more than one issue to address.

Carrie was adamant about coming with me to the appointment for support, but I refused. I couldn't get over the feeling of embarrassment about this completely medical and necessary test. She obliged and bowed out, knowing the test required me to be at some ease. At her test, I was there not only for emotional, but also physical support—to let her lean on me as we walked out of the hospital and to get her home and into bed. After performing my duties at the clinic, it was unlikely that I would need physical support. Maybe a nap would be nice, but walking shouldn't be a problem.

I left work around lunchtime and headed uptown to the clinic, which sat just off of Park Avenue in Midtown.

I walked into the office and was immediately taken aback. Opening the door revealed what appeared to be more of an old house than a clinic or medical facility. The floors creaked as I stepped forward, the hallway ahead promised to squeeze me with little clearance, and I could see the stairs ahead were each at least an inch taller than usual. I backed up and leaned my head out the door to check the address once more. It matched and I continued in.

I advanced up each step with a strong raise of my knees, cracking squeaks with each weight adjustment under my feet and a hand grazing the wall to keep clean balance.

At the top of the stairs, I turned to the left to find a middle-aged woman with short blonde hair filling out paperwork on a metal desk. She picked her head up and we greeted each other. "I have an appointment," I said quietly. It took me an extra moment to grasp what was so unusual about the aura of the place—which was the absence of something—noise. There was no ambient background noise. No air conditioner was running, no fan blowing, no hum of computers or resting copy machines. I could hear with great clarity the papers on the receptionist's desk as she moved them to the side, as clearly as I heard each of my footsteps on the way up.

After checking in with the receptionist, I walked slowly to a grouping of leather chairs so as to keep my noise to a minimum. A large tank of fish sat adjacent to the chairs with illuminated purple light and a variety of fish wandering around. As I sat near it, I could hear the motor bubbling air into the water, talking to me like an oblivious train passenger on a cell phone— no regard for the otherwise perfect silence around it.

I was called by name shortly and led through a few doorways toward the back of the office. The nurse handed me a single clear sterile plastic cup with an orange top, along with a pen. "Write your name on it, then you can go in there." She pointed to a door cracked open.

"Don't use any lubricants," she finished, without a trace of a smile, then turned and started walking away.

Through the partly opened doorway, I could only see a compact stained ivory sink. "When you come out," she continued, while walking with her head turned to her profile, "just give it to anyone over here," as she rolled her fingernails on a desk from pinky to index finger.

I took a deep breath and then pulled the cap from the pen. I lifted the cup in front of my face and awkwardly wrote my name on the rounded label, slipping the medium point off around the curve a few times. I put the pen down and walked to the door and pushed it open all the way so I could fit inside. I immediately turned to shut it behind me as quickly as possible.

*Now I'm alone.*

*Maybe not.*

The light was already on, but I searched the wall with my eyes and outstretched hand for a second switch. To my dismay, there were no more switches—there was no fan. My head slumped to the side and shoulders dropped. I could easily hear the nurses shuffling papers and chatting just outside my door. Clearly, they would be able to hear any noises from in this little room and it was not paper I was about to shuffle. I shook my head and investigated further.

Opposite the sink was a TV with a built-in VCR and headphones attached. Stacked atop were several colorfully named videotapes to help set the mood. One was already loaded into the machine and I pressed play. A slightly heavy woman with droopy breasts stared at me, bouncing. The camera zoomed out, exposing an Asian man behind her, lying back on the bed, arms stretched out. *Who was in here before me?* Enough. I shut it off.

To the left was a linen closet filled instead with a large variety of *Playboy*, *Penthouse*, *Juggs*, and other magazines. Most appeared at least two years old— for some reason I chose to look at the publish dates. Fortunately, I missed the April '99 edition of *Hustler* the first time around, so it was new to me.

An unfortunate thought dawned—*How many people have been in this room?* Not a helpful thought to imagine the past in here. I shook it off. Despite the thin door and lack of cover-up noise, the outdated nudie mags, tight quarters, Asian man and droopy-booby lady, and time pressure, all that really mattered was that I was a man. Who was kidding who? The environment was less than ideal, but I came to do a job and I was capable.

Fast forward.

I stood at the sink fully dressed with a plastic cup full of my swimmers. Actually, full is quite an overstatement. The office used urine cups, which were fairly large, making my non-urine fluid appear rather minimal in such a large container. *Will they think that's enough? Will they laugh at me?* I didn't know how much was "normal." *Have I been in the bathroom long enough? Or too long?*

I washed my hands one last time, grabbed the cup, opened the door, and walked slowly down the hall to keep the creaks down. I gradually peeked my head around the cubicle wall and offered the nurse a "hi."

"Oh, hi. You all done? Go ahead and put it in here." She tapped an opened plastic bag on the counter. I complied. "Did you get it all in the cup?"

*Really? Is it that difficult? Do people get so excited that they can't aim well enough?* I guess I could understand that, but I didn't bother to think of what happened if I missed. "Yes, I did."

We exchanged some more information, funds, "take-cares," and I was off.

A few days later, the results showed good count and good motility. My boys were swimmers. One less thing to worry about.

# 8. A PINCH OF HOPE

Early April rolled around and our hopes were rising. Dr. Blum had apparently found the issue that was holding us up. More importantly, Carrie was taking a drug that helps many women overcome PCOS and successfully get pregnant.

"J! Come here!" I heard from upstairs. I jumped. Carrie sounded alarmed.

I ran upstairs to the open bathroom door and looked in to find Carrie on the toilet. Her eyes were wide with excitement and she had an enormous smile on her face. Her right hand was raised out in front of her face, palm up. She saw me look in and reached her arm out toward me to show me the source of her outburst.

She pinched her thumb closed against her index and middle fingers, then reopened them, revealing a stretching, thick, clear goo.

"Egg whites!" she giggled. She pinched and reopened her fingers slowly, showing the mucus. "I have egg-white consistency!"

If accurate, her reading clearly indicated that the egg-white consistency of vaginal fluids was indicative of ovulation.

"Holy shit," I responded. "You've never had anything like that."

"I know." Carrie continued to admire the substance in her hand. "I think I ovulated this month. It's a damn good thing we've been doing it every other night."

"No shit."

We both calmed down but held on to the thought that this might finally be our month. All the stars were aligned. Carrie had ovulated even without the Clomid, we had plenty of sex recently, and nine months gave us the time necessary to move into our new house and furnish it.

What now? We hopped into bed and ensured fresh swimmers abounded.

# 9. WATCHING FOR LINES

A few days later but still several days before the various instruction booklets recommended, Carrie was raring to test.

"It's too early," I said. "We're going to get a negative no matter what."

"Then what does it matter—we get a negative. But if it's a positive," she slowed, "then we know for sure...earlier."

I sighed. Even though we both knew a negative test was almost a certainty, I sensed it would bring a modicum of unnecessary disappointment.

No matter.

Carrie woke early in the morning. "I have to pee."

I rolled out of bed. First morning urine, here we come.

We walked together to the bathroom. I removed the testing stick from the plastic cup I had placed on the vanity the night before and handed the cup to Carrie. She took it and sat. She dropped her head forward, flopping her hair nearly down to the floor. Watching closely between her legs, she positioned the cup underneath her and urine began to spray the bottom of the empty cup. The high pitch of the plastic cup started to drop as the cup filled.

The noise stopped. Carrie's head popped back up and she motioned the cup toward me.

I grabbed it and felt the warmth on my palm, pinky, and ring fingers. Quickly, I placed it back on the vanity, dipped the indicated end of the testing stick into the urine, and counted to five. I pulled it back out, replaced the plastic cap, and set it down.

Carrie and I walked back into the bedroom. "Five minutes," I said.

We waited in silence for three minutes.

"Go check it," Carrie suggested with a smile.

"It hasn't been five minutes," I said as I walked to the bathroom.

"It's negative," I said in a near whisper as I walked back into the bedroom holding the stick. I handed it to Carrie.

She confirmed my read.

We waited another couple of minutes and then reconfirmed the negative. We repeated this process for the next five mornings with no deviation. On the seventh morning, there was something different.

"Carrie?" I called.

"Yeah?"

"Come look at this."

She was in the bathroom with me in an instant. "Is that…?" Carrie squinted at the stick. There was a single solid vertical line which acted as the control. Just to the right of that should have been an identical red line if the test was positive. For the past six days there had been only an empty white space. This morning we could see the faintest hint of a line. Or maybe not. It was so soft that we went back and forth.

"Is it?"

"I can't tell. What do you think?"

"Not sure."

We passed it back and forth. We jumped into the bedroom to hold the stick directly under the brightness of our desk spotlight lamp. We squinted. We twisted it in our hand to change the angle. We held it up close to our eyes, far away. We blurred our eyes.

"Let's do another one," Carrie sparked. We were both getting excited. "The books say if there is any line at all, it must be positive, because the HCG is present in the body."

We grabbed another testing stick from under the sink, tore open the packaging, removed the cap, and dipped it. "One—two—three—four— five." I pulled it out, replaced the cap, and set it down. We then returned our attention to the first test, trying to decide if there was really anything there to see.

"If it is a faint positive, it could be faint because the hormones are just getting started and there are not enough to make it bright yet. If it's positive, it should show up stronger tomorrow," Carrie explained.

A very slow five minutes passed, and we looked at the second test of the morning.

"I can't tell again!" I laughed.

We closely studied the second test for any new information. We found none.

"Let's compare these to a test that hasn't been used yet," I suggested.

We grabbed yet a third tester stick from beneath the sink, tore open the package, laid the three sticks next to each other on the vanity, and stared.

We were quiet for nearly a minute—eyes jutting to and fro, looking for an answer.

Carrie looked up at my face. "J. I think we're pregnant. If there is even the faintest line, I must have the hormone. I think it will be stronger tomorrow."

We giggled at each other.

"I don't know. I hope so. We have to wait another day to be sure—but don't get your hopes up too high. We don't know anything for sure yet."

As she grinned ear to ear, she replied, "OK."

I didn't get the sense she heard a word I said.


Later on, Carrie called Dr. Blum's office to schedule a pregnancy test for the next day. We were both anxious to find out the news for certain.

The next morning, we tested again, ourselves. But there was little change. It was still very difficult to tell if there was actually a line present at all. We grew more skeptical, given that the hormones should only be rising, and the line, while perhaps still faint, should have at least been more pronounced than the previous day.

I readied myself for work, then sat softly on the bed next to Carrie. "If it doesn't happen this month, just remember, we haven't even started on the Clomid yet. We weren't supposed to be able to get pregnant yet."

"I know. But I'll still be disappointed if it doesn't happen."

I leaned in, wrapped my right hand behind her head, and lightly kissed her on the lips, then her head.

"I love you," I said as I looked deep into her eyes.

"I love you, too."

I left for work.


Two o'clock that day my phone rang with Carrie's cell phone showing in the ID window.

"The test was negative."

Dr. Blum had explained to Carrie that a slight line on the home test was probably indicative of a chemical pregnancy. In other words, the sperm and egg joined, but didn't successfully implant in the uterine lining.

That we could create a chemical pregnancy was good news, but it was little consolation at the time.

# 10. TRY, TRY AGAIN

The air was warming as winter drew to a close. The grass began to shout green, leaves started to bud on the trees. Easter and Carrie's birthday approached.

We boarded a plane to Michigan for the dual occasions, with a fresh jar full of Clomid pills in our black carry-on rolling suitcase. We had filled the prescription just before this trip. Carrie's room at her parents' house was not ideal for passionate make-a-baby lovemaking, positioned directly next to and sharing a wall with her parents'. No matter, it was time to start trying, this time with therapy and, for the weekend, quietly.

Carrie began taking the Clomid pills that weekend. Starting then and as we returned home, we were having sex every other day, even though we knew it was still too early in the cycle for ovulation. Neither of us deeply believed it to be true, but Carrie insisted on "using" sperm that was not much more than two days old. On the other hand, we never tried two days straight, opting to give my body a little time to regenerate.

Later in April, Carrie and I arrived at Dr. Blum's office for him to check the progress of her egg development.

Carrie assumed the position—legs up in the stirrups. Dr. Blum knocked and walked into the room. "So, how are we?"

We responded with some sort of positive pleasantry, but we couldn't focus on the small talk.

"All right. Let's see how the Clomid is doing for you."

He lifted the device to perform the intrauterine ultrasound. With one quick peek under the sheet, he inserted the device and shapes and shades of green quickly appeared on the screen.

"OK, here we are. Over here in your left ovary, it seems we have an egg developing quite well. He reached with his left hand over to the trackball on the keyboard, rolled it a few times, and a small crosshair moved across the screen. He slowed and stopped, deliberately positioning the crosshair at the edge of a green circle. He clicked a button, adjusted the ball to the left side of the green circle, and announced, "Eighty microns. That's not a bad egg at all. It appears as though the Clomid is helping your egg to fully develop." He pulled out the instrument and continued, "Now we have to wait and see if your body can release the egg." He estimated just a week or so until the egg would most likely be released and suggested that we have intercourse fairly regularly over the next two weeks or so.

We obliged, adhering to a strict schedule to have sex every other day. We ran into a small scheduling problem as Carrie's planned flight to Tennessee to visit her cousin for the weekend approached. It is not so easy to have sex from opposite sides of the Mason-Dixon Line. To compensate, we engaged the night before her flight and again early in the morning, before heading out for the airport. We now simply had to hope that ovulation had occurred already and that we would not miss it while she was in Tennessee.

Oddly, Carrie had planned a trip down to see her cousin Jamie on account of them having just found out they were going to have a baby. Jamie had started trying to get pregnant after us and they were successful nearly immediately. We were incredibly happy for them, but we also had to hide our jealousy.

Carrie soon came back to New York and we began "trying" again immediately.

As we neared testing time, Carrie noted that she was feeling tired and alternately hungry and nauseous. We looked for signs anywhere and these excited us.

Test number one was taken two days before the package recommended. We waited our five minutes and were greeted by a blank space next to the control line.

Test number two followed the next day, also with an emptiness.

Test number three was taken the morning of Carrie's official doctor's visit. Negative.

And so was the doctor's test.

# 11. THEY CALL IT THE AMERICAN DREAM

Early June and spring was in full bloom. We arrived a half hour early to the law offices for the closing on the purchase of our first house. We had little idea what to expect, but generally speaking, the process was fairly smooth, and we walked out of the office as homeowners, ready to nest.

We hopped into our car with house keys in hand, giggling and excited, and headed to Old Bethpage to wrap ourselves up in our new home.

With the intensity and time consumption of buying a new home, packing, and moving, we chose to pass on any reproductive therapies for the month.

It was a mad rush to unpack, hang shelves, connect the electronics, position and reposition the furniture, receive numerous deliveries, accept the phone guy and the cable guy, and stop only for quick meals. Perhaps it was a bit premature, but we had already invited our families. In all, fifteen people would be joining us in just a week for Father's Day. We were either overachievers or over our skis.

As we filled drawers with clothing and toiletries, clinked silverware pieces into their proper places in the kitchen, lifted books to the bookshelves, and peeled back newspaper from vases, empty brown boxes piled taller and taller in the front entryway. We worked into the night and eventually passed out in bed.

The approaching sounds of a large engine roaring interrupted by a loud brake squeal slowly worked into my dream. Each time it grew louder and louder, until I realized the sound was not part of my dream, and the early sunlight was directing the garbage man to our house.

"Garbage!" I shouted and leapt from the bed.

Carrie snapped up to consciousness. "What? Oh! Go!"

I ran downstairs and battled to open the front door, blocked by dozens of deconstructed cardboard boxes, piled over a foot high. I yanked at the door hard, each time gaining an inch until it was enough for me to squeeze my head and shoulders out into the fresh air. "Hi! Hey! Can I bring out boxes for you?" I said as they were gliding past our driveway offering nothing for their hungry truck.

"Sure," shouted back one of the men hanging off the back with two thick gloves and dangling one leg. The truck slowed as I battled to get the pile of boxes lifted and around the door I was pulling inward. I began swinging piles of boxes four or five at a time to the doorstep outside, until the door could finally move freely and I could escape. The garbage man and I carried piles of boxes to the back of the truck as I thanked him for stopping and for his help. He was nicer than I expected after being unprepared and slowing his journey.

Over the next few days, while we found homes for our belongings and tidied each room, Carrie's parents started their drive from Michigan for the long weekend.

After a twelve-hour drive split by an evening stop in Ohio, Matt and Nancy finally rounded the corner and parked in front, right as Carrie was calling out to me, "Up on the left. Good. That's perfect." I released the painting and we smiled at our favorite piece of art as it presided over the living room—a man at a lake house torn between the city and the country. We were done moving in just as Matt turned the key, silencing the engine.

Matt opened his door and waved while Nancy's door opened from the far side. She paused for a moment then stood and walked toward the front of the car, left hand outstretched. A leash pulled at her, leading down to a light blonde puppy with ears flopped to drag on the ground as her nose searched for information on the blacktop.

"Yay! Socks!" shouted Carrie.

Matt and Nancy had done a tremendous favor for us, stopping in Ohio to pick up a purebred Buff American Cocker Spaniel we had chosen from photos of a litter weeks earlier. Living in the city, we had both longed for a dog, but as renters it was always outside of the rules. At one point I had managed to talk Carrie into getting a parakeet, since that was not considered an animal in the lease rules. The bird chirped when we wanted peace, tore its own feathers out, and pooped on the wall next to the cage. Somehow, months after that decision, I convinced Carrie that a friend was really what Holly needed, so we got a second parakeet. They've since both been gifted to our dog walker.

Socks came rushing over to us to investigate and Nancy could barely keep up. The puppy was adorable, soft, quickly loving, and curious. She was also so much smaller than we expected, as evidenced when Matt and Nancy were laughed at by the breeder when they showed up with the leash we had mailed them that turned out to be several sizes too large for this baby's neck. We all stumbled into the house, full of excitement, with hello hugs and kisses all around and trying not to step on this tiny being.

We crowded into the kitchen and sat on chairs and the floor, letting Socks explore us. She bounded around the room as we all played and prodded. I grabbed for her and slid my hand along her smooth coat, lifted and gently pinched her ears between my fingers, felt her little paws, and brought her in close to rub noses and feel her small tongue explore my face.

The introductions went on for some time while we also caught up with Carrie's parents about the drive and shared all of the progress we had been making around the house. We eventually left the kitchen to give the tour and move on to some projects that Matt could help out with. His handy skills were much needed since I had little idea how to do much beyond changing light bulbs. For the rest of the day as we moved all around the house from one item to the next, Socks was alternately full of energy and exhausted.

Carrie and I had decided that we would crate train Socks. By all accounts from friends and family who had ever had a dog, the first couple of nights are the hardest. We can add to those accounts.

Bedtime rolled around and I coaxed Socks into her new crate with a small treat. The kitchen became her new bedroom for her first night in this strange place. We retired upstairs to our own bedroom for our slumber after a long day.

"Bark bark bark bark bark," Socks called, with the high pitch of a puppy but not as squeaky as one of those very small breeds like a Maltese.

"We just have to leave her alone and ignore her," I said. Carrie agreed, but dropped her lip into a pout. We went about our nightly routine, getting ready for bed as the barks continued steadily. Occasionally we would glance at each other, flashing a frown followed by raised eyebrows and a shrug.

The barks continued as we lay down to go to sleep.

"She'll get tired and stop soon," I professed.

Eleven o'clock. Twelve o'clock. The barks continued with only occasional and brief breaks. The breaks were great. "I think she stopped. She tired herself out."

"Bark. Bark."

"Shit. Jinx!"

Suddenly, Carrie sat up, grabbed the comforter off the floor, and headed out of our room and down the stairs.

I sat up and made no noise, listening closely.

A faint voice comforted, "It's OK, sweetie. I'm here. You're OK, Socksy. Shh. Shh. Shh. Go night-night."

The barking ceased, but Carrie's comforts continued.

After half an hour or so, the house had fallen silent. I slowly sat up and placed my feet gently on the soft carpet. I rose and walked toward the hallway raised onto the balls of my feet. I reached the steps and continued down slowly. As I stepped closer to the bottom, I leaned my head toward the wall on my left to see around the corner to the right and into the kitchen.

The soft moonlight revealed Carrie asleep, still with her fingers in the cage next to Socks. Socks lay on her side with a soft ear hanging over part of her face.

I reached down to Carrie and rubbed her arm. Her eyes opened and I whispered, "Come on back upstairs."

We looked at Socks, who appeared to be sleeping, but we weren't certain. "She's out," I guessed, and helped Carrie up.

The balls of our four feet carefully took us toward our bed. We only made it up three stairs when the barking started again. The calls were followed by our two long, harmonious sighs.

I turned back down toward Socks and grabbed the handle on top of the crate and lifted the whole contraption. I followed Carrie up, carrying Socks to the bedroom.

I set her down on the floor next to our bed and we got back under the covers.

Socks barked a few more times, then Carrie started whispering very softly, "It's OK, Socks. We're right here. Shh. Go to sleep. You're a good girl."

Just five minutes of Carrie's whispers and Socks' whimpering died out.

Day broke and we were weary from the long night. Neither one of us complained about the lack of sleep, knowing that we not only actively chose to bring a dog into our lives, but were spending time, money, and effort to bring a baby under the roof as well.

A couple more nights of whispering her to sleep in the crate in our bedroom and Socks grew comfortable. She won, forcing us to let her sleep in our room. We won, because at least she was willing to sleep in the crate. Life's a compromise.

The Sunday of Father's Day rolled around, and we woke early to attack some last items around the house and to prepare our long list of food and drink options.

There was somewhat of a mad rushing around the house to be sure everything was perfect for the first official showing of our house and to accept company in a good manner. Guest arrival time approached quickly.

"Can you just quickly hang this mirror?" Carrie pointed to a new decorative mirror she had bought on a shopping spree with her mother.

"Now?!" I replied. "People are going to be here any minute."

"Just do it quickly."

I grabbed a drill, tape measure, level, and two screws. Quickly measuring the distance between to the two hanging holes on the mirror, I transferred that information to the wall in the form of two dots, leveled perfectly. My parents' car turned the corner and pulled alongside the curb in front of the house. I rapidly drilled the two screws into the wall, grabbed the mirror, and centered it over the screws. I pushed forward and then slowly let go. I swiped my hands back and forth signaling my success right as my parents walked in the front door.

Father's Day 2003 was a wonderful day. Family was all around, the weather was beautiful, and a dozen hamburgers and a dozen hot dogs filled the grate of my new Weber grill. Conversations were free flowing, laughter abounded, and Hanna, our niece, was adorable as ever, dancing to the music.

For a few hours, we thought little of our attempts over the past few months and little about what we might need to do in the future, to have a family of our own.

# 12.  SPIRITS DRAINING

For the next few months, helped by the Clomid regimen, we tried. The disappointments at the end of each month came, sometimes in different ways. Often the home tests would remain blank, but occasionally the faint hint of a line on the dipstick drove Carrie to Dr. Blum's office for a test and more disappointment.

Neither of us were ever surprised to hear the negative result, but it was disappointing, nonetheless. We both had growing worries about how long it would ultimately take to get pregnant, but at the same time had unspoken monthly optimism. Any comment from Carrie that she was hungry immediately triggered a spark in my head. *Maybe she's hungry because she's pregnant.* Hunger, nausea, back pain, sleepiness, irritability—the slightest hint of anything at all made me think the same thing: *Could it be?*

Carrie went through some of the same thoughts—and in fact we even pointed them out sometimes in the beginning.

"I'm tired, J."

"Maybe it's because you are pregnant."

"You think? Nah. You think?"

But as the months drew on, these conversations retreated to our minds alone. Other new thoughts started to percolate but wouldn't escape our lips for a while. *What if we can't ever get pregnant? Would we adopt? Could I do that? Would I want to do that?*

I hold no negative feelings toward adoption. Rather, the thought of not ever being able to produce a baby is so permanent. I get one life, one body, one story—and it just may not include having my own child. This is true for many people, and many of them are extremely happy. But this is my life, and in my own head, I have no obligation to warmly accept paths that I do not wish for.

The months continued with the disappointments. Often the phone would ring at my desk in my office, and Carrie would only have to say "I got it," and we would sit in silence on the phone together for a few moments.

# 13. TIME TO TRY SOMETHING NEW

July kicked off with an assessment meeting with Dr. Blum.

"So, we've been through a handful of months with Clomid with no success. We can certainly try another few months on just the Clomid and see how it goes, or we can step it up just a bit."

Carrie and I looked at each other, then back at Dr. Blum. Carrie said, "I think we'd like to discuss what the next option would be."

"Sure, no problem. I would keep you on Clomid to help you to ovulate, which we think happened. But we can do something else to raise the chances that the sperm reaches the egg that's released. It's called intra-uterine insemination. It is a bit more intensive of a therapy on your part."

We followed, nodding.

"You would stay on the Clomid regimen and as we get close to the time that you should be ovulating, we'll have you come into the office every other day to check the progress of your egg development. When we are pleased with the egg size, we can force you to ovulate. We trigger ovulation by giving you a shot of HCG. The hormone tricks your body into ovulating. It's actually the hormone that your body starts to produce on its own when you are pregnant—and it is the hormone that pregnancy tests look for."

We continued to listen intently.

"The day after we trigger you, both of you will come into the office for the insemination. What we do is take your sperm," he motioned to me, "and separate out the best stuff in a centrifuge. Then we place that into a syringe that is attached to a long tube." All the while, the doctor was motioning with his hands, showing us the imaginary syringe and long tube.

"We insert the tube up past your cervix and into your uterus to deliver the sperm. We have had some very good success lately with our technique." He tapped his knuckles on the wooden desk. "That's basically how it works. Do you have questions?"

We had our list of questions on a notepad, which had become customary for us. He had already covered just about everything.

"So, if we want to move forward with IUI, when do we have to decide that by?" Carrie asked.

"Well, you don't have to decide right now. You should start back on the Clomid anyway, and if you decide to move ahead with the insemination, you should call the office in the next few days to set up your first ultrasound, so we can start following the development."

We thanked him, gathered up, and headed out.

It was just after 2 o'clock when we reached the lobby and walked outside, all the while chatting about what we had just learned. I needed to head back downtown to work but in our brief trip from the office to the subway, we had already decided to go ahead and give IUI a chance right away. We smiled. I kissed Carrie and descended to the 1 train.

A week later, Carrie came into the city again to see Dr. Blum for her first ultrasound and checkup on the egg development. I did not join her at the office for this meeting and good thing—it was fairly quick. Dr. Blum seemed pleased that the egg appeared to be immature, yet it was developing.

"We'll see you in two days," and he walked out of the room.

The same thing happened two days later and then two more days later and then another two days later. But two days after that, Dr. Blum seemed very pleased with the size and maturity of the egg.

He looked from the screen to Carrie. "I think it's time to trigger you." Carrie's eyes lit up, but nerves joined in.

Dr. Blum left the room and a nurse replaced him. She was holding a fairly sizeable needle and asked Carrie to stand, face the table, and lean forward slightly toward it. Carrie felt a cold cloth, an alcohol swab, then a prick on her right cheek. A deep burning sensation followed. Then the needle was out, and the triggering was complete. The hormone spread into her tissue and would cause Carrie to ovulate her well-matured egg within twenty-four hours.

That night, we lay in bed, staring at each other.

"I didn't envision my baby being conceived this way—with a doctor injecting your sperm into me," Carrie said.

"I know. Me neither. But if it works, then I don't really care. It's still your egg and my sperm. Our genes. Our baby. And it's how much we love him or her that matters."

"I know. It just feels weird." Her eyebrows lifted with a thought. "Oh, and Dr. Blum told me that we have to wait longer than normal to take a pregnancy test, because of the HCG shot. Since it's the same hormone we're testing for, we will definitely get an early positive no matter what."

"Ah. That makes sense." I raised my right eyebrow. "But you're still going to want to test before we're supposed to anyway."

She giggled. "Maybe."

I slipped out of work just after noon, as I had grown somewhat accustomed to overtime with the endless appointments. Not wanting to test the Midtown traffic, I walked over to the subway.

In Midtown, I climbed the stairs out of the subway at the corner of 59th and Columbus, where the traffic and construction were suffocating. An officer directed traffic around two street construction sites and construction barriers around the massive Time Warner Building that was rising a story a day.

I navigated my way across the street and around the barriers to get to the west side of the street, where I saw Carrie ahead of me.

"Sweet!" I called out for her.

She stopped and turned, smiling when she saw me.

I caught up with her and gave her a quick but soft kiss on the lips. "How are you doing? You get in with no problems?"

"Yeah. I was just getting a coffee. I got in early to be safe."

Of course she did.

I put my arm around her and we walked toward the office. "You feeling OK?"

"I'm good. Are you ready to make me some good spermies?"

I laughed. "I'll do my best."

We checked in at the front desk. "Hi, we're here for an IUI with Dr. Blum." The receptionist nodded. "Mandel, right? You can have a seat," she said to Carrie and then held out a urine sample cup to me and continued, "and you can go into the bathroom over there."

We were grownups. We were in a fertility clinic. This happens all the time, but I was still embarrassed, rushing off to the bathroom and quickly shutting the door.

Unlike the arousing palatial bathroom where I gave a sample a few months ago, this was a standard medical bathroom. No combo TV/VCR with headphones attached. No pile of old videotapes. No magazines. Really, there was no ambience at all. It was just that cup, my mind, and my hand—all alone.

Despite the sterile setting, it really was not much more than a few minutes until I emerged from the bathroom. Of course, I once again pondered if I was in there long enough or too long—either of which might draw questioning looks from the staff. I walked back to the receptionist and asked, "What do I do with this?"

She looked up from the paperwork she was completing and began to extend her arm until she saw the cup and quickly pulled back her arm to her body in a reflex. She was obviously distracted for a moment and smiled as she realized how that appeared. She had me place it down on the counter for one of the nurses to retrieve.

I rejoined Carrie out in the waiting room and nodded. *The deed is done.*

We sat in silence, both thinking about the potential gravity of the life-changing event that may take place in the next half hour. I thought about how excited and nervous I was to be a father. I wondered if I would be a good parent, as I had done many times over the past few months and came to the same place—I would be. I then thought about work, wondering by what time I could get back to my desk. It was not the sort of thing I wanted to be thinking about but could not avoid it. I had already been missing a few hours in the middle of the day in increasing frequency. I wondered what client, salesperson, or trader was waiting for my call back from an urgent voicemail they had left for me. At times, I wanted to tell some people at work the reason for my disappearances, but the opportunity never seemed to come up, and further, it wasn't really anyone's business but mine.

"Mandel," called the receptionist.

We popped up and followed her down the hall.

Door closed, Carrie followed the typical instructions. *Get undressed from the waist down, you can leave your socks on.*

After a knock, Dr. Blum opened and entered. "All right," he said as he smiled at us, alongside his nurse. "So, we're going to give IUI a try here. The sample was good, so we have what we need to do this." I smiled, proud of m'boys.

"Just pop your legs into the stirrups," Doc ordered Carrie.

I moved up by Carrie's head to make room for the professionals to work.

"We are going to take this tube and slide it up into you, to get it into perfect position. Then I am going to inject the sperm into you and remove the tube. It's that simple, really. You should stay here, lying down, for at least twenty minutes."

I grabbed hold of Carrie's hand and we squeezed tightly.

"Will this hurt much?" Carrie asked.

He tilted his head to the side. "It depends on how easy it is for me to get the tube in. If you have some pain along the way, at least that should be the only pain that you feel. Hopefully it won't be bad, though."

Carrie nodded in understanding.

He continued, "All right, I'm going to start by inserting the tube now," and ducked his head under the covering.

Carrie grimaced and squeezed my hand. I cried quickly to her in pain, "My thumb, my thumb! You can squeeze as hard as you need, but squeeze my whole hand, don't rip my thumb off." She readjusted her grip to my whole hand. Carrie is having a tube inserted into her and I'm the one whining in pain.

"Sorry it hurts," Doc said. "I'm just having a little trouble getting it up there. Hold on just a little bit longer."

Carrie sucked in a quick and deep breath through her clenched teeth and pulled my thumb back again. She moaned a few times, in more than moderate pain.

"All right, we're in. Sorry about that, but it shouldn't hurt anymore."

Carrie released her breath and my thumb, but her brow was still furrowed.

"Just relax. This will work best if your muscles are as relaxed as possible. I'm squeezing the syringe." He paused. "And now I am going to remove it."

As he pulled the tube back out, Carrie winced slightly again, then calmed.

"You are done," he said as he snapped the gloves off, one inside the other. "Just hang out here for a while, then you are free to get up and go about your business for the rest of the day."

'It still kind of hurts in there," Carrie said.

"I'm sorry. I had a hard time with your cervix. You may just feel a little sensitive for an hour or so."

We both thanked him for the effort and breathed another sigh as we locked eyes, now smiling.

He and the nurse walked out of the room and we felt a sense of anxiousness. That could have been the beginning of our little baby, but we would not be able to know that for another two weeks.

The next two weeks passed very slowly. We wondered each day if Carrie was pregnant. We wondered each time Carrie was tired or hungry or thirsty. We attempted to rejoin our regular routines and I struggled to focus on work while at the office.

Two weeks later, now late July, we began to take pregnancy tests.

We walked through the usual process for three days in a row, each with no sign at all of a line.

We lay in bed one night exploring our thoughts openly in a way we had avoided. We had avoided speaking aloud some of our deeper fears, but with the challenges, it felt like time to lift some weight off of my chest and share the difficult places. Carrie was on the same page. *What if we never get pregnant* was the question we pondered.

"Could you adopt someone else's baby and raise it like your own?" asked Carrie.

"I don't know. I never really thought that was a possibility." I slowed and then continued, "It's not as though I am against adoption. I think it can be a great thing to give a baby a chance and for someone to be able to become a parent if they can't have a baby. But," I paused again, "I just don't know if I could really raise someone else's child."

"I've always wanted to have my own child. Always. But I think I do have so much love in my heart that I would very quickly love an adopted child like my own. I mean, I have a stepdad who raised me most of my life and loved me like his own—one hundred percent. Maybe being a nanny for a while showed me how quickly I can fall in love with a baby and want to care for it. But yes," her voice drained into a sob. "I want my own."

I reached over and hugged her tightly for several minutes. I rubbed her back and whispered somewhat soothing thoughts. "We still don't know that we can't have a baby. There's more we can do. We just have to keep trying."

She pulled away, exposing her reddened eyes and teary face. "I feel defective. It's because of me that we can't have a baby." She sobbed harder and landed her head back into my chest.

"You are *not* defective. You are a wonderful woman. We just need a little help is all. We need to hang in with this and keep hoping that it will happen. You are *not* defective. You're not." I did my best to calm her, but I could understand her sadness and anger.

Through our efforts to have a baby so far, we had remained mostly calm, but for the first time I had stopped to really think about it. Some of the steps we had taken were just simply the "next step" and there was fairly little stumble to move forward. Reflecting on where we started and how far we had already come in the process brought a new perspective. The march forward just sort of happens pretty easily and suddenly you're far down a certain path and noticing that there may be more than just a little help needed.

*Defective.* Hearing Carrie say that word was an awakening for me. She was right. My sperm were in good shape and medicine believed I could have a child. Carrie was found to have PCOS and had been failing to ovulate. It wasn't until Carrie said she was defective that I began to really consider how she felt about the situation. I had never considered any fault in our circumstance, but I could see why Carrie would think she was disappointing me. As though she was the reason we might have to adopt.

I could see for the first time that she might think that and why she might. I never felt that way before and have never felt that since. We are a team through and through.

We held each other that night and talked more about how long it could really take to get pregnant and what we might do if we failed. It was not our first bad night, but it was our worst night so far. Many more tears were to come.

# 14. SECOND TIME'S A CHARM?

Early in August, Carrie started back on Clomid as we prepared for another shot at IUI.

Every other day over a few weeks, Carrie trekked into the city for Dr. Blum to keep tabs on the egg development.

At work, I looked up at the ringing sound and saw Carrie's cell phone number illuminate the gray display on my desk phone. I lifted the handset. "Hey, sweet."

"Hi," in a minor key.

"What's wrong?" She was not very good at hiding her emotions.

"I just left the office and Dr. Blum found a follicle that was nineteen millimeters and he triggered me for an IUI tomorrow."

"Wow, that's great. So what's wrong?"

"He told me that my uterine lining was a bit thinner than he would like."

"What does that mean?"

"He said that it could make it difficult for a fertilized egg to implant. It's a side effect of the Clomid for some patients."

"A side effect? It's a drug that's supposed to help you get pregnant. It helps us one way, but hurts us another?" I asked, almost growing angry.

"Yeah, J. He said it affects a small percentage of people that use the drug, which of course, includes me. Just my luck."

"Did he say what that means? Can we do the IUI?"

"We're still going to do the IUI tomorrow, but he seemed skeptical about whether it could work."

"I love you. Let's hope for the best."

"Love you."

That night we tried to comfort each other and go into the procedure with a hopeful view. We were both pretty quiet, though, having difficulty believing it could work.

I met Carrie at Dr. Blum's office, where I was once again sent into the sterile bathroom to produce a few million swimmers and where I once again did so with relatively little trouble.

Soon, Carrie was on the table with her legs in the stirrups, and I was holding her hand and kissing her head.

"Here we go," said Dr. Blum as he positioned the tube for insertion.

A wince from Carrie and she clenched her hand around my thumb.

"Ouch," Carrie said clearly enough to communicate her pain to Dr. Blum.

"I'm sorry. I'm just having trouble getting it in past your cervix. Just bear with me and try to relax."

*Oh sure, relax. With a tube being jammed up me.* That's what I knew Carrie was thinking as she squeezed her eyes shut and groaned.

"OK, I am in." A pause, then, "Now I am squeezing the syringe." Another pause, then, "All right. That's done. Now I am just going to remove the tube." He slowly pulled the tube out, while Carrie held her breath. "All done. I'm sorry about the pain. It's just that your cervix is tortuous."

We looked at each other and I raised my eyebrows, then bent over and gave her a long soft kiss on her forehead as she worked to regain her composure.

"Just lay there for about twenty minutes, then you're free to go about your day."

"Thank you, Dr. Blum," I said as he walked out the door.

Carrie remained laid out on the table as she explained her pain. "It still hurts. It's like I'm having little spasms in my pelvis now."

"Should I go ask about it?"

"No," she snapped quickly. "I'll be fine. It just hurts."

We eventually left the office, well aware of the long two-week wait ahead of us until we learned if the second IUI was successful or not.

That Saturday morning, we found ourselves philosophically challenged by an appointment we had thought little about in the previous month. It was a fairly routine event and sat innocently written on the calendar: "Spay Socks."

We had been spending the last few months intensely focused on conceiving a child and passing on our genes. Even the brief thoughts of adoption were not comforting. We wanted our very own blood-related child. There I stood, preparing to collar up Socks and deliver her to our veterinarian to ensure no pregnancy would ever occur. She didn't even know that our little trip down the road would mean for her what we feared for ourselves. I took her to the appointment.

During the two weeks between the IUI and the pregnancy test I began to notice with increasing frequency the comments and questions that others would innocently ask.

"So, you've got the wife, the dog, and now the house. When are you going to have a baby?"

All I could think was: *We're trying. Very hard.* Though all I would say aloud was, "We're not sure yet. We'll see."

The questions were asked innocently enough and largely by people who cared for us, so snappy responses would be entirely unfair. However, the annoyance and anger began to build inside. Each additional person who made a comment or asked "when" made us increasingly uncomfortable. There were many times when we wanted to simply blurt out, "We've been trying for a while now and are having trouble. But thanks for asking anyway."

After the long two weeks, a series of home pregnancy tests confirmed the negative.

# 15. BRING OUT THE BIG GUNS

It was early September and nearly a year since we started trying to have a baby. Carrie and I were growing increasingly antsy and at the same time skeptical of our chances. We arranged for a consultation to discuss our therapies and the forward plan.

Once again, I mysteriously disappeared from work to head uptown for the consultation. Carrie and I sat in the waiting room fairly quietly. We exchanged glances and wondered what lay ahead for us.

When we were called into Dr. Blum's office, we sat in silence and marveled at the volumes of medical books on his shelves, all of which were written on some uber-specific sub-topic of human reproduction. It is amazing to think about the innate desire to create and raise offspring. The wonder of life, which implanted each species with a drive to further its own likeness. Somehow, while I felt as though I was working at creating a family and a wonderful life for us, there was a larger force at work to roll this blob of the human race forward and upward.

Dr. Blum entered the office and my wandering mind immediately snapped back to the medical world of reproductive endocrinology.

We greeted him with soft and saddened smiles, which he returned.

"Hi, guys. So, it seems we're still having some trouble. I just want you to be reassured that I am very confident we will be able to get you pregnant. I don't see any good reason that we won't be successful."

We gave him tight smiles and nods.

"That being said, it seems that we're having some trouble with Clomid. Some people have a side effect that causes the uterine lining to thin, which appears is happening in your case. This makes it very hard for an egg, even if fertilized, to implant successfully. So I think we need to think about what comes next.

"There are two therapies that are meaningfully more intensive than anything you've done so far. The first is called injectables and the second is in vitro fertilization, or IVF.

"Going through a round of injectables consists of a routine of shots throughout the month that you will do *yourselves* at home. The purpose is to trick your body into maturing several eggs in a single cycle. We then finish off the cycle, once we see enough mature eggs, with a shot to trigger you to ovulate. Then we'll do another IUI and your chances of getting pregnant are better than they were with Clomid alone for two reasons. First, your uterine lining should be in better shape, because you won't be taking Clomid. And second, there will be multiple eggs released, raising your chances that one of them gets fertilized.

"Does that mean that we have a much greater chance of having twins or triplets?" Carrie asked.

"Yes. No question. The incidence of multiples with injectables is a lot higher. About one in three successful pregnancies through injectables is a multiple fetus pregnancy."

"Is there any way to control that? What if ten eggs come down?" I asked, growing concerned about this process.

"There is not any way to *directly* control the number of eggs that are released, but when we do injectables, we monitor very closely, doing ultrasounds every other day. Before we trigger Carrie, we can see how many eggs have developed. If there are just too many, then we'll have to trigger her and *avoid* fertilizing, because the risk is too great. That means no IUI and no intercourse during that time. Then we would have to try again the next month, tweaking the dosages of the injections to try and reduce the number of eggs that are matured."

Carrie and I traded worried glances.

"Then there is the complication of PCOS," he continued. "Because you have PCOS, there is a likelihood that the injections could cause you to mature and release a large number of eggs, making the process difficult."

We were able to defeat the PCOS through Clomid, but Clomid caused another problem. Now, with injectables, the PCOS returns to cause a new problem.

"Now, with the more intensive therapy of IVF, we still try to have your body mature as many healthy eggs as possible, but we can control the maximum number of fertilized embryos. IVF is just like doing injectables for the first step. But then, when we trigger you to ovulate, we do a procedure to go in and retrieve all of the matured eggs that have been released. We then fertilize those eggs *outside* of you with Jason's sperm, let them grow for a few days, pick the best two, three, or four, and replace them inside of you to implant.

"The reason we replace more than one is that the odds of an embryo implanting after we place it back inside of you is about one in three."

"How many would you recommend putting back in for us?"

"Given how young and healthy you both are and for your first attempt, I would be conservative and just put two back in. Of course, that gives you a chance of them both taking and having fraternal twins. But at least that's far more controlled than doing injectables followed up by IUI."

We pulled out our question notepaper and peppered him with whatever questions we were able to come up with ahead of time. He had already covered the truly hot topics and no major new insights came from our queries. We asked for a few minutes to talk it over, which he granted by leaving the office.

I started. "I'm not sure what you think, but doing the injectables just sounds more dangerous to me. Even if IVF is more intensive, I think it might be worth it to have everything more controlled."

Carrie responded immediately, "I think so, too. With the PCOS, I'm really afraid that we'll either have too many eggs and get pregnant with too many or have to scrap the whole thing and start again. And again. And if I have to go through a month-long round of daily shots, I want to be pretty sure that we are at least going to have a real chance at trying for pregnancy after that."

We chatted back and forth briefly, but were on entirely the same page.

Dr. Blum eventually stuck his head into the office, seeking our approval to reenter. We nodded and he walked in, closing the door behind him and sitting in his chair behind the desk.

Carrie declared, "We want to try IVF. We're worried about some of the issues with only doing injectables and IUI, especially with my PCOS. We just think it will be safer."

"I agree," he responded. "We'll have to set up some appointments. The first step, oddly enough, is to put you back onto birth control pills. We need to get your hormones back on track from having two months of Clomid. During the month, you are both going to have to come to the office one night to take a class in how to give the injections."

He reached toward the bottom of his bookcase, pulled out a videotape, and handed it to us. "Watch this video when you get a chance, before you come to the class. It will give you a primer on how the injections are mixed and administered. In the class, you'll get a chance to practice mixing and injecting into a sponge ball."

He rose to his feet and we followed. He led us out of the office to the front desk, where we signed up for an injection class during the month. He reassured us that everything would eventually work out and saw us off.

# 16. WE HAVE MUCH TO LEARN

A few days later, and before we had a chance to watch the video, Carrie was off to the airport, headed to Tennessee for her cousin Jamie's baby shower. While she was happy and excited for Jamie, it would still prove to be a bit difficult to see the festivities around her for a baby on the way. Life goes on around us.

With Carrie back in town and after catching up on a *Friends* episode, we prepared ourselves to dedicate full attention to the screen. I pushed the black videocassette into the front of the VCR, which sucked it in and rumbled some low mechanical noises until the screen came to life with a doctor seated at his desk. Paraphrasing, he began something like this, "Hi. I'm Dr. So and So. For the next half hour you will learn how to open and use mixing syringes, properly mix medications, draw them with injection syringes, inject them into your body, both subcutaneously and intramuscularly, and how to properly dispose of used needles."

The screen populated with block white text of each phrase below his face as he ambled through them.

The scene changed to a close-up of a vial, a syringe, and what looked like a wet-nap. The bottom of the screen glowed "Lupron."

"As we prepare this first shot, you will learn some safety procedures that you will repeat each time you prepare and give a shot.

"The first step is to prepare the needles you will need. Remove the syringe plunger from the packet, then remove the syringe needle from its packet. Be sure to leave the plastic cap on the needle until you are ready for the injection." The hands on the screen were unwrapping the two parts of the needle and began to line them up and screw them together following the voice-over instructions.

"Place the needle aside, then remove the protective cap from the vial. Open up the alcohol swab packet and wipe down the top of the vial to ensure it is entirely clean." The voice went on to explain how to withdraw the Lupron into the syringe by turning the vial upside down, plunging the needle into the rubber, injecting some air to create pressure, and pull back on the plunger until the fluid reached the prescribed dosage. It instructed us to remove the needle and flick the syringe while holding it upright and squeezing the plunger to evacuate any air.

The camera panned to a woman who lifted her shirt up above her belly button. The pair of hands opened another alcohol packet and reached toward her stomach, choosing a spot a few inches to the right of her belly button, and wiped the area clean several times.

"Be sure to sterilize the entire area and allow the alcohol to dry fully. You can now pick up your syringe and prepare it for the subcutaneous injection. The goal is to inject the medication just under the surface of the skin. To do this, pinch the skin and insert the needle at an angle."

The man in the video picked up the syringe, removed the protective hard plastic covering over the needle, and pinched the skin on the woman's stomach in the spot he had just swabbed clean. He positioned the needle an inch or so away from her skin and paused for a moment.

"Be sure to stick the needle with enough force to break the skin," suggested the voice-over.

With that, the man jutted the needle forward, plunging it into the skin of his wife. She twitched ever so slightly. Then he squeezed the plunger and removed the needle from her.

"If you don't have a partner, you can give these shots to yourself in just the same way," said the voice.

Carrie's head whipped toward me. "I'm not giving these shots to myself. I can't stick that needle into myself."

I half-giggled, "OK, OK. I'll be here to give them to you."

"But what if you are out of town? I am going to have to give them to myself then!" She was clearly worried about the shots and began to chuckle out of fear. "I can't do that!" she repeated.

"Just relax. We'll do what we have to do."

"We? *You* don't have to do anything. It's all *me*," as she slightly chuckled. "Why am *I* always the one that has to do this stuff? It's always *my* body."

"Shh," I offered back, mirroring her nervous chuckles as I attempted to calm her. The chuckles at her mouth were soon joined by tears in her eyes. The unwelcome smile on her lips faded as her bottom lip quivered and her head tipped down into my shoulder. A full sob.

I held her for a few minutes. "I'm here for you now and always. We'll get through this together. I know that it's always your body that gets exposed and probed and tested and injected. You're so brave and amazing for being willing to endure all of this so that we can have a baby. I appreciate that. It's all going to be worth it."

It was a few more minutes until composure was regained.

I reached for the remote and rewound the video that had been playing unwatched all this time.

The video next tackled the subject of intramuscular injections—larger needles, deeper injections.

"Insert the needle into the vial and draw out the required amount of progesterone. Note that this medication is oil-based and as a result, the solution requires greater pressure on the plunger to move through the needle." The gentleman on the video pulled back on the plunger and filled the needle with a golden-colored liquid. The voice instructed the man to find a spot for the shot on the upper, outer quadrant of one of his wife's buttocks, where there is typically sufficient muscle tissue for such a shot. He cleaned the area and pinched the skin, but this time he plunged the needle directly into the skin and slowly forced the medication as the voice-over highlighted, "The oil-based medication will require more force to inject and will likely burn as it is injected."

"Oh, come on!" Carrie belted. "I have to do that every day?" she shouted and began to laugh.

He finished and removed the needle, quickly covering the spot of the injection with the gauze pad in his other hand and rubbing. The voice continued, "Rub the spot of the injection in a circular motion to help disperse the medication. You may notice a bulge in the area for some time until the oil spreads completely."

With a release of emotion, we laughed together at the events that lay ahead of us.

# 17.  IVF SCHOOL

A few days later, oddly on the second anniversary of the tragedy of September 11, we headed back to Dr. Blum's office for a final checkup and the actual injection class.

After work, I rode the subway up to 59th Street and met Carrie outside of the Starbucks on the corner. Our hands clasped into one another and we drifted toward the office.

We opened the frosted glass doors we had passed through so many times already, revealing a greater number of patients in the waiting room than we would expect for an evening appointment. After checking in, it became clear to us that tonight was IVF night. Everyone waiting along with us was waiting for Dr. Blum to give a quick ultrasound and then commence the class.

While we waited, others were called into the examining room one by one. Mishi (pronounced MEE-shee), the head nurse in the office, was pushing around a small plastic filing cabinet on wheels. Mishi was an older, short black woman, with an accent sounding of the Islands. We had come to like and respect Mishi, who seemed to know all the ins and outs of this office.

A few of the drawers of her rolling cabinet were partly opened, with papers and small packages leaning out; generally it appeared well used and fairly unkempt. She began to drag available chairs around the room into a semicircle.

"Mandel," called one of the nurses.

We rose and headed back to the examining room.

"Hello, Carrie. Hello, Jason," greeted Dr. Blum, awaiting us. "You know the drill—get undressed from the waist down and I'll be back in a second."

Carrie hurried to undress and hop on the table as things seemed rushed and a touch chaotic.

A knock and then Dr. Blum was instantly at the ultrasound, grabbing for Bob Barker's microphone.

"OK. We're just going to check to be sure everything is as we expect so we can begin the IVF cycle."

With that, he inserted the device into Carrie and watched the screen. He moved around the uterus and scanned the ovaries with some speed and then pulled out.

"Everything looks fine. Let's get you out to the class and get started."

Just a minute later, we, as the last ones to enter the circle, claimed the two remaining seats. Mishi walked over to us with a blue folder, blank except for the "Mandel" label printed on the front. She quickly took it back, opened it up, read with her index finger for a moment, and handed it back. Without saying anything, she turned and walked back to the rolling file cabinet, opened a few drawers, pulled out a handful of items, and walked them back to us. Again, without saying anything, she moved to the head of the class.

In her lovely accent, she began. "Good evening everyone. All of you are here to learn how to mix and give injections for IVF or injectable cycles, correct?" Everyone nodded. "Good. Then we can get started. I'd like for everyone to get familiar with the objects I have given to you.

"You should all have a blue spongy square, which we will use to practice giving injections. You have two packets with needles and another with the plunger part of the syringe. You also have a vial of saline to practice with. Then you have some alcohol swabs as well.

"Let's begin by opening up the syringe and learning how to assemble it. For practice, I have given you just one syringe, but most of you will be using different sizes depending on the portion of the treatment you are giving yourselves. There are different-sized plungers and different-sized needles. The needles go by gauges for the thickness of the needle. A higher gauge indicates a *smaller* or *thinner* needle. Each needle also has an indicated length—in inches. Again, your papers will tell you what types of syringe to use with which medication. The lowest gauge needles, which are the *thickest*, are typically used for mixing the medications, not for injecting.

"Everyone open up the two needles and the plunger to get started."

The noise level rose around the room as people reached for their packages. One lady to our left opened her package and then removed the hard plastic covering that protects you from inadvertently sticking yourself or someone else with the needle. We saw this happen, looked at each other, and thought simultaneously, *There's always one.*

Mishi, catching the mistake, quickly rushed over to her. "No, no! Don't take that off. You don't want to stick yourself." She carefully took the exposed needle from the somewhat embarrassed lady and replaced the plastic cap for her.

"I'm sorry. I thought we were supposed to take that off, too," she said to Mishi.

The miscreant turned her head to the two women accompanying her—

she was the only one in the room without a man by her side—and said, "I don't know if I can do this." She then spoke for others near her to hear. "I tried this a couple of years ago and just couldn't do it, but I'm back again to try."

I wondered if her guests were her mother and sister. I wondered about how painful it must have been for her to get all the way up to IVF two years ago and then quit. She probably spent the last two years continuing her failed streak of trying to get pregnant and was back again for another shot. Oddly, it also made me question just how much she wanted a child. To avoid IVF, a treatment with quite impressive success rates, simply because you fear needles. On the one side, I thought, *Who am I to judge?* But on the other I thought, *I can judge anyone I want.*

"Everyone pick up the twenty-five-gauge needle," Mishi started again. "This is your mixing needle. Take the plunger part of the syringe and screw the two of them together."

I took the two parts, lined up the plastic threading on the needle with the hole in the end of the plunger, and twisted until tight.

It felt strange to be holding a full-fledged syringe. There are no doctors in my family and I've never used heroin, so this was a new feeling. My head filled with a quick flash of the scene in *Point of No Return* where Bridget Fonda puts together a massive gun in the bathroom of a hotel in New Orleans during Mardi Gras. Back to reality.

"Now place the assembled syringe back down on the table and pick up the two vials. The one with the saline and the one with the medication."

I looked at the vials, confused, seeing one with liquid and an empty vial. Murmurs spread throughout the small class as others struggled with the same issue. We soon realized that we were playing make-believe. There *would* be medication in the real vials when the time came, but for now, we were in Fantasyland.

I followed her instructions and pulled the tops off, revealing another metal top, but this one had a small white circle of a material that allowed the needle to pass through to withdraw the medication.

"Open the alcohol packet and use the swab to clean off the top of the vials. You should do this every time before you insert the needle.

"Now," she looked at the miscreant, "pick up the needle and remove the hard plastic covering, exposing the needle."

As I removed the cover, it exposed a needle that looked to be so thin and sharp that the smallest wrong move or touch and I would have it under my skin. I continued to follow the instructions with very great care, especially now.

"Turn the vial upside down with one hand and with the other, take the needle and pull out on the plunger with your thumb, taking in some air. Then push the needle into the vial and press the plunger, forcing the air into the vial. This creates some pressure that makes it easier to pull the plunger back out, drawing out the medication."

I pushed the needle in, watching closely to keep the needle below the surface of the liquid. I pushed the air into the vial and the pressure quickly forced the plunger back out, pulling liquid in through the needle. I looked closely at the markings on the needle to slow the intake until I had the right amount.

"Now, pull the needle out and pick up the other vial, the empty one with the make-believe medication. "Inject the liquid into that vial slowly. Tilt the vial and lay the needle along the inside of the glass, letting the liquid slide down to the bottom of the vial."

I held the vial and needle up nearly over my head to watch the liquid leak out of the needle inside of the vial.

"Remove the needle, replace the protective cap, and put it down. Now take the vial and roll it back and forth at an angle, between your thumb and index finger, to mix. Don't shake the vial. You want to be sure the medication is fully dissolved and the liquid is clear. If not, throw out everything and start again."

I rolled the liquid in the vial back and forth, pretending to be mixing. I handed it to Carrie so she could pretend too.

The class paused for a few minutes as Mishi walked around to help the slower children in the class. One couple was still trying to figure out the right way to get the liquid drawn from the vial. We took that time to leaf through our folders, which exposed dozens of pages of explicit instructions. There were a few blanks on a series of pages that described how much of which medication to take, and when. We shrugged at each other. "We'll ask her after about how to know what to take," I said.

The class resumed. "Your instructions will tell you how many ampules of medication you need to use. If it calls for two, then you just redraw what's in this ampule and inject it into another with more medication. If it calls for three, you repeat it again."

We were growing confused about how much of what we would be using, but reserved our queries for the moment.

"Now, if we've got what we need in the ampule, it's time to inject it. So, unscrew the mixing needle from the syringe and replace it with the injecting needle."

Everyone complied with little difficulty this time.

"Before you remove the safety covering from the needle to do the injection, you need to prepare everything else. You would clean the area with an alcohol swab and let it dry. You should also have a gauze pad ready to cover the area of injection after you remove the needle.

"Pick up the needle and hold it upwards. You want to flick the side of the syringe several times to get any air bubbles up to the top." I had known this step from watching *ER*.

"Then squeeze the plunger very slightly, pushing out the air, until you get a bead of liquid to come out.

"Here's how to do the injection now. Take the practice cube in one hand. You will be using this hand to pinch some skin, which makes it easier to break the skin with the needle—just like it's easier to pop a full balloon than one that is largely deflated."

That mental picture filled my head and seemed like a surprisingly good analogy. Then I pictured failing to pinch Carrie's belly and the needle bouncing off of her stomach creating nothing but pain and anxiety. I decided pinching was a good thing to remember.

"Hold the needle in your other hand like a pencil—between your thumb, index, and middle fingers. Then you want to jab the needle quickly and with force into the body to be sure you break the skin. Push the plunger and remove the needle. Immediately place the needle down on a table. You do not want to be trying to cover up the injection site or shuffling for the gauze with a needle still in your hand."

Mishi demonstrated the injection into her blue spongy cube.

I looked at Carrie and then down at the cube as she watched closely. With one smooth, quick motion, I plunged the needle into the cube. I placed my thumb on the plunger and pushed, then pulled out the needle. I quickly dropped it on the table and covered the block with my gauze pad. I looked up at Carrie, who nodded approvingly.

Then she took a turn, repeating all of the steps.

Mishi walked around the class, helping people having trouble changing the needle or getting the bubbles out or understanding how to hold the needle for the injection.

When everyone seemed to finally understand, or at least when people just gave up asking questions, Mishi announced, "All right. Now that we all know how to give the injections, I need to meet with each of you to give you the list of medications to order." She handed a red plastic container with a white plastic top and a Biohazard symbol on the side to the first couple to her right. "Please put your used syringes in this container. You will all get one of these with your medication order when it comes."

As she passed the container, she invited the first couple down the hall to the offices.

While we waited for our turn, I asked Carrie, "Do you feel like you know what you are doing?"

"No. I mean, I understand how to give the injection, but each medication is given differently," she replied, concern on her face.

"That's what I mean. I'm not sure when we mix, with which needle, injected into where."

Our concern grew greater as another couple was pulled in and the first couple left. Mishi appeared rushed, trying to get everything finished up to go home for the night.

Another couple in and another couple leaving.

Finally, she came for us.

We walked into the office and she shuffled several folders around the desk. "Mandel, right?"

"That's right."

"Give me your folder." She took it from Carrie and opened to an order form, where she began to fill out numbers in blanks next to various medications, syringe sizes, needle gauges, and boxes of alcohol pads and gauze pads.

"These are all of the supplies that you need to order. You can order them from a place in the city, who will deliver. They are very helpful," Mishi said, looking up at us only intermittently as she hurriedly finalized the form.

Carrie jumped in. "How do we know how much to take of what? And when? And which needle to..." pausing between each question in confusion until Mishi interrupted.

"I am going to fill that out in your folder for you to keep. You should read this entire folder. Dr. Blum wrote it himself and it is very detailed." She turned the pages and began to fill in the blanks on the instructions with numbers and names of medications.

"Just follow these instructions and you should not have a problem. If you are ever unsure of an injection—call the office."

With that, she led us back to the waiting room. Carrie and I looked at each other and mouthed a quick silent conversation, "Do you understand?"

"No," Carrie replied silently, with her eyes widened.

I shrugged, raised my eyebrows, and held the folder up in the air, indicating that we should give the manual a shot before bothering Mishi anymore right now.

We gathered our belongings and disappeared.

We were on our way to beginning our cycle of IVF.

The next day, I faxed in the list of supplies to the pharmacy Mishi recommended and the drugs showed up on our doorstep two days later. Perfect.

Carrie was tested at her OB's office for GC/chlamydia, a requirement before beginning IVF. After so many negative pregnancy tests, it wasn't so bad to be able to be happy about a negative result.

A few days later, Carrie went in to see Dr. Blum for her last ultrasound prior to beginning the IVF therapy. He was happy with her insides and granted a bright shining green light.

"You can start on the Lupron tonight. Take the shot every night until I tell you differently. You will come in for blood and an ultrasound in about two weeks. We'll go from there. Good luck." He smiled and Carrie was on her way.

# 18. LET US BEGIN

After eating dinner and watching some TV to relax, we felt the tension beginning to build.

"Carrie. We have to go upstairs to do the shot soon."

She let out a moan, then, "I knoooow." She paused and looked at me. "I'm scared."

I tilted my head downward and gave a sympathetic smile. "I know, sweetie. We just need to keep thinking about what it's for."

We slowly made our way up the stairs toward the bedroom.

I opened the folder with all of the detailed instructions, which we had already read through several times.

Lupron, our first medication, is given to suppress ovulation. For IVF to work properly, we want to be able to control, with the greatest amount of accuracy, everything in the process of creating eggs and releasing them.

We neatly lined up the ampule of Lupron, the proper needle, a plunger, a gauze pad, and two alcohol swabs. Carrie read aloud the instructions and I followed very slowly, step by step. I tore open the needle and plunger and screwed them together to form the syringe, the smallest of the needles we would need for the process. Following her instructions, I placed the needle down on the countertop and then removed the cap from the Lupron ampule. I cleaned the top with an alcohol swab. Then I reached for the syringe and removed the hard plastic covering on the needle. I lifted up the Lupron and turned it upside down, then inserted the needle. I watched closely, keeping the needle below the surface of the liquid. I plunged air into the bottle and then easily drew back, filling the needle with 1 cc of Lupron. I pulled the needle out of the bottle to a quick, soft sucking sound. I held the needle up to eye level and flicked the side to force the air bubbles to congregate near the top and pressed the plunger until a thin stream of Lupron was visible squirting from the needle. I replaced the cap and put it down.

Carrie and I both exhaled, as it seemed we had completed the first part successfully. Unfortunately, the first part was the easy part.

"Are you ready?" I asked.

"No," she said and started to laugh and cry at the same time.

"We'll just do this and it will be over. Real quick."

"I know, I know. Just give me a minute."

Carrie was never this way with needles at the doctor's office, but the gentleman or woman giving the injection had typically had more experience than watching a home video and taking a couple of practice shots into a blue sponge in the crowded waiting room of a doctor's office. This, however, was my medical resume.

"I'll do it quick and you'll barely feel it."

"OK, let's go," she said tentatively.

I picked up the second alcohol swab and Carrie lifted her shirt, exposing her belly.

"Which side do you want to start on?" I asked her.

"I'm not sure," she said as her hand started to pass across her belly as though she was seeking a divine numb spot. Not finding it, she said, "I guess over here," as she rubbed her hand over a spot to the left of her belly button.

I lifted the alcohol pad up to her belly and rubbed the spot in a circular motion a few times, then blew on it to help it dry.

The time had come. I picked up the syringe with my right hand and removed the plastic cap. I held the syringe like a pencil just a few inches from her belly. With my left thumb and index finger I gently pinched the sterilized area.

"Not yet. Give me a second."

"OK. Just relax. I won't do anything until you tell me to," I replied.

She took several deep breaths.

"Whenever you're ready. Just stay calm. It will be over quickly," I tried to comfort her.

"All right. Go ahead."

I steadied my right hand, angled the syringe, and pulled back ever so slightly for a running start.

"Wait!" Carrie cried out.

I stopped and looked up at her.

She whimpered, "I'm sorry. I'm sorry. OK, I'm ready. Go now."

Before she could get another chance to stop me, I jabbed the needle into her stomach. Carrie flinched slightly, but was able to hold steady for the most part. I moved my thumb to the plunger and forced the Lupron into her body, then pulled the syringe out. I quickly placed the needle down on the countertop and grabbed the gauze pad and covered the spot of the injection.

"Are you OK?" I looked up at her.

"You did that fast. I think it's OK. It didn't really hurt. "

I pulled the gauze pad away to see the spot and found nothing.

"It's not even bleeding," Carrie marveled. She bent over to examine. "I don't even see where it went in."

We breathed a sigh of relief. One down, countless additional shots to go.

We repeated this process for the next several nights and while I slowly got more comfortable with the procedure, Carrie remained understandably uncomfortable.

# 19. A GOOD WORK IVF BALANCE

For several months, I had been skipping out of work in the middle of the day to doctor's appointments. On occasion, such as when we were doing an IUI or some test, I would not return to work. For the most part, I kept the mysterious absences just that, a mystery. However, the intensity of the treatments for IVF would require me to be home every night to administer the shots. Though it was possible for Carrie to give herself some of these shots, the idea did not go over terribly well with her—nor should it.

Travel to see clients typically picked up in the fall and grew heavy into the winter in advance of voting by clients for the best research analyst in a poll conducted by *Institutional Investor*, a financial trade magazine.

Unfortunately, the demands of my job and of our desire to have a baby were on a collision course. I felt forced to share our private struggle with my boss in an attempt to draw some sympathy and gain some leeway.

I knocked on my boss's door and he invited me in. I closed the door behind me and sat in one of two chairs facing him as he drew his eyes from the screens to my presence. Jon was a short, thin man. He was nothing much to speak of from his physical stature and I would bet he was enjoying the laughs now at the bullies who used to knock his books over in school.

"Jon, I wanted to tell you about something that's going on at home with me, and to ask for some leniency in travel."

He looked concerned, and maybe a little frightened that I would share more with him than he cared to hear.

"My wife and I have been trying to have a baby for some time now, unsuccessfully. We've gone through a series of treatments including pills and some other procedures. My point is that we are now going through a cycle of in vitro fertilization, IVF. I don't know if you know much about the process, but it is actually very intensive. It requires daily shots that I have to give to

Carrie and sometimes two or three shots per day. "

He looked uncomfortable, nodding quickly and saying *yeah* and *mm-hm* several times, as if to hurry me to my point and skip details. It reminded me of the discomfort male teachers would exhibit when a thirteen-year-old girl asked to go to the bathroom for a "woman thing," and this reaction was likely helpful to my cause.

"The point of me telling you all of this is that, as I said, we are just starting this cycle, which means that I will need to be around for the next few months. I understand that we are getting into an important time for travel, so I need to ask for your understanding if I am unable to travel much, or if I need to return home from a trip early."

"Yes, sure. That's no problem. Whatever you need." He was nervous and ready for me to thank him and leave his office.

With the upper hand in this discourse, I stood tall and reached out my hand. Jon stumbled to his feet to match and shook my hand. "Thank you for understanding," I said confidently.

"Of course—sure. No problem," he said and caught me as I turned. "And of course, good luck."

With the boss's permission to avoid much travel, I felt better, but still felt the need to attend groupwide regional visits. For these trips, it would seem very strange for someone to miss the trip, barring a solid and known excuse.

One such regional overnight trip was approaching and would force me to miss a night of giving the Lupron shot. So, several nights before I was to leave, Carrie insisted on practicing—making the effort to administer the shot herself.

We assembled all of the necessary supplies on the night table next to the bed, just as we did on the nights preceding. This time, though, Carrie walked through the process of preparing the needle from start to finish. She had never up to this point really handled the needle, even to prepare the shot. She moved slowly, but followed procedure perfectly.

With everything ready, there was only one thing left to do—inject herself.

She wiped a portion of her belly clean and held it pinched with her left hand. She lifted the syringe and pulled off the cap with her mouth, spitting it out on the floor. She lowered the needle, lined it up with the target and took a deep breath.

"I don't know if I can do this," she said.

"I know you can. Just relax as much as you can, count to three, and then jab it in. It'll be over before you know it. The hardest part is waiting and staring at it. Just go."

"All right, all right! Give me just a second." Another deep breath.

"Go ahead. Count to three," I encouraged.

"Stop it!" she shouted. "You don't have to stab *yourself* with a needle. Give me a second."

"I'm sorry. Just trying to help. I know it's not easy."

"OK. Here I go." She successively took three deep breaths, then held the last one, paused, and jabbed quickly toward her stomach.

The needle depressed the skin on her belly, then bounced off.

"Ouch!" she shouted. "It didn't go in!"

Surprised that the needle bounced off, I tried to calm her. "Just relax. Take a minute and we'll try again."

She released all of the muscles in her body that had just been tensed up for the failed shot. She moaned, took another deep breath, and froze her body. A pause. Then her hand jabbed toward her belly again.

Bounce.

Her body released and collapsed back to a slumped sitting position on the bed as she screamed out.

"Are you OK?" I asked quickly.

"That fucking hurt. And why won't it go in?"

"I'm sorry, sweetie. You want me to do it?"

She whimpered, "Yes. Just tonight, though. I want to try again tomorrow night."

I took the needle and gave her the shot.

After we removed the gauze from the successful shot, Carrie examined her stomach to find two marks, each with a spot of blood, where she had partially stabbed herself.

The next night, Carrie tried again. On the first shot, the needle bounced off again.

"I think your natural reaction is to pull back on your hand as you jab. You just have to fight that and push all the way in. Don't worry, it's not possible to go in too far."

She lined up the shot, held her breath, tensed up, and rammed the needle toward her belly.

This time, the needle penetrated and slid into her. She squeezed the plunger and yanked it out. She smacked it down on the counter and exclaimed, "Yes! I did it!"

# 20. THAT COULD'VE BEEN BAD

As the end of September neared, so too did the first of our regular every-other-day appointments to allow the doctor to monitor Carrie's condition very closely.

We drove into the city together on a cool Sunday morning and found a spot on the street. As an aside, a spot on the street is a huge treat since parking in a garage is about twenty dollars a pop for her many appointments to date.

Our understanding was that Sunday mornings were reserved primarily for bloodwork and ultrasounds for people going through injectable or IVF cycles. To beat the rush, we arrived at the building fifteen minutes early for our appointment.

We pushed open the frosted doors to the office to find nary an available seat. Apparently fifteen minutes early was not enough to do the trick.

We checked in at the desk, but quickly got the sense that things were disorganized and that this would be a long wait.

Carrie was quickly called to have her blood drawn, but soon returned to her seat next to me.

We then sat in the crowded waiting room for more than an hour with little action. People drank coffee, read novels, the newspaper, medical pamphlets, anything to keep busy. Husbands would be dispatched to get coffee from downstairs "quickly" so as not to miss being called—only to rush back for another half hour of waiting. Occasionally, the nurse would emerge from the hallway with a file and fumble with it for a moment. Everyone looked up from their distractions and the room fell silent. Finally, she would call out the lucky winner. The others returned to their reading materials.

Eventually, a coated, work-bag-carrying Dr. Blum burst through the frosted doors into the waiting room. His face showed obvious surprise at the number of people waiting and probably at the number of coffee cups and sections of the *New York Times* that had already been read and discarded at the feet of his patients. He quickly disappeared down the hallway.

Carrie and I looked at each other. "Did he just get here?" I asked her.

"I don't know. Have we been waiting for an hour without even a doctor being here?"

After about fifteen minutes of heightened frustration, we were called in. The nurse led us into the examining room, where Carrie was instructed, as usual, to strip from the waist down.

We waited another ten minutes in that room until a knock at the door was followed by the entry of a tall man in a white coat.

Without even pulling his eyes up from the file in his hands he began, "Hello, I am Dr. Jansen." Pronounced *YAN-sen.* "Let's do a quick ultrasound."

Carrie and I looked at each other and shrugged.

Without much finesse, the new doctor inserted the device into Carrie and his eyes moved to the screen. I was not sure if he had seen our faces yet. So much for eye contact and building trust.

"All right. Everything looks in order. You should begin your shot regimen tonight. You've been on Lupron up to now, right?" he said as he replaced the device in the holder and returned his eyes to the chart.

"Yes. Lupron every night," I said.

"Can we just ask you a couple of questions?" Carrie followed.

"Sure, sure," he said, though with pen in hand marking our chart, it wasn't clear if he was listening.

"We're a little unsure about the doses. It says we take five ampules of Repronex and five ampules of Follistim. Does that sound right to you? We aren't sure."

"Whatever Dr. Blum wrote for you to take in your file is what you should follow. OK?" he asked, as if ready to leave the room.

"Wait, I have more questions," Carrie spat out, worried he was about to grab the doorknob.

"I'll see you in the office in a few minutes." With that, he did then grab the doorknob and disappeared.

"J, what are we going to do? We need to get these questions answered." Carrie was moving from frustrated to nervous, and I could see tears well up.

"Hang on. I know we have questions. We are not leaving here until we know what we need to do—until we get them all answered. Just get dressed and let's go wait in the office for him."

Carrie dressed quickly, just in time for the nurse to come into the room to prepare it for the next patient. We asked her which office to wait in and were directed down the hall.

We plopped down. I continually peered down the hall to be sure he was coming. I spotted him in short order, knocking on the exam room door we just left, entering to see the next patient.

We got up and walked down the hall to a nurse standing with a patient. We interrupted and asked her if Dr. Jansen knew that we were waiting in the office for him. She couldn't answer the question, and the scene grew more intense. There was an air of rushing and intensity in the hallways and behind the main desk.

"Can we talk to Dr. Blum? We're supposed to start our shots tonight, and we don't know what we are doing," I said, voice level now rising.

She began to answer us, as the other patient tried to regain the attention of the nurse. Then Dr. Jansen emerged and I aimed at him with strength. "We need to ask some questions. We do not know what we are doing."

Carrie's welled up tears began to drop from her eyes and she added, "We don't know what the right dosages are—we are afraid I'm going to be taking too much."

With the scene escalating, Dr. Blum emerged from an adjacent office and quickly looked toward Carrie's scared face. "What's wrong. What's the matter?" he asked as he pulled her into his office—I followed.

He pointed to the two empty seats, shut the door behind us, and sat at the desk.

In a shaky voice, with tears rolling, Carrie started, "We don't know what we are doing. And then we come in this morning and waited forever and Dr. Jansen is here and he didn't even seem to want to answer our questions and—"

"All right. Calm down. We can talk about whatever you guys need to. Don't worry about anything. *Dr. Jansen,*" he pronounced his name with emphasis, "is new to our practice. We've been growing so fast that we need to bring on someone else. I wasn't even supposed to come in today, but I just thought I should come to check everything out."

"Good thing," I said.

"I know." He paused and handed a box of tissues to Carrie. "Now, why don't you tell me what is going on."

I put my hand on Carrie's leg to allow her a break. I took over. "We are unsure of the correct dosages to take when we begin the real shots tonight. Our file says we take five amps of Repronex at night and five amps of Follistim in the morning, but that sounded high to us and when we told Alyse, she said it sounded really high."

He jumped in. "No, no. You are not going to take five of each." Shaking his head softly, "That is just what Mishi ordered for you in total."

"*No,*" I said with appropriate authority as I lowered and twisted my head. I was beginning to feel confirmed in our concerns and I was certain we read the sheets correctly. I pulled out the order form from our folder, showing him the order for forty amps each of Repronex and Follistim that was given to us by this office.

As he shifted his head to see the page, I could sense the chaos and continuous motion of the office that morning come to a sudden halt. His body seized motion.

I then flipped our instructions open to the page showing blanks next to "Follistim" and "Repronex." In each space, there was a "5."

Dr. Blum's eyes, fixated on the order form, switched to the instruction sheet, where his index finger settled under the first "5," then the next.

We looked up at Dr. Blum's face, which had fallen pale and silent.

After a few moments, he said slowly and clearly, "No. This is not right. Do not, I repeat, do not take five amps of each. Hang on." He hopped to his feet and lunged for the door, yanking it open. "Mishi! Mishi, come in here. I need you."

Within seconds, she appeared in the doorway.

"Mishi, you wrote on their instructions to take five ampules each of Follistim and Repronex every night. Why did you do that? Have I ever, in all the time we've been doing this, prescribed a dosage that high? No. This is very dangerous."

Her expression changed from hurried to fear. She reached for the file and mumbled about copying his orders into the instructions. She flipped pages of doctor's notes, her hands shaking. We tried to avoid looking at her, feeling guilty for getting her in trouble. It was not our goal. Dr. Blum handed the file to her and told her to look for it and come back later.

She closed the door behind her and Dr. Blum regained his composure. "I'm very sorry about that."

"We weren't trying to get her in trouble, we just wanted to be sure of the right dosages," I said.

"No, it's all right. She needs to be very, very careful about this kind of thing. I will write out the instructions for you very clearly—take *one* vial of Repronex tonight and *two* vials of Follistim in the morning. Take this same dosage every day until we tell you to do otherwise. I'm glad you asked—never be afraid to ask us anything when you are here or to call us when you are not here. This can be a confusing process, which is why we try to detail exact instructions in your packet."

Mishi opened the door and walked in, pointing to a scrawled instruction in the notes. "I thought you meant…" Her voice became inaudible to us as she got closer to Dr. Blum and lowered her volume.

He shook his hand and responded with a quiet comment, then motioned for her to leave the office. "We'll talk about this more later on."

He turned his attention back to us. "Is that all clear? I'm sorry about this confusion."

Carrie responded, "Yes. I feel better. Thank you for taking the time to talk to us today. I'm sorry I broke down, but it was just very stressful today, with our confusion and seeing a new doctor that we don't know." She wiped the last of her tears away.

"Can you just write the correct dosages in our chart as well?" I asked.

He agreed and made the appropriate cross-outs and new markings.

We all got up and walked out of the office. Carrie and I headed down the hall, passed the remaining patients, and went out the door. I presume the long wait combined with Dr. Blum rushing in just twenty minutes earlier and topped with a husband consoling a sniffling, red-eyed wife walking out the door was less than comforting to the others seated, staring us out the doorway.

We held each other and walked slowly to the car to head back home.

# 21. TRIGGER HAPPY

Hours after we calmed from the jarring office experience, night fell and we began the preparations for the more complicated portion of the injections regimen. We carefully mixed the liquid with the single vial of Repronex and injected the solution into Carrie's belly, just as we had been doing for the Lupron, which also continued. So, each evening, there were two shots and each morning we would mix the two vials of Follistim and inject that into Carrie's belly. Carrie had started a practice of staring at pictures of babies that she had cut from magazines for motivation and to distract from the pain. Finding fresh spots on Carrie for the injections grew increasingly complicated as the days passed, but like everything else so far, we managed.

As we proceeded with the shots, September grew into October and Carrie was commuting into the city every other day for a checkup given by Dr. Blum.

Carrie would catch a train and commute nearly an hour and a half each way for what was typically a twenty-minute appointment. Each appointment called for a blood draw and hormone check. The levels never moved outside of the boundaries, allowing us to continue the same doses. Then Dr. Blum or his partner would perform a fairly quick ultrasound to check for egg development. And after each appointment Carrie called my work line and passed along the updates on follicle sizes. The sizes meant little to us without the commentary from the doctors, who seemed pleased with the growth. The goal was at least three eggs measuring eighteen to twenty-one millimeters, but with the intensity of the treatment regimen, we hoped for well more than three mature eggs.

On a cool Saturday morning, the first weekend of October, Carrie and I woke early, dressed, and hopped in the car. We stopped at the local bagel place for bagels and juice, then hauled into the city to beat the Saturday morning rush at Dr. Blum's office.

Now experienced with this process, we were among the first ones to arrive, but the office was not yet open. There were two other couples sitting on the floor, outside of the frosted doors. We assumed our place in line and waited.

It was an interesting dynamic. Each couple at the clinic had a story. In fact, each story was probably quite interesting and I was quite certain most would be willing to discuss their trials—sharing with others in similar situations can be a relief. That said, sharing in the office was quite rare, since nobody wanted to ask the question—*What are you here for? What is your story?*

When the first nurse arrived and unlocked the door, we flooded toward the desk in an orderly fashion to sign the register.

After a modest wait, we were called in for Carrie's regular ultrasound.

The office was moving efficiently for once. We waited only briefly in the exam room with Carrie naked from the waist down until Dr. Blum entered.

"Hey, guys," he said and we all kept the small talk to a minimum and went straight into business.

He looked at the screen. "All right. We are getting close now." He took a few quick measurements and declared, "We've got some good ones here. This one is sixteen. Another is fifteen and a half, fourteen, another sixteen. I think you guys should come back in tomorrow morning to get checked again. We're going to be triggering very soon."

Carrie and I smiled at each other as Dr. Blum removed the device, holstered it, and yanked off his rubber gloves.

We thanked him as he left the room, then gathered our belongings and headed back out to Long Island.

We were back home by around ten o'clock and went for a walk around the block with Socks. "So, if he tells us to trigger tomorrow," I began to ask, "then we'll go in for the retrieval on Monday?" I was still a bit uncertain of the timing, and was trying to gather my thoughts on which day I would need to miss work yet again.

"No, it's thirty-six hours after we trigger. So, if he tells us to trigger tomorrow, then we take the shot at night, and we'll go for the retrieval on Tuesday morning."

"Ah." It was just early enough in October to be out of work ahead of earnings season when things get very busy, but still causing me angst over my numerous absences.

Socks started to bark and off in the distance, we spotted Rob, our extremely friendly neighbor. Since we moved to the area, he was one of the only people to speak to us, let alone endearing himself quickly as a good friend. We had been sharing our tribulations over the past few months with him and his wife, Chris, both of whom had been very supportive.

"Hey, guys. Hi, Socksy!" said Rob, as we got closer to him.

I greeted him. "Hey, Rob. What's going on?"

"Not much. You guys are up and around early," he replied.

I looked over at Carrie and smiled. She started, "Actually, we just got back from the city."

"You guys stayed in the city last night?"

She laughed, "No. We went into the doctor this morning, and now we're back."

"Wow. That was fast. It's only," he looked at his watch, "a quarter after ten."

"Yeah," I replied. "And we're going back in early tomorrow again."

"Again?"

Carrie jumped in. "They think we're getting close. We're going to be ready for the egg retrieval soon."

"Great. Well, good luck."

The next morning, we repeated our routine from Saturday and arrived at Dr. Blum's office at about the same time as the prior day.

After the expected wait, we were called into the examining room.

A knock at the door and a short, stocky man with a half-bald head entered, to our surprise.

"Good morning, I am Dr. Matz, Dr. Blum's partner. I don't believe we've met yet." He extended his hand to Carrie first, then to me.

"Hi, Dr. Matz. It's nice to meet you," said Carrie. "You actually helped Adam and Alyse Mandel to get pregnant. Adam is Jason's brother."

"Ah, yes. How are they?" asked the new doctor.

"They're great, and Hanna is adorable."

"They are such a nice couple. I'm really glad things worked out for them," he replied.

"We were in yesterday and Dr. Blum told us to come back today because he thinks we're getting very close to triggering," said Carrie with an excited smile.

"Well, let's take a look." He grabbed the device and carefully inserted it, shifting his eyes to the glowing screen. "Looking pretty good. Here's a fourteen. Here's a sixteen, and a seventeen."

Carrie's hand squeezed in mine at the excitement as he rattled off a series of high numbers.

He snapped off the gloves, stepped on the garbage can pedal, and flung the rubber ball off the backboard and into the bucket. "I think Dr. Blum was right. We are very close. I think we could use one more day, but I don't think there is any need to have you come back in tomorrow. Let's have you trigger *tomorrow* night, for a retrieval on Wednesday morning. How does that sound?"

"Sounds great," we said with big smiles.

He turned toward the door and said, "Get dressed and meet me in my office."

As the door closed, our hands squeezed each other's tightly and we grinned ear to ear, with our faces nose to nose. Carrie flared, "We're gonna do this!"

"I know, I know. Wednesday morning." I took a deep breath, "Here we go!"

Carrie dressed and we walked out of the examining room and wandered down the hallway seeking his office. We found an open door with the good doctor sitting behind the desk and scribbling away.

He looked up and saw us. "Come on in. Sit down." We slid into the two seats across from him and he began to speak as he continued to write. "I am filling in the exact instructions for you to follow for the next couple of days."

He turned around the page he'd been scribbling on so we could see. He pointed at the instructions with the pen. "Tomorrow night, between seven and nine p.m., you are going to trigger—mix ten thousand units of Pregnyl—this is the HCG hormone—with one cc of the diluent. The timing is very important, so be sure to follow these times exactly." He paused, then said, "This is an intramuscular shot. It's oily and heavy, and a bit tougher than the shots you've been doing so far."

Carrie let out an uncomfortable laugh. "Well, if I want it this bad, I'll just deal with it."

He smiled and moved his pen to the next blank that he'd filled in. "Then, the next night, Tuesday night, between nine p.m. and midnight, take the first doxycycline pill and then keep taking them every twelve hours until they are gone—you should have enough to get you to three days after the retrieval. This is just to prevent infection from the procedure."

He moved his pen again and continued, all the while with us nodding our understanding. "Starting the night before the retrieval, eat or drink nothing at all."

He paused and looked up at us directly. "Now this is very important. We don't do the retrieval at this office. You must meet us at the clinic on Park Ave and 74th at no later than six-thirty a.m. The retrieval must be done within thirty-six hours of the Pregnyl shot, so that timing is crucial."

Then he continued with yet more steps. "The day after the retrieval, you will begin shots of fifty milligrams of progesterone each day. These are also intramuscular shots."

Carrie raised her eyebrows and smiled.

He continued, "Over the next few days, the lab will fertilize the eggs with Jason's sperm and let them mature. The lab will call you with a date and exact time to return to the clinic for the transfer. The transfer is the process that involves replacing the best embryos into the uterus." He released his intense forward pose and dropped his back against his chair, pushing a short swoosh of air, and finished, "Then it's just cross your fingers and hope."

After answering what few questions we had left that he hadn't managed to answer already, he wished us luck and we were on our way.

The next night, we read and reread the instructions. Make one mistake and we could destroy the whole process so far and potentially even put Carrie at medical risk. I carefully chose the correct syringe and mixing needle. I mixed the appropriate amounts of medication and liquid and slowly rolled the vial between my fingers to allow it to fully dissolve. Carrie watched very closely. After it was fully mixed, I replaced the hard plastic cap over the needle and unscrewed it from the syringe. Double-checking the length and gauge of the injecting needle with the instructions one more time, I screwed it onto the syringe and put it down.

I looked up at Carrie. "You think you are ready for this?"

"I'm nervous. Just be really careful."

"I will. I'll do it quickly and carefully." Oddly, I had grown to view the subcutaneous shots in the belly to be rather routine and brushed off any winces by Carrie. However, this shot in the butt, with a bigger needle, reminded me to be sympathetic.

I picked a cheek and then chose a spot in the top outside quadrant of the buttock, just as that old, grainy VHS video had instructed. I wiped it down with the alcohol pad and then lightly blew on it to dry.

Framing the target with my left thumb and forefinger, I grabbed for the syringe with my right. I carefully positioned the needle in the center of the bull's-eye, an inch off of Carrie's skin.

"Are you ready?" I asked in a calm voice.

"Just give me a second," she said. I paused and waited. "OK, do it."

I jabbed the syringe forcefully forward. In an instant, the tip of the needle broke through the skin and sunk all the way up to the end of the needle. I quickly repositioned the thumb of my right hand onto the plunger and forced the Pregnyl into Carrie's tissue. The oily liquid in the syringe required notably more pressure than the smaller shots. I pulled the needle back out, dropped it down on the dresser, and grabbed for the gauze, covering the puncture and massaging gently to disperse the oil.

Softly, I asked, "Are you OK?" looking around her side and up at her face.

"Yes," she said with strength but discomfort in her voice. "It hurt a little, but I'm all right."

I offered a comforting thought. "Well, you're triggered now. We're gonna go get pregnant in a few days," as I smiled at her.

She tried to remove the discomfort from her face, looked me in the eye, and smiled back.

# 22. THAT COULD'VE BEEN BAD, TOO

At around four thirty a.m. on Wednesday morning, my alarm clock blared to life, immediately waking both of us from a light sleep. Fearing the prospect of oversleeping, we had set three separate alarm clocks on high volume. The thirty-six-hour cutoff after triggering for ovulation was serious business. If we failed to show, Carrie would likely ovulate all of those matured eggs on her own, rendering useless the entire month's shots and doctor's visits, not to mention money.

We spent no time dawdling in bed; rather, we rose immediately and prepared to leave the house, headed to the clinic in Midtown for the retrieval.

Ironically, the day was also Yom Kippur, the Jewish day of Atonement. Normally, a full day's fasting from sundown to sundown wipes clean the year's sins. Given our immediate need for healthy sperm, I avoided fasting the night before and indulged in a bagel with cream cheese breakfast from our local shop as we departed for the city. On the other hand, Carrie was fasting, but on doctor's orders, not God's.

Leaving the house at five a.m. allowed for smooth sailing all the way to the city. We arrived at the clinic on Park Avenue more than half an hour early and opted to look for a hard-to-come-by spot on the street. That lasted about ten to fifteen minutes until we pulled into a local parking garage for a hefty fee instead.

We walked across the street and found the door matching the address on our instruction sheet.

The plaque outside the door read, "Park Avenue Medical Complex." Below the plaque was a smaller sign reading, "If locked, please ring bell for assistance." We rang, then waited patiently.

After a minute or two, I rang again, then cupped my hands on the glass of the door and leaned in with my face to see inside.

"It's dark in there," I said.

Carrie pushed up her sleeve to look at her watch; the time was six ten a.m. "It's still only ten after."

We sat ourselves down on the sidewalk, with our backs propped against the Medical Complex.

We sat quietly for a few moments and then Carrie said, "I'm nervous."

"I know, sweetie. We just need to keep thinking about *why* we are here. I know neither one of us pictured having a baby being this difficult." I planted a kiss on her cheek.

"I know. And what ever happened to Fertile Myrtle?" She lifted her hands into the air.

"Guess that didn't pan out."

After a few more minutes, I rose, recupped my hands on the glass and peered in. "Do you think they come in this way, or maybe some back way?"

"I don't know. Ring the bell again if you want," Carrie said.

I rang the bell, waited a few moments, then spun back around and sat back down.

"Do you think this is going to work?" Carrie asked.

"I hope so. Dr. Blum seemed to be very optimistic about it."

She turned and looked at me. "He was optimistic about Clomid and IUI also."

I smirked and shrugged.

The day grew brighter as the sun rose higher off of the horizon. I rose as well and began to pace.

"It's six thirty now," Carrie announced.

I walked back over to the window on the door and rang the bell several times. Peeking in revealed nothing new.

We waited, with me pacing, for another ten minutes.

"Do you think we should call?" I asked.

"I don't know. I don't even know who to call. They don't turn the phones on at the office until eight."

After a few more minutes of pacing, a heavyset gentleman dressed in a sharp doorman's outfit with white gloves and a cap appeared from around the corner. He looked at us a few times. I looked at him, smiled, then put my head down and continued pacing, counting the blackened gum marks on the sidewalk to keep busy.

"Are you waiting for the fertility clinic?"

Excited, I popped my head back up and responded, "Yes." Realizing he came from around the corner, I figured he was about to lead us to a side entrance.

Instead, he said, "They're usually here by now."

My smile disappeared. "We were supposed to meet here at six thirty."

He motioned to the door. "They're usually here by six. You tried the bell? The door's locked?"

I responded, "Yes. I don't think anyone's inside. Thanks." With that, he turned and drifted back around the corner.

"I think we should call, Jas," Carrie said. We were both growing nervous with each passing minute.

I pulled out my cell phone and called the main office, hoping to reach someone, but rather finding several rings, then the answering machine. "You think I should page Dr. Blum?" I asked Carrie.

She nodded and I dialed the office phone again. As the machine rattled off the phone number of the answering service to call, I called out the digits for Carrie to remember. With Carrie repeating them to me, I dialed.

"Reproductive Endocrinology Associates," said the voice on the other end.

"Hi. We have an appointment at the clinic this morning and nobody has shown up yet."

"This is just the answering service." which we knew already. "Do you have an emergency that you need to have me page someone?"

"I guess not. Do you know what time the office opens up?" I struggled with whether or not to consider this an emergency. I still expected Dr. Blum to come walking around the corner any second.

The voice droned back, "The office opens at eight a.m."

I thanked the unenthusiastic individual and ended the call.

"What should we do?" I asked Carrie.

"I don't know. Maybe we should have him paged if they're not here by seven."

I agreed and we paced for another ten minutes.

"It's five to seven. Let's page him," Carrie said. I agreed and dialed back the answering service.

"Reproductive Endocrinology Associates."

"Hi. We called a little while ago about an appointment this morning. We need you to page Dr. Blum."

In a deeply bored voice, "Is this an emergency?"

"Yes. It is now an emergency," I said firmly.

"If it's just a missed appointment, can't you just wait for the office to open in an hour?" Clearly the answering service was under strict instructions to filter all calls to emergencies only. I could certainly understand that. With the volume of hormones raging through the patients of the office, I could imagine that emergencies would commonly be perceived.

"No. We can't wait. This is now an emergency and we need to speak to Dr. Blum."

"Dr. Matz is the doctor on call. I will page him for you. What is your name?"

"No!" I barked back into the phone. "You need to page Dr. Blum. We need to speak with him directly."

"All right. What is your name?"

"Jason and Carrie Mandel." I gave him the phone number and he promised a call right back.

I clenched the phone in my hand as I paced rapidly.

"Jas, thirty-six hours is at eight forty-five. If they don't get the retrieval done by then—that is a major problem."

"I know. Just stay calm. He's probably just running late." With that, the Flintstones theme began chiming from my Nokia cell phone.

"Hello," I said.

"Mr. Mandel, I have Dr. Matz on the line for you." My blood boiled. The damn idiot at the answering service pooh-poohed my request and went ahead and called Dr. Matz.

"Hello, this is Dr. Matz."

"Dr. Matz. We are at the clinic waiting for the retrieval and nobody has shown up. You told us to be here at six thirty a.m."

"All right. Um. Let me check to see what's going on. I'll call you back in a few minutes."

Before I could muster any response, he was gone.

I immediately dialed back to the answering service.

"Reproductive Endocrinology Associates."

"Hi, this is Jason Mandel, we just spoke—you got Dr. Matz on the line for us," I said firmly.

"Yes," he said calmly.

"Please page Dr. Blum immediately," I said slowly and clearly.

"Dr. Matz is on call today," replied the operator in a frustratingly calm voice, as though we had not been through this five minutes before.

"I know. But this is an emergency and we need," I paused, raised my voice, and spoke slowly, "Doctor ... Blum."

"OK, sir," he said, frustrated. At least there was some sort of emotion being raised.

A few minutes later, the Flintstones rang again. "Hello," I said.

Dr. Blum's voice, sleepy, confused, and perhaps annoyed, answered me. "Hello, this is Dr. Blum. Did someone page me?"

I was relieved that I finally had the right doctor on the phone but began to sweat in fear. I had hoped he would be calling from his cell phone and shouting about the awful traffic. I explained, "Dr. Blum, this is Jason Mandel. Carrie and I are here at the clinic waiting for our retrieval."

"What retrieval? You aren't scheduled for a retrieval today," he said, confidently.

"Yes, we are!" I shouted back, in shock that we truly were waiting in vain. "Dr. Matz had us trigger on Monday night for retrieval this morning."

"You triggered Monday night? Let me just check this out. I'll call you back in a few minutes," he said. His voice still projected confidence but began to contain some doubt.

As I hung up the phone, Carrie immediately asked what happened on the call. She was anxious, hearing only one side of the conversation, and picking up that we were all alone on the corner of Park Avenue and 74th Street.

"He said he doesn't know about any retrieval for this morning. He sounded sleepy like we just woke him."

"Oh, fucker!" Carrie shouted. "Jas, if we don't get this retrieval done soon, we're going to lose all of the eggs. And I don't think it's safe for me to ovulate all of those eggs!"

"I know, I know. They'll have to get it figured out. If anything, Dr. Matz will have to come up here from the office to do it." I tried to offer a solution but was growing fairly certain that we would not be having the retrieval today.

The Flintstones rang. "Hello," I said quickly and loudly.

"Hi, Jason? This is Dr. Blum."

"Hi."

"I just called the office and they told me that Dr. Matz did tell you to trigger, but he never told me." He paused for a moment. "That's something for me to deal with him about later. But for now, just stay put. I'll call the staff and have them get there right away, and I will jump in my car and be there as soon as possible. Just relax and tell Carrie to relax. We *are* going to do the retrieval this morning."

"You think you will still be able to get here in time?"

Hurriedly, he answered, "Yes, I'll be there. And the rest of the staff lives near the clinic, so they'll be there soon and can get everything ready. Just stay there and keep Carrie calm."

"All right. We'll be right here. Thank you."

The instant I hung up, Carrie asked, "What happened. He's coming?"

"Yes. He said that the staff will be here soon and he's on his way. Where does he live?"

"Jersey, I think," Carrie said.

I thought, then looked at my watch. "It's gonna be interesting. He has to come in from Jersey and it's nearly seven thirty. He's definitely going to hit some good traffic."

"Oh, shit." Carrie dropped her head into her hands.

"No, no. He said to just relax. The staff will be here soon and they can get everything ready. He only really needs to be here for the last part, to do the retrieval."

I grabbed Carrie and hugged her tight for a while. Then we both paced for the next twenty minutes.

"Hi, guys," said a young Latin fellow as he approached us. He pulled keys from his pocket and headed for the door to the clinic. "Exciting morning, huh?"

"Yeah, I guess so. More than we'd hoped," I responded.

"We'll get it done, don't worry. Come on in."

He unlocked the door we'd been waiting by and led us to a couch in the waiting room to relax, where we waited some more as two other people showed up and prepared the facilities.

Then one of the nurses came out and handed me a cup. "Go ahead and fill this," she said.

I kissed Carrie. "I love you. I'll see you in a few."

I walked toward the back, where despite the stress of the morning, I was able to pleasure the cup in a fairly short period of time. This time, I had no cares for what others might think about the amount of time it took me, and rushed right out of the bathroom.

"Hello?" I called as I wandered back down the hallway. As I reached the front of the building, Carrie was gone from the couch and I heard noises coming from upstairs. Near the entrance, there was a landing and an old, steep, wooden stairway, which I decided to try. Each stair creaked with my steps and I heard the noises grow louder as I climbed. When I reached the top, there was a series of closed doors. Before I had to guess, a nurse thankfully emerged, saw me, and grabbed the cup with her gloved hand. "She's in there getting prepped. Just wait here and they'll roll her out in a second."

In an instant the nurse was gone, disappearing through another door.

I looked around. The doors were all old, with aged doorknobs and some cracked paint near the ceiling. It felt like a quaint bed-and-breakfast built in the early 1900s—not like a medical clinic.

One of the doors opened and a bed rolled into the hallway. Carrie was lying down under a white sheet and Dr. Blum, pushing the bed, nodded to me.

"Better late than never," he said. I managed a smirk in acknowledgment. He continued, "We are just about all ready to go." He stopped rolling Carrie and I grabbed her hand.

"Everyone's here now and you are going to do great," I said, trying to ease her worries.

She took a deep breath and squeezed my hand. I leaned in to kiss her lightly.

"I'll see you when I get out," she said. With that, Dr. Blum rushed her into the next room and the doors shut behind her. A nurse pointed me downstairs to wait for the procedure to be finished.

The stresses of the past fifteen minutes of rushing combined with the prior hour of waiting impatiently melted me into the couch in the waiting room. My head flopped back and my lungs released an audible sigh.

For the next twenty minutes, I stared at the colorful fish swimming aimlessly around in the tank across from me. Finally, a nurse emerged from the stairway and said, "You can come back up here. We're all done."

I hopped to my feet and scurried up the stairs. I was directed to the only room with an open door.

I walked in and rounded the curtains to see Carrie lying quietly in the bed.

"Hi," she said, with a very soft smile. The drugs were apparently still with her.

"Hey, sweetie," I said as I glided to her side. "You're all done. How did you do?"

"I don't know," she said.

"She did great," called out Dr. Blum's distant voice as he appeared from around the corner. Fully audible, he repeated, "She did great. We got nine mature eggs. There were two more hidden behind the ovaries that I couldn't quite get to without puncturing the uterus, so I had to leave them. But nine is pretty good. We should have enough to get a good fertilized embryo."

Dr. Blum walked around me toward Carrie's head and stroked her forehead once, "You did great. We're going to get these eggs fertilized and get them back into you."

Carrie reached out slowly and placed her arm on his. She lightly rubbed his hand and said in a slow, sweet voice, "Thank you so much, Dr. Blum. I want to tell you that you've been so nice to us and we really appreciate it. I think you are wonderful."

He handled a somewhat strange situation with grace, offering back, "Oh, it's not a problem. I just want to see you guys get to where you want to be—pregnant. And I'm sorry we had a problem this morning. The practice has been growing so quickly. Even though we try hard to avoid any miscommunications, we still have some kinks to work out." He appeared genuinely apologetic and somewhat embarrassed by what took place.

He continued, "Do either of you have any questions?"

Carrie jumped in. "Yes. When can we have sex again?"

My eyes widened and my head cocked back. Those were some good drugs.

Dr. Blum handled the question smoothly. He smiled and said, "You should really wait until a few days after we do the transfer. It would just be safest that way."

The medication administered to ease the pain of the procedure had left Carrie in a cloudy wonderful place. She nodded slowly and smiled again.

I pulled Dr. Blum aside so that I could be more direct with him. "Dr. Blum. I want you to know that we think that *you* are doing a great job and we feel we can trust you. However, we have little faith in your office. Dr. Matz told us to trigger and then somehow he never told you that we would be here waiting this morning. When we were getting ready to begin our Follistim and Repronex, we were hours away from starting to overdose because we were given the wrong instructions." He nodded along with my concerns and I continued, "Again, it is not *you* that we are concerned with, but this whole process is stressful enough that we don't want to have to worry about the processes and communication happening correctly at your office. I'm glad the office is growing quickly and that's great for you, but we still need to feel comfortable."

He finished nodding in agreement and said, "I completely understand. These are things that should not happen, even though we are growing quickly." He stopped and turned around, searching the room. He retrieved a pen and turned over a piece of paper in his hands to write on the back. "I am giving you my home number and beeper number. Feel free to use it if you need me and you are not getting what you need from the office. I want you both to feel comfortable and don't want anything to go wrong that doesn't need to."

I took the paper and thanked him sincerely. "I have no plans to use this, but I appreciate it very much."

He leaned to my side to bring Carrie back into his line of sight and said with some speed, "I do have to run, though. I am illegally parked. You guys did great. Hang out here until you feel up to getting up and going home. The clinic will call tomorrow to talk about the instructions for the transfer. I'll see you guys back here for the transfer." He stopped his motion and slowed his speech. "I promise I'll be on time." With that, he nodded and disappeared around the corner again and we were alone in the room.

Carrie turned to her side slightly and let out a low moan. "They only got nine? He couldn't get to the two others?"

I walked back over to her and put my hand on her forehead. "He said he was pleased. Nine is more than enough. We're only putting two back in."

I leaned in and kissed her softly and moved my hand down to her face. She shut her eyes for a moment and relaxed.

As if to awaken from a dream, her eyes opened again. "What did I say to him?"

I paused and smiled. Through my grin, I slowly squeezed out, "You asked him when we could have sex again."

Her eyes opened wider, more alert now. "I did not!" she insisted.

"Babe, you did. You also stroked his hand and told him he was wonderful," I informed her, giggling.

She snapped back louder and even more alert, "I did not! Did I say those things? Oh," she groaned. I laughed.

As Carrie regained normal consciousness, she began to feel the pain of the procedure setting in and growing by the minute. It wasn't long until the pain was debilitating, causing her to double over. I comforted her as best I could and suggested we get prepared and out to the car as quickly as possible—to get back into the comfort of our home.

The ride back out to our house was not comfortable, as she felt the pain in her cervix with each bump and pothole. The Long Island Expressway was not a place to find a smooth ride.

It was hours until Carrie began feeling meaningfully better. The craziness of the day was behind us, leaving us both physically and emotionally drained. Yet, we couldn't help but relive it—we walked through the events of the day and our disappointment in Dr. Blum and his office. Had we not strongly advocated for ourselves, forcing a way into the doctors, the day could easily have wound up effectively a disaster.

While I wanted to commiserate and bash our doctors, I eventually decided it would be best to take the calmer road and to reassure Carrie. "He took me aside after it was all over. He apologized about the mix-up and took responsibility." I pulled the card from my pocket. "He even gave me his home and beeper number, which nobody gets."

We let the negativity lapse and melted the day away alternatively talking about recent events and meaningless topics and drifting to naps.

The next day back at work, too anxious to wait for a call from the embryologist, I started calling the clinic to find out how our babies were doing.

After leaving a few messages, the phone in my office rang with "Clinic" in the caller ID.

I snatched up the handset. "Jason Mandel."

"Hello. Can I speak with Jason Mandel?" said a man's voice on the other end.

"This is."

"Hi, Jason. This is Marcus, the embryologist from the fertility clinic. I was just returning your call."

"Yes. Thanks for the call back. I was hoping to find out how our eggs are doing?"

"Sure, sure. We went ahead and fertilized the eggs with your sperm yesterday. Six of the eggs fertilized successfully."

"Is that good?"

"Well, it is certainly fine if you are only putting in two or three."

"Yes, we are putting two back in. When do we have to decide if we are going to freeze any of them?"

The benefit of freezing the embryos is quite simple—they are already fertilized and can be thawed and used later. In the event that the IVF procedure fails, we would be able to do IVF again without having to go through all of the shots and the retrieval.

He answered, "We should wait to see how they develop. Some of them may develop better than others, and it is still possible that one or more may cease to develop. You are going to want to use the best two available."

"All right. That's great. Thank you again."

I called Carrie from my office to let her know the good news.

"Hi. It's me," I started. I continued with an upbeat tone, "I just spoke to Marcus, the embryologist, about our babies. He said that six of the eggs fertilized successfully."

"Six?" she answered. I sensed the surprise was negative. "Just six? I just spoke to Alyse. When they did IVF, they got twenty-eight eggs out. She thought that nine was really low. And now we are down to just six." Her emotions spilled through the phone.

Up to now, we really had little frame of reference as to what we were looking for. Now, it seemed, our odds were dropping.

I tried to comfort her by saying that we would let them mature and then pick the best two, and we'd just have to leave it to nature after that.

It was of little consolation to her, nor to me.

That night, we began the progesterone shots. Progesterone is a hormone the body produces which is necessary for establishing and maintaining a pregnancy. But it's a bitch of a shot.

The needle is the longest of the bunch and the hormone itself is dissolved in oil, which makes it thick and more painful. When injected, the medication leaves a lump under the skin because of the oil, which has to be dispersed by rubbing the area. I injected the hormone into Carrie and rubbed to spread it. The process was clearly more uncomfortable and painful than the other lighter shots.

On top of the shot, Carrie would need to supplement with a vaginal suppository of progesterone in the mornings. What a trouper—and pincushion.

The next morning I again called the embryologist to check in on the progress. Perhaps these calls were my first taste of fatherhood. I called several times, each time leaving messages, and I avoided leaving my desk for fear of missing the call back. I need to know—how were my babies doing?

Finally, the phone rang, with "Clinic" on the caller ID.

Again, I snapped my claw at the phone and yanked it to my ear. "Jason Mandel."

"Can I speak to Jason Mandel, please?"

"Yes, that's me."

The woman's soft voice chimed back. "Hi, Jason. This is Tara. I work at the fertility clinic and was calling you back from a message you left for Marcus."

"Yes, thank you. I wanted to find out about our embryos, and to find out about freezing."

"Yes. We fertilized nine eggs, and six fertilized successfully." Yes—I knew that. "Of those six, five look very good, and are maturing well." There was the news.

"All right. Good. When do we have to make a decision on freezing embryos?"

"Well, I don't really think that you should freeze any. After another couple of days, we will be able to see more differences in them. This way, we can pick the two best out of the six." She continued, "Also, the odds of a frozen embryo thawing successfully are about half. So even if you decide to freeze a couple, it is possible that even fewer will make it out OK on the other side."

I thanked Tara and we hung up. I paused to consider if this was good or bad news. We had just assumed there would be embryos to freeze should this time around fail.

I called Carrie to relay the news and I could sense some disappointment on the lack of freezing opportunity.

"I just feel like there is a lot of pressure on us," Carrie said. "We've gone through this whole process and came out with just enough embryos to go through IVF *one time*. If we fail, we have to start again—*from scratch*."

There was little I could do to add comfort, as I felt the same way. We would pretty much have to cross our fingers and pray, as we had done so many times before already.

# 23. THE TRANSFER

The big day arrived. Four days after the retrieval, with our little embryos growing all the while, we arrived at the clinic at eleven thirty, hoping to become pregnant. Just as a failsafe, I had called the office the day before to be completely sure the doctors knew with no doubt about our procedure this time around—they did.

By the time we arrived at the clinic, Carrie had already finished off a bottle and a half of water, and when we got there they offered more. For this procedure, Dr. Blum could not use the transvaginal ultrasound, and instead had to do an external ultrasound, through the belly. However, in order to see clearly, Carrie's bladder must be full.

We sat in the waiting room as Carrie drank more water and tapped her fingers and bounced her knees. Nerves were getting the best of her and she was forced to ask a nurse if she was allowed to make number two.

"Can you do it without making number one?" asked the nurse.

"I don't know. I think so. I'll try." Carrie paused as the nurse was thinking, and looked behind her as if hoping to see Dr. Blum down the hall for help. "I really have to go. I can do it without peeing."

"All right. But keep drinking water when you get out," said the nurse.

So off Carrie went, as I waited, staring at the fish.

Within two minutes, Carrie was back, with her little problem solved and urine retained. She grabbed the bottle and polished it off.

Shortly after, we were guided upstairs. It was time.

Carrie and I were ushered into the recovery room that Carrie had been in once before. The nurse drew the curtain, motioning to the gown on the bed. Carrie undressed and we talked for a minute. "It's going to go great. I have a really good feeling about this. They said the embryos looked good and everything else seems to be in place," I said.

All Carrie could really do was keep looking me in the eye, nod, and smile, while her eyes slowly filled with tears. Her excitement and fear were showing through clearly, as I stroked her forehead until they came to get us.

The nurse wheeled Carrie's bed into another room, which looked nothing like an operating room at all. In fact, there was little to make it look medically related, except for the spotlight, ultrasound machine on wheels, and a unit that appeared to be an incubator at the back of the room.

"Mr. Mandel, please come over here," the embryologist called out as he motioned for me to approach the incubator. "Please take a look," he said.

I bent over and positioned my face over the two eyepieces of the microscope, looking into the contraption.

"He asked, "How does that look?"

I could see a petri dish and two small circles sitting inside.

"They look great," I said with a smile and pulled away from the scope. He clearly wasn't certain I gave the answer he was looking for and rephrased, "Is it right?"

I reengaged the microscope and realized he wasn't asking for my medical opinion, but to confirm the last name scrawled in black marker on the bottom of the dish was mine. I guess double-checking that you're putting the right fertilized embryos into the right people is not a bad idea. I quickly recovered, saying, "Yes. That's us," and pulled away in slight embarrassment.

By the time I turned around, Carrie's legs were already up in stirrups. There were several people in the room, all preparing for their role in the procedure. Much hustle and bustle.

I moved near Carrie's head and grabbed her hand. She smirked at me, understanding what I had just done.

"All right. We are just about ready to begin," said Dr. Blum, sitting on a stool at the foot of the bed, between Carrie's legs. He continued, "I am going to place a speculum into your vagina for this procedure. Then you will feel a little pressure, as I work to put the blastocysts back into you. I have a technique with positioning that has been working very well, so I need you to stay as still as you possibly can during the transfer."

He looked to us for our understanding—Carrie nodded.

As Dr. Blum inserted the speculum into Carrie, the embryologist prepared what looked like a long, thin straw, complete with our little babies. He carefully handed the device to Dr. Blum. A nurse placed the ultrasound sensor on Carrie's belly and the monitor sprung to life. With another doctor we had never met observing, Dr. Blum explained his procedure and placement in terms we did not understand, nor did we care to.

Dr. Blum announced that he was about to begin and then stopped talking. The whole room silenced and held its collective breath. Carrie froze in position. I held her hand tightly.

Dr. Blum inserted the straw and then focused his attention on the ultrasound screen. Quietly, Dr. Blum updated the room. "I'm almost in position. Carrie, just stay as still as you can."

She didn't even respond, holding her muscles in place.

"All right, I'm there." He paused.

"Releasing." He paused again.

"Slowly pulling out." He paused again. Then a heavy sigh of relief from the good doctor. "All right. We're all done. Perfect placement." The rest of the room exhaled and Carrie's now sweaty, tightly gripped hand released mine. The tension of the room was released in an instant.

Dr. Blum pulled out the speculum and made a loud clang, dropping it onto a metal tray, and followed with an aggressive snap-snap as he tugged off his rubber gloves. "OK, guys. The transfer went beautifully. Carrie, you just have to stay lying down for at least half an hour."

"Thank you so much, Dr. Blum," Carrie said, smiling at him, then turning and smiling a wide grin at me, which I returned.

The room's hustle and bustle that had entirely disappeared for just a few moments was back in full swing. Suddenly, Carrie was being rolled back out of the room, into the hallway, and back into the recovery room. The nurse pulled the curtain and reminded Carrie to just stay put.

We were suddenly alone. "Congratulations, baby," I said, as we kissed and squeezed hands.

"Time to pray now," she responded. "But I'm just glad we got to this point. We could have lost everything a few days ago. He seemed happy with how it went, right?"

"Oh, absolutely. It was a little tense there for a minute, but it sounded like he thought he nailed it," I said.

I laid the top half of my body down over her in a horizontal hug for a minute and we just held each other.

"I have two bubbies in me!" she said with silly, great excitement.

For just this moment—even if only for this moment—we were pregnant. We felt the joy. We clenched our hands together and stared into each other's eyes, smiling.

"I have to pee," Carrie said, interrupting our silence.

"Um. All right. Um. I think you're supposed to stay lying down for a little while longer. Can you hold it?"

She squinted her face. "I don't know. I really have to pee. They made me drink so much water."

I looked around the room, searching for an answer of some sort. "Uh. I guess I can go ask someone. Do you want me to go ask?"

Carrie was never one to bother people for more than was absolutely necessary. "No. Forget it. I can hold it."

She took a deep breath, then clenched her fists and released them. Clenched and released.

"Carrie. Let me just go ask."

"No! I'm OK."

I tilted my head and raised my eyebrows. "Just let me ask someone." I smirked. "You stay right here."

She chuckled back.

I stepped through the opening in the curtain and walked out of the room. Searching, I could find nobody. The whole place was alive with commotion minutes ago. I continued to wander, then walked downstairs where I heard voices, then found a nurse. "Hi. My wife really has to use the bathroom. Is she allowed to?"

The nurse tightened her lips, then put her four left fingers over her mouth and her eyes turned skyward as she thought and hummed. "She only had the transfer about ten minutes ago, right?"

I nodded.

"She really shouldn't get up, then. I'll let you know when." I thanked her and returned to Carrie's side with the bad news.

"But I really—I really, really have to go," she said.

I walked out of the room again and this time found a different nurse and asked for help. She turned and reached into the supply closet, pulling out a large silvery metal object and handing it to me.

"A bedpan?" I asked.

The nurse shrugged, turned around, and walked away.

As I pulled the curtain back and revealed the bathroom solution, Carrie yelped, mixed with a chuckle, "A bedpan?!"

"Beggars can't be choosers," I responded.

Laughing in near pain now, Carrie said again, "A bedpan?! I don't even know how to use a frigging bedpan!"

Now we were both getting giddy.

I explained, "You just slide it under you and go," as though it were that simple.

"Have you ever done it?" she asked, laughing more.

"Well. No. But you don't have a choice. You have to stay lying down. Here, just take it and do it."

"Help me!" she shout-laughed. "Hold it."

"Only guys have something to hold," I joked back.

She clenched her eyes shut in laughter and pain. "No, you jackass. Hold the bedpan."

"Oh. But you have to just sort of sit on it." I helped her try to position the mobile urinal as we continued to giggle like two idiots. "I hope nobody walks in on us right now," I said as Carrie's gown was pulled to the side and her rear lifted in the air to position the bedpan.

She laughed and let her butt collapse onto the bowl. "OK. I'm gonna pee."

Her face turned from clenched to relaxed for just a moment.

"It's running up my back!" she shouted.

I started to laugh uncontrollably at this point.

She laughed and panicked. "J—go get something. I'm peeing all over myself."

My eyes began to tear as I pictured what we would look like to an outside observer. I burst through the curtain and went to the supply closet. Searching quickly, I grabbed the first thing that looked like it would help—another paper medical gown.

"Here!" I shouted, as I handed the gown to Carrie.

"This is not a towel—it's a g-g-gown!" She could barely finish the sentence, being overtaken by her laughs.

She grabbed it anyway and tried to wipe up her back, which had become drenched with her own urine. "Take the pan!" she ordered.

I pulled the bedpan from under her and looked in it, barely able to see from the tears now flowing from my eyes. "Carrie—there's almost nothing in the bedpan."

"I know!" she shouted. She was quiet for a moment as she tried to regain her breath. "It's all on me. I need more to wipe it up."

I grabbed another two or three gowns and handed them to Carrie, who attempted to wipe up more of the urine. She continued, with each syllable broken up into its own word, "These things don't absorb anything." She struggled to maintain composure. "They're like wax paper." Another deep breath. "I'm just spreading it all around."

Both laughing uncontrollably now, I took the wet gowns from her, stuffed them into the bedpan, and slipped it under the bed. Sensing that even without getting vertical, Carrie's movements to urinate and then clean herself were too much, I said, "Carrie, you need to calm down." I forced the smile off of my face and wiped my eyes. "You really need to calm down and stay still." As hard as I tried to keep a straight face, a few bursts of chuckles forced their way through.

"I know, I know." She took deep breaths to chase away the laughter and held a straight face—still breaking into brief uncontrollable chuckles. "It's like when you are in church and someone does something and you know you aren't supposed to laugh, but you just can't keep it in."

It was another minute or two until we were both able to calm down and fight off the giggles.

"We were like Lucy and Ethel," Carrie said. "We're just a couple of idiots."

After another fifteen minutes or so, I left to get the car, met Carrie at the front of the building, and we headed for home.

# 24. BATED BREATH

For a few days after the transfer, Carrie was ordered on bed rest to give our little babies a chance to hang onto the uterus wall and fully implant. Two weeks. That's how long we had to wait after the procedure to take a pregnancy test. The trigger shot I had given Carrie was synthetic HCG, which is the hormone present during pregnancy that tests look for. So, if tested too soon, we would likely get a positive reading no matter what.

"Do you think I am pregnant?" Carrie asked.

"I don't know, I hope so. I guess I think so."

"Why?"

"Because you just ate your third pickle since we've been talking." Through the phone at my office, I could hear the snapping of the pickle and subsequent slurping of juices. She laughed as I said that, causing a bigger slurp to save the juices.

"You think I'm craving pickles?"

"Let me ask you this—the last time you went to the fridge to get a pickle, did you take a drink of the pickle juice?"

She laughed again. "Yes."

That night, we were getting ready for bed, and Carrie took off her shirt. "Holy shit. You're showing already," I said. If I had thought about this comment before saying it, I probably would have either reserved it or been more tactful. But the size of her belly caught me by surprise.

"I know, right?" she said. Thankfully she agreed with me rather than taking it a bad way. She turned her body sideways to the mirror and let it all hang out. "I swore earlier that I was showing. "

"You look like you're a couple of months pregnant already," I said.

"I do. And I've been really crampy down there all day."

I responded, "Do you think you are OK?"

"Yeah, I guess so. Just some cramping."

We dismissed the issue, but our internal excitement grew.

"J!" Carrie called from the bathroom. I ran in, given the tone of the shout. "I gained three pounds in the past few days."

"Yikes," I said, nervous to say much.

"That's a lot," she said.

"Maybe we should be calling the doctor. Your belly is swelling, you're crampy, and you've gained weight quickly."

Early the next morning, Carrie called the office and we set an appointment for that afternoon. Again, I left work to meet her at the office.

After a modest wait, we were called in to see Dr. Blum.

"Hey, guys," Dr. Blum said, with a large smile. "How are you feeling?" as he looked at Carrie.

"Big. I feel big and I've been crampy low in my belly." She smiled and chuckled. "But otherwise, I'm great."

"Well, let's just take a look to be sure everything is all right."

He inserted the transvaginal ultrasound and watched the screen. He diagnosed very quickly. "Yup. You are definitely hyperstimulated. You have a lot of fluid in your uterus, which your body is trying to figure out how to deal with."

"Is that why I am always craving pickles and miso soup?" Carrie said with a laugh.

We were surprised to find a serious answer. "Yes, actually. Your body is craving salt to deal with the excess fluid, so that manifests in whatever you associate with salty. In your case, pickles and miso soup."

Carrie and I looked at each other, impressed and surprised.

He continued, "You should try to drink a lot of Gatorade, to be sure that you stay well hydrated."

With that, a nurse walked in and handed Dr. Blum a small piece of paper.

He smiled and looked up at us. "Well, I don't want you to get excited, but your urine shows a very faint positive for pregnancy. Also, hyperstimulation is an indicator. But I don't want you to get too excited until we take the beta blood test in a couple of days."

Carrie and I smiled at each other with no control over our facial expressions. My eyes welled up and I blinked repeatedly to reabsorb. I grabbed her hand and squeezed, then leaned in to kiss her on her forehead.

"So, I need to see you back here for your appointment in three days to do a blood test. If, in that time, your discomfort grows a lot or you gain more than two pounds in a day, you need to come back in. Got it?" he finished.

"Got it," we said together.

As he left the room, I leaned over her to grab for a hug. We embraced for a moment, then pulled away and reminded each other *nothing's for sure yet*.

Two days later, Carrie woke with my alarm for work. I dragged myself into the bathroom to begin getting ready, but Carrie beat me to the toilet. She placed a large red plastic cup under her and filled it halfway, finishing into the bowl.

"What are you doing?" I asked. "We're not supposed to test yet. You still have HCG from the shot in your system."

"I want to test. I think the shot is gone by now," she said, defiantly.

"So, you think the doctors lied to us, just because they don't want us to take a test at home?"

"J—just let me do it." With that, she plunged the tester strip into the urine and counted slowly to five, when she yanked it back out, replaced the cap, and laid it flat on the vanity.

She got back up and walked to the bed to lie down. I grabbed my toothpaste and toothbrush to begin my daily regimen.

As I swished the last mouthful of water around and spit it into the sink, Carrie said, "It's five minutes. Check it."

I leaned over the tester stick and squinted my eyes. I picked it up and walked into the bedroom to hand to Carrie, who turned to her side and leaned up on her elbow. I pulled the string on her lamp, lighting the room.

Carrie's face filled with a wide grin, and I said, "Don't get too excited. We knew it would probably be positive anyway."

"I know," she said, still grinning. "But it's a positive."

While I didn't want to get too excited, I also believed that we were really pregnant. After our trials to this point, I certainly did not want to step on Carrie's excitement, so I sat on the bed, leaned over, and we shared a tight hug. We spoke no words, but understood each other clearly—*we're pregnant, but we need to hear it from the doctor.*

I showered and dressed for the day and left for work with an extra hop in my step.

Two days later, Carrie traveled into the city, peed in a cup and had blood drawn, then traveled back out to our house and waited.

I was deep into a document at work when my phone rang. Without picking my face up off the page, I grabbed the receiver, "This is Jason."

"Hi. It's me," Carrie's voice sang.

"So? You hear?"

"No. Not yet. I'm really anxious."

"I know, me, too! Don't call and make it sound like you know something." She laughed. "I'm sorry."

We chatted about other stuff to fill the air, but there was only one thing that actually mattered that day.

"I'll talk to you later. Call me when you hear—and don't call and make me think you know something again!" I said.

I attempted to get some work done, but there was little I could do that would take my mind off of the tests being done uptown on my wife's blood.

The phone rang again, with our home number on the caller ID. I snapped up the receiver. "Hello."

"We're pregnant!"

"All right!" I shouted out, then quickly lowered my voice. "Congratulations, baby! What did they say?" This time my eyes welled and droplets formed. I felt a tinge at the back of my nose.

Carrie started again, and I could hear her smile through the phone. "They called and said that the test was positive. "

"That's all?"

"No. They said that my HCG number was very high, four hundred fifty-seven, which is much higher than normal. It probably means that we have twins!"

"Twins?!" My eyes turned to full moons.

"Yes. But that's just an indication. They can say for sure that we're pregnant, but they won't know if it's one or two until we go for our ultrasound."

"That's fantastic. I feel like it's been forever—waiting for a definitive answer."

# 25. SURPRISE YOU. SURPRISE ME.

With the good news firmly in hand, we began the exciting process of telling our families.

Carrie's parents:
Two rings and then Carrie's dad's voice popped onto the line. "Hello."
"Hi, Dad," Carrie said.
"Hey, Doo." Carrie is affectionately referred to as Doo by her family, with the exception of her grandparents, who would have no part of calling her anything outside of her proper name.
"Get Mom on the phone, too," Carrie demanded.
While we had kept Carrie's parents up to date on all of our appointments and developments, they were under the impression that we would not be tested by Dr. Blum's office for another week. A little white lie.
"Hello." Carrie's mom's voice joined the line.
We chitchatted for a minute or two, then Carrie blurted out, "We wanted to let you guys know that you are going to be grandparents!"
I don't even recall what they said, or even if there were real words, but their reaction was delight and excitement.
We could almost feel their tears of joy through the phone.
Carrie's mom said, "Oh, I wish I could give you a big hug right now."

My parents:
We sat across from my parents at Tenjin restaurant, a great local sushi place that we frequented.
I flashed back for a moment to the fall of '99. We were in the process of planning our wedding and tensions were beginning to rise. Everyone seemed to have a different idea of how the wedding day should go, including everything from the location to the band to whether or not the bride and

groom should see each other before the wedding ceremony. We had asked my parents to this restaurant so that we could hash through some of the issues. To break the ice and defuse the tension back then, I blurted out a lie in the middle of our miso soup. "Carrie's pregnant." Carrie spit out her soup and coughed in shock. I can still picture both of my parents with spoonfuls of soup approaching their mouths. The spoons stopped moving instantly and their heads tilted upward to look at me with deep fear in their eyes. I thought it was a good icebreaker. Nobody else did.

Back to the story at hand. We sat, sipping our miso soup once again, and I reached into my coat pocket, pulled out a card, and slid it over to them.

"What's this?" my dad asked.

"Just a Halloween card," I replied. We had never in our lives exchanged Halloween cards, but what the heck?

He picked up the card, and with my mother looking over his shoulder, he opened the envelope.

On the outside, the card simply read, "Boo." He opened it and found just "We're pregnant" written inside, the original card's message crossed out.

Their four eyes immediately shot up from the card in confusion, but with a shine of excitement that was not there the last time I told them Carrie was pregnant.

"What do you mean?" asked my dad, confused. Just as with Carrie's parents, we had lied to my parents, telling them it would be another week until we knew anything.

Carrie beamed. "We kind of lied to you. We found out yesterday for certain. I was already tested at the doctor."

Their eyes filled with tears and smiles adorned their faces as they got up to walk around the table for hugs.

My brother and sister-in-law:
A day later, we went into the city to visit my brother and his family, Adam and Alyse and their beautiful daughter, Hanna. The apartment was hectic. It was bath time for Hanna and the two of them were trying to bathe her at the same time she was trying to play. After fifteen minutes of chatting while bathing, Alyse finally blurted out, "So, are you guys pregnant or what?"

Our excitement was difficult to contain. We wanted to share our good news with the world, but knew that we should really be waiting a few months before telling all but the closest family. At this point, we didn't even know for sure that we were having twins, though it seemed like a certainty only waiting to be confirmed at next week's appointment.

To let out some of our pent-up excitement, we went shopping. After all, you can tell salespeople that you are looking for supplies for twins—they don't qualify as people that you can't tell.

We went to Bellini's to search for twin furniture. Our question list began to form. Do we put them in the same room? Are you allowed to put them in the same crib? Would we even want to? Do we put them in separate rooms and give them very different furniture and decorations to allow them to have their independence?

Then we went to BuyBuy Baby to look for twin strollers. More questions. Do we get a side-by-side or a front-and-back stroller? If we get a stroller with front and back seats, will the one in the back feel left out? If we get a side-by-side stroller, will it fit through doorways?

We went to Baby Fortunoff and ran into a couple with newborn twins. "Hi, your babies are beautiful," I said to them.

They thanked me and I continued with the real question, "Do you like that twin stroller? My wife and I are having twins and we're trying to decide on strollers."

"Oh, congratulations," they offered. They extolled the stroller as best of the bunch. It was a front- and back-seated stroller.

Carrie walked over from looking at stuffed animals and I made the introduction. "This is my wife, Carrie."

"Are you sure it's just two?" the mother of the twins asked. We laughed, knowing that just two eggs had been put back into Carrie. "Yes, we're sure of it," Carrie replied.

We congratulated them and they us. As we walked away, Carrie whispered to me, "I'm still not sure about the front and back strollers."

A few days later, now into early November, I met Carrie at Dr. Blum's office for our confirmation ultrasound.

Carrie and I walked back into the examination room for what we believed would be one of our last visits. She undressed, assumed the position on the table, and then Dr. Blum knocked.

"Hello, everyone. How are we feeling?" a jovial Dr. Blum asked.

"Good. Excited," responded Carrie.

"Great, I think you should be. Are you still feeling very bloated?"

"Yes, but no more so than before," she replied.

"All right, well let's take a look, then."

He inserted the ultrasound into Carrie. The screen popped to life. Carrie grabbed for my hand and took a deep breath.

"Is that? Do I see two sacs?" Carrie shouted out.

"That is definitely two sacs. You guys are going to have a set of fraternal twins for sure," he said, smiling at the screen.

We turned to each other and smiled widely. Tears filled our four eyes and I leaned over to kiss her. We both looked up at the screen again to focus on the two small circles near the sides of a much larger ring of green, which was otherwise filled with black, the large volume of fluid in Carrie's uterus.

He finished up and told us, "Everything looks just great. Go ahead and get dressed, then meet me in my office."

As he left the room, I leaned on top of Carrie and we embraced in a long, tight hug.

"I can't believe it's true. We are having *two* babies!" I said.

Sinking in a bit more, now with confirmation from the doctor, Carrie said, "Can we handle two?"

"Can we handle *one*?" I chipped back and laughed.

We then quickly gathered up and headed down the hall and into his office. Shortly after, Dr. Blum entered and shut the door behind us.

"So, I guess congratulations are absolutely in order," he said as he walked around to his side of the desk and reached out his hand to me for a shake and then leaned into Carrie for a kiss on the cheek.

"Well, I'd bet you guys are going to be busy for a while," he said and we chuckled. "You guys are going to need a high-risk OB. I'm not saying there's anything wrong, but having twins by nature means closer care and more experience is necessary."

"Can you recommend one to us? Out on Long Island?"

"Well, Dr. Boris Feinman is very good."

"No way!" Carrie jumped. "He's a partner in the practice we are already seeing. That's perfect."

"You already have one issue taken care of. See how quickly you are moving along? You should make an appointment with him very soon to talk about his recommendations on what to do and what not to do during your twin pregnancy. What is the same as with a single, and what is different. You are going to come back here just one more time for a final ultrasound, then you are all his. Some people feel a bit abandoned when they get to this stage, because we get used to seeing so much of each other, and suddenly that ends. But it was my job to help you along to get pregnant and now it is your OB's job to get you to the end of your pregnancy safely."

We nodded in understanding.

After a few more minutes of discussion and some questions from Carrie's regular question sheet, we were headed out of the office and into the elevator, where we had a moment alone.

We faced each other and with my hands locked around her, I looked her in the eyes and said, "Congratulations, baby. I love you so much and couldn't be prouder that you are having my babies."

She shuddered for a second, then said with a huge smile, "Babies. We're going to have babies. Not a baby. Babies!"

We embraced. The doors opened.

# 26. THEY NEED NAMES

We lay in bed together that night, giddy about the recent slate of news. Pregnant first, and now twins.

"How about David?" I asked.

"No. That's become a little too common . What about Owen?" Carrie put back to me.

I jumped straight into character with a deep and labored woman's voice with a lisp, "Owen doesn't have any friends because he's fat and he's stupid!"

"What the hell?" Carrie asked back.

"Sorry, it's from a movie," I closely but inaccurately quoted *Throw Momma from the Train*. "Still, I don't like Owen."

Carrie suggested others and I shot down some. I suggested a few and Carrie nixed some of those. We continued this way and began slowly to build a list of possible names. We needed a bunch of them. Not knowing if the twins were boys, girls, or one of each, we aimed for a list of four names— two each. We flipped through a name book Carrie had bought months before, but that we had left unopened until now.

We tested each idea to make sure we weren't creating bad initials, a name that sounded strange if shortened by friends, or names that rhyme with bad words. It turns out that if you're creative enough, all names rhyme with some bad word.

It took a few days of building lists and then culling them to come up with our four: Madelyn Elizabeth, Maya Brynn, Chase Anderson, and Asher Devin.

# 27. A STRESS HEAD FAKE

As I sat in my office, reading through an earnings release, my phone rang. I answered and Carrie's voice, deeply frazzled, crackled back. "J—I just went to my regular doc to get that rash on my butt checked out. He said that because it's only one buttock he didn't think it could be caused by the progesterone shots I'm taking every day."

"OK," I said, listening for the part where we go downhill, which was clearly coming.

Carrie continued, but her voice cracked into a whimper as she barely eked out, "He asked me if I have ever had herpes."

"Herpes!" I responded in a whispering scream.

She tried to regain composure in order to speak. "He asked me if I had ever had a rash or warts in my vaginal or buttock area. Then he took a scraping to test me for herpes," as her voice trailed into a cry.

I took a deep breath and tried to center myself. "Why the hell does he think it's herpes?"

Her anger at the situation showed through as she yelled, "I don't know!"

I asked, "Well, how long will it take to get the results?"

"He said we should have them within a day or two. For now, he gave me some pills to start on for treatment, but he's not sure if they are safe for the babies."

Surprised, I responded, "Not sure?! He prescribed pills for you that he's not sure are safe for the babies?"

She had trouble catching her breath, then could only whisper, "What does this mean for the babies? Did I give our babies herpes?"

"I don't think YOU have herpes, so I certainly don't think you gave it to our babies. Let's not get to any conclusions yet. Call Dr. Feinman's office to find out if the medication is safe and call Dr. Blum to ask about the rash and if he's ever seen it before in patients taking daily shots of progesterone in the butt. And just hang in there. This is crazy."

As we hung up, I felt all of the energy drain from my body and my stomach sink to depths unknown. *Herpes? How could that even be? What?*

A very long ten minutes later, the phone rang again, with Carrie on the other end.

"What did you find out?" I asked.

Slightly more composed now, Carrie replied, "The OB said that I should not take the pills because the medication is a type B drug, which means they are not certain if it is safe. And given that we don't know if it is herpes, we might be treating something that does not exist."

"That sounds right," I responded.

She continued, "And I spoke to Dr. Blum's office. They asked me if I could come in today. So I called your mom and she's going to go with me."

"All right. Then get going. And Carrie," I paused, "just stay calm. Hang in there. We're going to be fine."

Nearly two hours later my phone finally rang again. "Hi."

"I just left Dr. Blum's office. He looked at the rash and said he's seen similar rashes with other people on progesterone, but that it was strange that it only manifested on one side. So he took me off of the shots and is just having me use suppositories."

"OK. So he seemed to think herpes was not likely?" I asked, anxious for an answer.

"Well, he wasn't certain, but he sure didn't think so."

The next day, Carrie called me. "It's not herpes. The test was negative."

Instantly, my stomach bounced back from great depths, though my energy managed to drain once again.

I let out a huge sigh. "Thank God." Then some of the stress transformed into anger. "What the fuck was he doing diagnosing you with herpes? None of the other doctors thought that made any sense at all." I stopped to let Carrie speak, but jumped back in. "*And*, he was going to start you on a drug that wasn't even for sure safe for the babies."

"I know. He's an idiot."

A stressful lesson for sure, but a lesson nonetheless—*get a second opinion.* Doctors are not always right.

# 28. MEETING THE GREAT DOCTOR

A few days after the herpes fiasco ended, I left work early, yet again, to meet Carrie at the offices of our OB for our first meeting and examination with the great high-risk OB, Dr. Boris Feinman.

We were brought into a small examining room, where we waited fifteen minutes for signs of life. After the long wait the door burst open in a sudden shot revealing a short man with messy hair and a scrunched face. He had an obvious confidence in his manner and comfort in his own skin. He opened his mouth, revealing a relatively high pitch for a man of supposed power. "Hello there. I am Dr. Feinman. I understand that we have twins to take a look at."

"That's right," Carrie said with a smile on her face.

We were both on our best behavior, holding Dr. Feinman in high regard. We had done some research ahead of the appointment to find out he was not only the top dog in this office, but viewed generally as one of the top OBs on Long Island—and for that matter even in the country.

His voice squeaked on, "Well then. Let's have a look. Go ahead and lie down."

"Do I need to undress for a transvaginal ultrasound?" Carrie asked, used to Dr. Blum's office.

"I don't think so. We should be able to see what we need from the top. If not, we can do that instead," he said.

As Carrie lay down and lifted her shirt to expose a growing belly, he grabbed for a white plastic bottle that looked like a ketchup squeeze bottle with a cone top.

He turned it upside down and squeezed a stream of blue jelly onto Carrie's belly.

She shivered. "Cold," she whispered.

Dr. Feinman had no response.

He replaced the bottle and grabbed for a rounded device not much larger than a fist, which was attached by wire to a stand with a keyboard and small monitor—maybe nine inches diagonal.

The little TV woke with a weak display of undefined green specks, lines, and circles.

"OK. I see one. I see two. Everything looks good to me." With that, he replaced the device and offered Carrie a towel to wipe up with.

It was a quick exam, but the man knows how to do his job.

"Follow me back to my office and we can talk about what to expect and I can answer any questions that you have."

He said the magic word, *questions*. Carrie had her list.

We walked into his office, which was well larger than the others throughout the hallway. The walls were covered with floor-to-ceiling bookshelves stocked to the brim. His desk boiled over with files, papers, books, and figurine caricatures of twins and triplets. The few spots on the wall that were not covered by the bookshelves were covered with diplomas and certifications.

As we sat down, he began by more formally introducing himself. He detailed his schools and degrees, hospital affiliations, and special distinctions. "With the exception of one guy in Nevada, I have delivered the most triplet pregnancies in the country." We were impressed. Quite a distinction indeed. We sensed his dislike for the leading doctor—merely because he was leading.

Next, he began to rattle off a series of do's and don'ts. Do continue to exercise, but nothing too strenuous. Don't eat pond fish due to high mercury levels. Do drink plenty of fluids. Don't lift heavy objects. And on and on.

Then he launched into a list of frequently asked questions by mothers of multiples. Are there greater risks because I have twins? Yes, but for the most part no. Does this mean I will need to have a C-section? Not for certain, but there is a greater chance we will need to.

It was a solid ten minutes of listening to his prepackaged FAQs before he opened up the floor. "All right. Now that I have covered all of that—what questions have I not yet covered?"

Honestly, a good section of our list was obliterated, but there were a few stragglers. His answers were mostly quick and he was more than ready to send us on our way when it seemed we were nearly done. Given our degree of respect for this doctor, we were sensitive of his time.

# 29. THANKFUL

The weather was turning colder and Carrie's belly was growing larger. Nearing ten weeks pregnant and Carrie was already carrying a noticeable bowling ball and wearing maternity clothes. She glowed. Her smile was constant.

The week before Thanksgiving had become our own traditional pre-Thanksgiving Thanksgiving. Rather than battle the airports on the actual national holiday, Carrie's parents would fly into New York the weekend before to celebrate. This year, we had much to be thankful for. It was a full house, with Carrie's parents, my parents, my brother, Adam, and his wife, Alyse, and their daughter, Hanna, and of course, Socks—all crammed into our home. We talked, laughed, told stories, posed for pictures, and had a few drinks—those of us who were allowed to. Alyse rubbed Carrie's belly for luck. We watched as Hanna and Socks took turns chasing each other.

For that evening, all seemed right. It was a scene out of a Rockwell family holiday portrait.

We eventually settled at the dining room table for the feast. With great pride, I carved the turkey and sat at the head of the table—just as I had pictured when I was five, watching my father do the same.

My mother began, "I am thankful for my two boys. I am thankful for the girls they have brought into my life—Alyse and Carrie and of course, Hanna. I am thankful for my husband. I am thankful that Matt and Nancy could be here for this tonight. And lastly, I am excited and hopeful for the two little ones on the way." Tears dropped from her eyes, painting two clear lines down her face. She grabbed for her napkin and began to wipe when Nancy jumped in. "You're not supposed to make us cry!" and the two of them sniffled and laughed and wiped away their tears.

We continued around the table, offering our thanks.

The circle reached back to Carrie. "I am thankful for everyone at this table. I am thankful for my husband." She started to choke on her words. "And I am thankful for the two little babies inside of me that I have wanted so badly. I am doubly blessed." I leaned over and kissed her, with my hand slowly rubbing her back. She choked her breath a few more times, still wiping at her tears.

Lastly, it was to me. "I am thankful for all of the same things that everyone here has already said. I am truly grateful and ecstatic that we can all be here together, celebrating Thanksgiving. It is not something that we have really had the opportunity ever before to do. And, of course, I am deeply thankful for my gorgeous wife and that she is having my babies."

We ate and laughed and drank—enjoying the presence of each other and celebrating this holiday in a way that Carrie and I had never known before. I was thankful for so much but felt a nagging worry for what could still be to come.

# 30. JAW DROP

A few days later, I sat in my office at work, reading through an earnings report from one of the late-reporting companies that I follow. Carrie was headed into the city with my mother for her final visit with Dr. Blum. It was just a simple final checkup before we were handed off fully to our OB. In tow, Carrie had a box full of the leftover injectable drugs that we had over-ordered thanks to the dosage mix-up. We figured the doctor may be able to use them to help cover part of the costs for another couple trying to get as lucky as we were, but who may not have had such strong insurance coverage. The drugs accounted for a huge portion of the cost of fertility treatments.

At around two thirty, just as expected, my phone rang, with Carrie's cell phone number in the light.

"Hey, babe, how'd it go?"

Carrie's voice returned, with her words difficult to understand—she was crying and working to catch her breath between nearly each word. "J—we have a serious problem."

I pushed myself upright into the seat in which I had been slouching. "What's wrong?" I shot back.

"He looked at the embryos…"

"Yes. And?"

"And they both split. We have quadruplets."

I could feel the blood drain from my face. I froze my body—not even breathing—listening closely to Carrie.

"He said that they both split and that one of the fetuses doesn't have a…" Her voice trailed off into a whimper.

"I didn't hear what you said," I responded.

"A heartbeat. One of them does not have a heartbeat."

I stumbled on my words, starting and stopping a few times before getting out, "Where are you right now?"

"We're on our way to your mom's apartment," she said as she wept.

"All right. I'm leaving right now. I'll meet you there in a half hour."

I hung up the phone and stared blankly at the wall for a minute. My fingers tingled as they lay flat and spread on the desk. I swallowed a massive lump in my throat and tossed myself out of the chair. I tore open the door to my office and hustled across the office to Jon Franc's office. I popped my head in the doorway and rapped my knuckles on the open door behind me to get his attention. "Do you have a sec?"

He pulled his head up from the document he was reading and the fingernail he was chewing. "Yeah, sure."

I quickly shut the door behind me and didn't bother to take a seat. "I have a major problem. My wife and I were successful at getting pregnant and in fact we had twins. But she just called me and told me that the embryos both split and we now have quadruplets. I really need to go—and I'm not really sure what it means for the next few days either."

His eyebrows rose and he raised his hands to flail them uncomfortably in the direction of the door. "Yes, of course. Go. Go ahead. Do what you need." His words were hurried and he wore his discomfort with such personal detail on his face.

In a flash, I was downstairs and in a cab headed to the Upper East Side. I took a few deep breaths and stared out the window, thoughts flying past me faster than the buildings and cars.

Then I twisted my body to reach the cell phone in my pocket. I hit the speed dial.

"Hello," Carrie answered.

"Hey, babe. I am in a cab and I should be there in twenty minutes. Where are you?"

"We're in the apartment now."

"So tell me what he said about them splitting and the fourth with no heartbeat," I said.

Slower and a bit calmer now relative to our conversation ten minutes earlier, she explained, "When he started to do the ultrasound, he just stared at the picture without saying anything for a long time. I was looking at the screen, too, and I saw four circles. I asked him, 'Did they split?' He didn't answer and just kept looking at it. I asked again and then he pulled out the ultrasound thingy and told me to get dressed and meet him in his office—that we have to talk."

"My mom was there with you, right?" I asked, immediately feeling guilty for not being there. This was one of the only real appointments that wasn't one hundred percent routine I had ever missed.

Carrie responded, "Yes. And she said she saw the same thing. By this point, I'm crying and your mom is trying to comfort me. So we go into his office and he tells us that both embryos split and that we have four fetuses now. Two sets of identical twins."

That phrase, *two sets of identical twins*, resonated in my head.

She continued, "He said that the fourth baby either has no heartbeat at all, or is just too small for him to see."

I cut her off. "Carrie, I am pulling up to the building. Just hang on, I'll be up in a minute."

I charged past the doorman, who appeared to recognize me and waved me past. I hammered at the elevator button. Up eighteen floors, around the corner and pushed open the door marked 18G, with a Mezuzah pointing me inside.

I walked straight for Carrie and we embraced tightly. We held without words for a full minute.

We released. My mother walked over to me and gave me a tight, short hug and a kiss on the cheek.

Carrie and I sat on the couch to talk.

I started, "So tell me if I understand this correctly. Both embryos split, so we had two sets of identical twins—and one of the babies does not have a heartbeat."

"Well, he wasn't sure. He said it was either too small to see, or there wasn't one."

I dropped my head for a moment, then pulled it back up. "So, what do we do now?"

"He said I can't carry four babies. He said he thought we would need to have a reduction and gave me the name of two fetal reduction doctors."

I shook my head. "What is that? A fetal reduction? Is that like an abortion?"

"I'm not really sure. I think so, but they don't take them out. He said he thought we should probably reduce the single baby whose twin died, because there must be some sort of genetic defect that caused that death—and if they are identical, then its twin must have a problem too." She finished the commentary weary, unsure of herself and unsure that she fully understood what she was told.

"Sounds like it makes sense," I replied. "So we should call these guys for an appointment right now, right?"

I took the names and phone numbers to call for consultation appointments. I booked one appointment and then the other, but both a full week away. An eternity.

I then called Dr. Blum, just to get a little more clarity on the situation.

Carrie and I called Alyse together to break our news. She was dumbfounded and could only share her deepest sympathies and prayers.

I called any friends of mine whom I believed were related to doctors who might be able to offer advice or help—I called those doctors. I asked my parents for any relevant physician they knew. It was a quest to get information and advice immediately from any source. To get it from many sources. It seems strange looking back that these conversations would help at all, but we had never heard of anything like this before and just needed to circle the wagons around us.

After twenty phone calls, some with Carrie at my side and some alone in the bedroom, I sat, drained, on the bed. Carrie walked into the room, hearing the silence, and sat by my side. We looked at each other, leaned in, and rested or foreheads together, then sat motionless.

Minutes later I pulled away and leaned further down, resting my lips calmly against Carrie's belly, kissing our four babies.

Later that evening, we headed back home to Long Island. We were both beat—mentally and physically.

After pulling into the driveway and greeting Socks at the door, we checked the answering machine. The number one blinked in red. I pressed the button.

"Hi, it's Grandpa." The voice belonged to my dad's dad. "I just wanted to call to congratulate you, Carrie. Best of luck to you and Jason. Mazel tov."

As my grandfather's voice stopped and the machine beeped, Carrie and I stared at each other, stunned.

"How did he know?" Carrie asked. We were only a handful of weeks pregnant and had told only the smallest group of immediate family. Generally, we were planning to wait until three months to go public.

I stopped to think how he found out, then realized what must have happened. "I bet my father forwarded the pictures from Thanksgiving to Uncle Steven, not realizing that you were obviously pregnant in them."

It was a sweet message from a man who did not often exude sweetness, so we could not be angry. However, the message was difficult to hear right at that particular time. Perhaps calling him back would have been the right thing to do, but I did not really know how to handle the conversation. We didn't want to discuss the latest but also didn't want to just thank him for calling and act like all was well. I asked my father to take care of it—which he promptly did, after apologizing for sending the pictures. We were not angry—he sent them as a proud dad, not to break news.

# 31. BACK TO THE GREAT DOC

The very next day, we essentially forced ourselves onto Dr. Feinman's schedule, despite push-back from the office.

Still shaken up, we arrived at Dr. Feinman's office and sat in the waiting room. Two women across from us were chatting and embracing their exciting pregnancies. They discussed how wonderful it is to be pregnant despite some of the complications—nausea, backaches, cravings. Nothing that rose to the level of complication we were waiting to discuss.

We were called into an examining room and greeted by Dr. Feinman several minutes later.

His squeaky voice started out, "So, we've had some changes, huh?"

Carrie explained the situation as Dr. Blum had explained it to her, while Dr. Feinman rolled the ultrasound over her belly, staring at the screen.

"Yes, I see. There are definitely four fetuses in here and as you suspected, the fourth does not have a heartbeat." With that, he replaced the ultrasound wand and asked us to join him in his office.

"Thank you for seeing us so quickly, Dr. Feinman," I said. "We are obviously still in a bit of a state of shock, and we could really use your advice."

"Well, you have three live babies in you right now. I have delivered the second most sets of triplets in the country, so while this is new and shocking to you, I deal with it all the time."

I thought about how lucky we were to be sitting in chairs opposite this doctor.

Carrie asked, "But with the complications of having a fourth that has died already and the worries about having triplets to begin with, we don't know what we should do."

Matter-of-factly, Dr. Feinman began to answer, "Well, if you had one baby, I would tell you to keep it. If you had monochorionic twins, I would tell you to keep them." Monochorionic twins are twins that share a single placenta. "If you had quadruplets, I would almost always recommend reducing. But with triplets, it can be a tough decision. It's more case by case."

"OK," I said. "If we did decide to reduce, is there any reason to reduce the singleton or reduce the twins?"

"The twins definitely are riskier," he said quickly. "First of all, there are two of them, obviously, which is riskier. But you also have monochorionic, diamniotic twins. That means they share a big sac and placenta, but have a membrane separating them. Being diamniotic is good, because they can't get their cords tangled, which would otherwise be a big risk. However, they do share a placenta, which means there is a small chance of developing what is called twin to twin transfusion syndrome. That's where the babies share some blood flow and that can cause serious problems if they aren't sharing equally. For serious problems, there's a doctor in Florida that's had some success with fusing the shared flow, but that surgery is very risky too."

I asked, "We spoke to Dr. Blum at our fertility clinic, who directed us to two reduction specialists—we're in with them. Is there anyone else we should talk to?"

"Yes." He lunged forward for a pen and piece of scrap paper. He started writing a name and phone number on the paper as he wrapped up our consultation. "I want you to go see Dr. Jain. She can do a very detailed ultrasound and offer some more advice. Good luck with your decision."

On our way out the door, we were already jabbing away at our phones to make an appointment for a consultation with Dr. Jain.

# 32. PRISONER'S DILEMMA

Two days later we arrived at Dr. Jain's office. We had since found out that she was another high-risk OB affiliated with the same hospital as Dr. Feinman.

A nurse led us into the examining room, where Carrie lay down and prepared for the ultrasound. We both gawked at the machine to her right. Compared to the machines we'd grown used to at the fertility office and the tiny TV at Dr. Feinman's office, this machine looked to have been developed at NASA. The screen was oversized, the base was sprawling—with a full qwerty keyboard, large trackball, and dozens of other functional buttons. The side held multiple different ultrasound devices. The whole computer sat atop a sturdy wide base on wheels. The large TV screen showed a colored "General Electric" screensaver bouncing off the virtual walls.

Dr. Jain entered. She was very trim, with smooth, dark skin and carried a young but impressionably professional appearance.

"Good morning, I am Dr. Jain." Her moderate accent revealed her Indian heritage. As she grabbed for the bottle of blue gel and squeezed the lubricant generously onto Carrie's belly, she asked for the history of our pregnancy. Carrie didn't jump at the gel—it had been sitting on the NASA machine in a warming station. While Carrie explained the details, Dr. Jain kept her eyes fixated on the shapes forming and dancing on the screen, nodding every so often. The TV was full of color, rulers, and motion.

Shortly after Carrie finished explaining the history of the pregnancy to date, Dr. Jain completed her ultrasound and faced us to say, "I can confirm from the ultrasound just what you are saying. There are four fetuses—two sets of monochorionic diamniotic twins—and one of the fetuses clearly has no heartbeat. Why don't you go ahead and get dressed and come into my office so we can talk?"

We complied.

We took our seats in her office and waited a moment for her. She entered and closed the door behind us, signaling that we had her undivided attention.

"I sympathize that you are in a very difficult situation. We know where you stand right now factually but let me just share with you some of the risks of your alternatives.

"If you keep all three of the babies, you are at relatively high risk for a number of problems. The first and most obvious is early delivery. Average gestation periods for triplets are around thirty-three weeks, well short of the forty-week singleton normal gestation period. In your case, originally having quadruplets adds a risk factor, which probably skews the risk towards the earlier end of that benchmark. Preterm delivery brings about a whole host of risks. Just to give you an idea, the most common are underdeveloped lungs, risks of infection, the potential for having a brain bleed, cerebral palsy, and risks of permanent developmental delays."

We both sighed, listening to these awful potential outcomes. I asked, "The risks that you list—they are related to having multiples and ultimately really risks of preterm delivery, right? Are there other risks related specifically to our type of pregnancy?"

She nodded, responding, "Yes, that is correct. These are issues that people face with preterm delivery with singletons, twins, triplets, whatever. It's just that the risk of preterm delivery is significantly higher than with twins and certainly with singletons. Now, I also can't say that if you reduce one or two that you will carry to full term, because you will still have some risk factors— those being that you started with four and that you have had your uterus poked for the reduction. So I would guess that you would still not carry to full term, but you *are* more likely to carry longer than without a reduction."

Carrie asked, "So do you think that we should have the reduction?"

Dr. Jain sighed and collected her thoughts for a moment. "Well, it's not that simple. By reducing, you will be creating a new risk. The reduction in and of itself carries risks to it. There is the possibility that you could lose the entire pregnancy as a result of the reduction.

"There is also another issue that you need to understand."

As she began a new topic, I felt comforted by the generous amount of time that she had already taken with us to this point, and by her desire to arm us with all the information we could possibly need. There was no sense of rushing, that our allotted time was ending or that our questions were bothering her.

She continued, "With the type of twins that you have, there is a real risk of what is called twin-to-twin transfusion syndrome."

I nodded. "Yes, we have heard a little bit about that and we've done some research, but please tell us whatever you can."

She nodded, apparently pleased that we had been doing our own work already. "TTTS can be a life-threatening problem, or it can be benign. If it develops, you have a donor and a recipient. It is usually the recipient who is actually at greater risk of heart failure. Shared blood vessels in the single shared placenta allow blood flow to be shared between the two. One fetus will be the donor and grow very slowly, and the recipient will grow very quickly, putting great strain on its heart.

"In about forty percent of cases with the kind of twins you have, TTTS develops spontaneously. We have no way yet of predicting when it may occur until it does occur. Then, in about forty percent of the TTTS cases, the condition is severe—life threatening."

I quickly calculated the statistic. "So, in about sixteen percent of cases of our kind of twins, there is a life-threatening TTTS?"

She nodded but dodged her head side to side at the same time. "Yes, I suppose that is right."

I continued, "Is there anything that can be done once it is detected?"

"Well, if we discover TTTS, but it has not evolved into a problem, then we don't really want to do anything, because it's the doing that could cause a loss. And if it develops into a problem, it usually happens at a fairly rapid pace. There is a doctor in Florida who does some fetal surgery where he fuses the shared vessels to close off the shared blood flow, but the outcomes are fairly mixed."

We both sighed, feeling overwhelmed with the decisions ahead of us. "So, what do you think of our options?" I asked.

"Well, if you reduce the twins, then you are reducing currently healthy twins for the benefit of a greater chance at having a healthy outcome. If you reduce the singleton, then you could potentially save the twins but face the risks of TTTS as well as elevated risks of preterm delivery. Lastly, you could leave the pregnancy as is, and attempt to carry the triplets."

Carrie spoke in a timid voice. "So, what are we supposed to do here?"

Dr. Jain released a sigh of her own. Her head shook faintly and her hand rose to cover her mouth for a moment. I could tell our agony was being shared, if only for this moment. "I honestly wish I could tell you. I wish there was a clear-cut answer. I think this would be an easier decision if there was already a problem right now and you were forced to do something specific, but that is not the case. I cannot tell you that you are unable to have three healthy babies. I *can* tell you that the odds are not in your favor for that to occur. You need to decide for yourselves. There are only so many statistics and risk factors that I can talk about. In the end, you also need to look within yourselves at the emotional situation you are facing. Before you make any decision to reduce, you might think about what it actually means and if you can live with your decision. You should talk about this with your support system and with each other." She again shook her head and dipped it forward slightly, with a soft shrug. "I wish I could help more."

We walked out of the office mostly in silence. I was not expecting an answer as to what we should do, but the stark realities laid out by Dr. Jain left us far more informed, though also more uncertain. Her honesty about the physical realities, combined with her tender acknowledgment of the emotional and moral side, was extremely powerful.

# 33. A SPECIALIST

I met Carrie on the Upper East Side, where we grabbed hands, walked through the hospital entrance, and went up the elevator.

"Mandel. We have a consultation with Dr. Hofmann," I said, as we reached the reception desk.

"All right. You will need to watch a video first."

She guided us into a small cubicle about the size of one of those picture booths at a mall. There were two school chairs and a small television and VCR sitting on a shelf at seated eye level. She started the tape for us and then pulled the curtain.

The video kicked off with a man in a white lab coat seated behind his desk. His expression was serious and his words heavily scripted. "If you are watching this video, then you are probably facing some very difficult decisions. Multiple fetus pregnancies can be dangerous to the unborn fetuses as well as the mother, and in certain cases, one should consider the possibility of having a fetal reduction. This is without a doubt a very difficult decision—in addition to the obvious emotional issues, there are numerous medical criteria and statistical facts to consider."

Over the next ten minutes, the procedure of a fetal reduction was explained. A syringe filled with potassium chloride is injected into the mother's uterus through the belly. With the help of ultrasound, the tip of the needle is directed into the target fetus, and the injection administered. Death of that fetus occurs nearly instantly.

For the next fifteen minutes, we were deluged with a long series of statistics from many possible permutations of reductions. These covered reductions from two fetuses to one. From three fetuses to two. From three fetuses to one. From four fetuses to … and on and on.

Then each was broken down by timing of the reduction—at twelve weeks; at thirteen weeks … and on and on.

Then those were broken down by degrees of success—lost pregnancy; birth between twenty-five and twenty-eight weeks, birth between twenty-nine and thirty weeks … and on and on.

Then each of those outcomes were explained by survival rates and health of the baby.

It was a dizzying volume of painful statistics. At times, I scribbled notes furiously into our little blue notebook.

The video was closed out with the same doctor behind the same desk adding his understanding that the decision we faced was a difficult one, but that he hoped the hospital's research on the subject might help.

As the movie faded to black, I looked down at my notepad—scribbles of figures, readable headers, and scratches. We were both overwhelmed. Exhaustion was the best description at the end.

We stood and opened the curtain to our private viewing booth and were ushered into a fairly sizeable examining room. An ultrasound technician entered after us and dimmed the light.

In a moderate Russian accent, she asked about the history of the pregnancy as she performed the ultrasound. For several minutes, she explored Carrie's uterus on the screen, all the while taking screen prints. The printer hummed on and off as images scrolled out on waxy paper.

As she neared completion, the door opened and a clean, tall, handsome gentleman entered.

He greeted us. "Good afternoon. I am Dr. Hofmann."

We returned the greeting.

After snapping on rubber gloves, he subbed in for the technician at the ultrasound machine and watched the screen as he asked for us to repeat our history. He finished swiftly and asked us to join him in his office.

After cleaning off her belly, Carrie and I headed down the hall. Dr. Hofmann's office was fairly small, with a filled floor to ceiling bookshelf on one wall. Not surprisingly, most of the book bindings related to pregnancy. I eyed one in particular that stood out as less likely to be in the office of an expert in the field of high-risk pregnancy—*Pregnancy for Dummies*.

He caught my gaze. "My partner, Dr. Steel, co-authored that book." It immediately struck me as odd for a specialist in fetal *reductions* to co-author a book on pregnancy.

He turned his attention quickly back to the issue at hand. "Given what I am able to see from the ultrasound, you are clearly a candidate for a fetal reduction. It is my medical opinion that the greatest chance for a healthy outcome here would be to reduce babies A and B, the live identical twins, leaving baby C, the single baby.

"Now, I am here to help with your medical questions about making this decision. I understand there is a meaningful emotional component, and I would encourage you to talk this over with your families. Now, what questions can I answer?"

Carrie nodded at me and began, "Actually, when we were talking to Dr. Blum, our fertility doctor, he thought we should reduce the single baby whose twin died, because he was worried that whatever genetic defect its twin had, causing it to die early, is likely also carried by its twin."

He cocked his head and chose his first words carefully so as not to entirely quash Dr. Blum's credibility. "Well, actually, I think there *is* a small chance of that being the case, but really most likely it is not a genetic defect. Most people don't realize this, but there are a huge number of pregnancies that spontaneously terminate within the first several weeks for reasons unknown to any of us. And in many of those cases, the woman may not even know she was pregnant to begin with. What we believe to be the case with spontaneous early miscarriages is congenital defects that develop during the first few crucial stages of development—which are *not* genetically related. I would argue that if Baby C's twin died at around seven weeks due to a *genetic* abnormality, then Baby C should have died as well—which was not the case."

He made a compelling point and we nodded.

After a pause, he continued, "To be more confident, we can do a CVS test on that baby's sac. The test involves inserting an instrument into your belly and taking a very small sample of tissue from the baby's placenta. We can run genetic tests on the tissue to determine if there are any genetic abnormalities. It is like doing an amniocentesis, but we can do a CVS even earlier in the pregnancy."

Carrie continued to her next question. "Outside of twins being riskier than singletons, is there any other reason that you would recommend reducing the twins instead of the singleton?" Carrie was priming him for the TTTS answer but wanted to hear his viewpoint without muddying the waters with ours.

He jumped right in. "Actually yes—and that is a very good question. Your twins are monochorionic, diamniotic. That means that they share a placenta but are separated by a membrane. Being diamniotic is good, because the risk of cord entanglement is eliminated. However, sharing a placenta opens them up to a potentially serious condition called twin-to-twin transfusion syndrome. In this case, the twins share blood vessels that run through their umbilical cords and through the placenta. In other words, they share blood supply. This condition can show up at any time and then either be benign or become an issue that can threaten both of the twins' lives."

I followed up. "And there is nothing that can be done about it?"

He flopped his head back from left to right. "Well, there is a doctor in Florida doing some experimental surgery where he actually lasers the shared blood vessels to close them off, but that's not something you would hope to deal with."

I quickly dismissed the idea of experimental surgery and returned to my sixteen percent figure. Then we asked him about the actual procedure.

"I would insert a needle into your belly and direct the tip into your uterus and into the heart of the target fetus, all guided by ultrasound. Then I inject potassium chloride, and the fetus dies instantly."

"So, the fetus feels no pain?" Carrie asked anxiously.

He nodded. "The baby dies instantly." Then he scrunched his face. "But I can't really say for certain if they feel or don't feel anything, to be honest."

We understood—and appreciated the honesty.

# 34. ANOTHER SPECIALIST

Carrie and I met again in the city midday, this time for an appointment we had procured with fetal reduction specialist Dr. Matthew David, thanks to the help of the head physician at my company. On our call alone, we were unable to get an appointment with Dr. David, and our timeframe was relatively urgent.

We were directed to a cold and dreary waiting room. The flooring was reminiscent of an elementary school, with oversized faded brown and green tiles arranged in diamond patterns that had been disrupted by the occasional wrong-colored replacement tile. There were two rows of plastic bucket chairs in a variety of faded colors attached to silver metal legs. The chairs were arranged against the side walls, and thus facing each other, forcing you to trade uncomfortable, fleeting glances with the other waiting patients. The room was otherwise barren and nearly silent, making any conversation north of a whisper general knowledge for the others.

Fortunately, we were called in to Dr. David's office after only a brief wait.

His office was very small, with piles of papers, folders, books, and magazines covering his desk and the credenza behind him. Standing atop his credenza was a high hutch bookcase, filled solid.

He turned toward us from his computer screen and rose to greet us, offering his hand for a shake. "Good afternoon, come on in. Please have a seat," he said as his jowls shook. Dr. David was an overweight man, with an unkempt partial beard and uncombed hair. He wore blue scrubs.

"Thanks for squeezing us in on such short notice. We've really been caught off-guard by our news and are looking for expertise and advice," I said.

He shook his head and his jowls followed after. "Not at all. Let me just tell you a little bit about me, and then I'll turn it over to you to tell me about the situation."

While we were already well-versed with his background from online biographies, we acquiesced. When he got to the part about Wayne State Medical Center, Carrie interrupted. "I am from Michigan."

A smile came across his face. I've come to notice an affinity that Midwesterners transplanted to the East Coast have for each other. I believe it to be a greater and more friendly immediate bond than the reverse case of New Yorkers meeting each other in the Midwest.

Some small talk about Michigan ensued, followed by his explanation that the Wayne State hospital's desire to help the poor overwhelmed the system and didn't allow the moneymaking centers to flourish and support the rest. Voilà—he moved to New York.

Back to the topic at hand—Carrie explained our history to Dr. David, who followed along closely.

"First of all," he began, after Carrie finished, "I don't believe that Baby C necessarily has any genetic defect just because Baby D passed away sometime before seven weeks. There are so many things that can go wrong developmentally in the first few weeks to cause a normal singleton pregnancy to terminate, many times before you even know you are pregnant. On top of that, we can simply do a CVS test to check for genetic abnormalities. To be frank—you are both young, both healthy—I would not expect to see any genetic defects.

"And secondly, without yet having seen the ultrasound, from what you are telling me, I would definitely recommend reducing the twins and keeping the singleton. By doing that you greatly reduce the risks of material preterm delivery, which raises the chances that your little baby will be healthy. Also, with identical twins, there is the chance of something called twin to twin transfusion syndrome."

We interrupted him and explained that we were already aware of TTTS.

"Let me show you something," he said, as he turned to his computer and clicked at the mouse. A PowerPoint presentation opened up and he scrolled through the slides, settling on one titled, "Risks of Cerebral Palsy in Multifetal Pregnancies."

We leaned in to read the numerous table headings and figures, but he quickly pointed to a few items we could not see clearly and translated for us. "The risks of having a baby with cerebral palsy or another lifetime debilitating physical or mental condition is about a third *per baby* in pregnancies with more than two fetuses. By carrying three babies, the chances of you having at least one baby with a serious long-term problem is really very, very high."

He continued his pressure to reduce the twins, suggesting that we go ahead to take a peek inside (ultrasound) and set up a CVS test.

"Can I just ask about timing?" I timidly began to ask. "Health comes first, but it would be a very big deal to get home to Carrie's family for Christmas, especially so soon after the reduction. So, would the time it takes for the CVS test results create a problem for us?"

He jumped right in. "Oh, that's not a problem at all. We can schedule you for the CVS test ASAP and have the results in a day."

Confused, I responded, "But we were under the impression that it takes a full week to get the results from the CVS test."

Ready to answer, he replied, "I can do something called a FISH analysis on the sample that we get, which is almost fully as accurate as the full analysis and will give us what we need."

Learning something new, we nodded, interested in his method.

A few minutes later, Carrie and I were led into an examining room. Well, not quite a room, as there was no door, just a medical curtain. Carrie lay out on the table and exposed her belly for the technician.

In a heavy Russian accent and with a cold voice, she asked Carrie, "Please explain for me—history."

Carrie took a deep breath and walked her through the events to date. The entire time, no words or expressions were emitted from the Russian. Typically, at the very least, we get sympathetic "awws" during the explanation. Not here.

As Carrie completed the story, the Russian's eyes remained trained on the screen, studying closely. Moving the device, then holding it and studying.

Carrie and I grew increasingly uncomfortable and began exchanging glances and short shrugs as if to say, "Is something wrong?" This continued for an eternal five minutes.

Eventually, Dr. David popped through the curtain and took the device from the Russian, who explained to him everything she saw. None of it was news to us.

To conclude the consultation on the table, Dr. David one more time advocated heavily for the reduction of the twins. We thanked him for his time and found ourselves on our way.

## 35. DECIDING WITH A GUN TO YOUR HEAD

That night, we lay in bed, facing each other. Socks was flat on her back with her legs hanging open, exposing her belly for mommy to give rubs. As Carrie slowly dragged her hand back and forth on Socks' smooth underside, we talked decisions.

"I just don't know how I can live with myself if I kill two of my babies," Carrie said, eyes already red with exhaustion and frustration.

I nodded back. "I know. On the one hand, it just seems like we will be improving our odds of having a single healthy baby by reducing, but as Dr. Feinman said, 'If you had one, I would say keep it, if you had identical twins, I would say keep them, and if you had triplets, I would say keep them.'"

After a pause, Carrie started again. "At the same time as I say I can't imagine reducing, I also don't even understand how we could handle three." She began to get worked up as her ability to plan and prepare was being challenged severely. "I mean, we don't even have enough room for three. How do I go anywhere by myself? How do I go to the grocery store? How do I feed three babies at the same time?" Her words drifted into a stressed laugh.

I smiled and interrupted. "I know, I know. The answer is, I don't know. But what I do know is that other people have done it before—somehow. We'd probably have to get help—a nanny."

Her eyebrows rose. "But I never wanted to have a nanny or a nurse. I want our babies to get attached to me, not them."

"Well, we have to figure out a way," I said.

Her eyes drifted to the ceiling in deep thought. I asked, "What are you thinking?"

She came back to me. "We're going to have to get a minivan!" I laughed and she continued, while chuckling, "We're going to need a triple stroller and three highchairs and who gets which room? There are two rooms—is the one who has to sleep alone going to feel lonely? Or are the two who have to share going to be jealous that they don't get their own room? And they're always going to be waking each other up." She drifted with a laugh and a whimper into a light-hearted sob.

I reached around her and pulled her head onto my chest to calm her. "It's all right. People have done it. We'll do it too."

We decided. It would be three.

"Do we keep the appointments?" I asked. We had already set some upcoming meetings with other doctors for second, third, and fourth opinions.

"I guess we should. It's just more information and…I guess we should just in case," Carrie said hesitantly.

"Probably right, but we should set a date. A final decision date. Even though we've made the decision to be happy and excited about our decision, we should just set a final date for after the extra meetings."

We shuffled through Carrie's calendar to find a spot after our last scheduled appointment and well before the twenty-four-week legal cutoff for a reduction.

It would be three. The extra meetings were just for information.

# 36. PREPARING FOR A FULL HOUSE

The next day, full of excitement and nervous energy, we sought out the few stores that carried a selection of triple strollers. This was the sort of purchase that required a test drive.

I tracked down a salesperson at the first store and exclaimed, "Hi, we need to see some triple strollers. We're having triplets." The nice gentleman dropped an unintentional glance down at Carrie's belly and then gave a small chuckle.

"Right this way," he directed us.

There were three kinds of triplet strollers on the rack, assembled and ready for testing. When I pulled the first one down, the first thing I noticed was its weight. These things were going to be very heavy and hard to handle. The stroller was limousine-style, with three baby seats lined up single-file, facing backward at the driver and stretching out more than six feet forward.

Carrie took the handle and pushed, walking straight ahead and turning to go around the island display rack. "Holy crap. This thing is hard to turn!" she soft-shouted to me. I chuckled back, watching her force her hands right to swing the heading left.

"What about the baby right in front of me versus the other two? The other two are jammed in there, with the cover of the other baby's seat right in their faces."

I reached to grab another model while she came around the far turn. This one was more of a double stroller for two to face forward and another seat placed on top, facing back to the driver. It was equally heavy.

Carrie set aside the limo and came to see my new toy. "One gets to see me and the other two face forward? That doesn't seem fair," she said while grabbing a hold of the handle. She pushed the vehicle away from me to test and craned her neck back. "Is this thing even going to fit through a doorway?"

She continued forward to the front of the store and lined up with the open door, pushing ahead slowly, looking back and forth to each side, assessing the clearance. She pushed through, with small touches to the sides, and then pulled backward, swung it around gracelessly, and drove to me. "Well, it fits, but not by much."

I slid the last model toward her, a triple-wide. This stroller was simply three seats side by side by side. "Well, that thing sure as hell isn't going to fit through any doorways!" she laughed to me.

I smiled and shook my head as Carrie took over and drove it right back to the same doorway to illustrate the obvious. The stroller was at least a foot too wide for the standard doorway.

We spent the next ten to twenty minutes taking turns pushing each stroller, turning, and then battling the complicated efforts of folding them up and feeling the weight in our arms. Driving the massive strollers was already difficult and made worse when I reminded Carrie, "Don't forget—these strollers are *empty* now." She responded only with a quick exhale and laugh.

Taking three babies with us anyplace was obviously going to be an event. How do simple tasks like grocery shopping work? Which stroller is easiest to handle and fairest to the babies? Do we rotate babies around positions in the limo and double-decker strollers to be fair or is it best to let them get comfortable with their own seats? We both noodled these issues, but at the same time prayed silently that these would in fact be the biggest challenges to handle. Having a first baby brings up a million questions in your head. We were having three. We needed help—more help—the most help we could get.

"MOST," suggested the nurse practitioner while Carrie waited for her regular doctor to come into the room. Carrie was sitting on the checkup table at her primary care physician's office for a regular checkup, as she discussed the pregnancy with the nurse practitioner checking vitals.

"What is that?" Carrie asked.

"You should look up MOST. Mothers of Supertwins. It's sort of a support organization for people having multiples. It's really for triplets and more, but I know about them because I had twins."

The advice sure was timely, and immediately after the appointment and back at home, Carrie jumped on the web to search it out. She found the site and ordered a starter information packet.

As I walked in the door from work that night, Carrie excitedly explained all she'd learned and the connections she'd made.

"I spoke to this lady, Maureen, today. She founded this thing called MOST—Mothers of Supertwins. I joined and we're getting a packet with tons of information in the mail. I found support groups through MOST and have been chatting with other moms of multiples and pregnant moms."

The development was very comforting and calming for me as well. Aside from going to work during the day, I was by Carrie's side step-by-step. But I'm a guy and I'm not pregnant. Talking about things we've been through and fears of what could be ahead with other women who can truly sympathize mattered—a lot. In a short period of time, Carrie learned much about what could lie ahead of us before and after birth. She learned of new resources for specific conditions. She learned of other manufacturers for strollers and other items that Mothers of Supertwins could need. Perhaps most importantly, Carrie found support in this group of women—unfettered support for our decision to take the risk and save our babies.

# 37. NO HIDING THIS

Weeks ago, we had made plans for dinner with three other couples that I was friends with from high school. The day had come, and Carrie stood sideways in front of the mirror preparing. She shouted to me as she swung her head around, "J! Come here. Look at this!" she demanded. A small stunned smile adorned her face.

"Well then," I said calmly. "It seems you are really not going to be able to hide that." Carrie was unsuccessfully trying on outfits to camouflage the pregnancy. To date, only family knew anything.

"Hide it? No way! I am not supposed to be showing like this. Most people don't show until they are three or four months," Carrie said incredulously.

"I know, but you are carrying triplets."

"Yeah, but I didn't think we wanted to tell people until we were three months. There's no way your friends aren't going to notice this weekend."

"That is most certainly true," I said, the whole time lightly chuckling. "I'll call them this week, so that they are not surprised."

We both stared as Carrie turned and twisted a few times. It was fair to say that Carrie's belly was not growing gradually.

That week, I called each of the couples to tell them the good news, that we were pregnant. I left out the number of babies. While Carrie and I had decided *against* the reduction, we were still inside of our cutoff date for our final final decision, so sharing our news of triplets was still a bit tender.

The week faded and the weekend was upon us. We were nervous. This dinner represented our first "out" appearance. All of our other ventures out of the house were either to medical appointments or for anonymous shopping trips. We had yet to see friends with Carrie's belly just starting to show.

"J—come here!" I heard coming from the bedroom.

I ran upstairs to find Carrie lying on the bed with her back propped up against the headboard. "What's wrong?"

Her head did not rise up to meet my eyes and her hands were spread on either side of her belly. "I can see the bottom of my belly button."

"What?" I asked.

"My belly button! It's always been so deep that you can't even see the bottom of it. But it's starting to flatten out with my belly getting bigger. Come look." She waved me over in great excitement.

I knelt over the bed to look into the black hole. She was right. The black hole had turned into what could more accurately be described as a normal-looking belly button. "Wow. It really is flatter. What's that?"

She flicked her nail at a darker spot in the corner of her belly button and a small piece of lint popped out.

Immediately, Carrie broke out laughing heavily. After a few deep, uncontrolled laughs, her eyes refocused on her belly button and suddenly her laughs snapped significantly louder as she lost the ability to speak.

I was laughing along—it was awfully contagious. I barely made out her words—"Do you know how long that lint must have been in there?"

She tried to speak a few times, but failed miserably as tears began to roll out of her eyes. A minute in, she forced herself calm enough for me to make out words, but only one at a time, with breaths in between, "You…have…to look…at…my…belly…button…when…I…laugh." As soon as she finished her words, she lost control again, but keeping her watered eyes trained on her own belly.

I turned my eyes back south and saw a near puppet show. With each burst of laughter, her belly button inflated outward. It looked like the tip of a long balloon on a clown's last breath. Poking out and quickly disappearing back in. On the "ha," the tip poked out and catching a breath it suddenly retreated in. Carrie's belly button had become a living being all in itself—and we were greatly amused by it.

We drove to the local diner and pulled into the lot. I parked, shut the engine, and, in the silence of the car, turned my attention to Carrie.

"Are you all right?"

Carrie took a deep breath, looked me in the eyes, and said, "Yes. I am. I love you."

With that, we walked to the door to the diner, hand in hand.

We found our friends already waiting for a table.

We all greeted each other warmly with hugs and kisses. Smiles and congratulations were offered and surprised looks accompanied quick points to Carrie's belly.

"I know. I'm showing so much already," Carrie responded. I looked at Carrie closely in the face. After being together for years, I could easily discern between the false happy and the true happy. Her smile and demeanor were genuine. She was basking in the focus on her and her belly. For so long before we got pregnant, talk of babies was bittersweet and since getting pregnant our emotional roller coaster had drained much of the joy. This was an escape and a relief.

We were seated at a table and quickly the hum of several separate conversations filled the evening. Soon after, we were prompted for our drink order by the server—club soda for Carrie. The ordering provided a nice, natural pause. Carrie looked to me and I nodded at her with a hidden smile—permission granted.

She looked around the table and took the floor. "J and I have been through a lot to get to where we are and we considered you guys special enough to want to share our news with you. We're sharing earlier than we planned—we were going to wait until I was three months along—but partly the size of my belly and partly our excitement knocked that out. The news that you don't know is that we are having triplets."

Eyes lit up and jaws dropped around the table. Shock led to "congratulations," which very quickly led to concern. "Are *you* all right?"

"Yes, I'm fine and the babies are fine," Carrie responded, smiling. Her head dipped to the side as she continued, "Things have been a little bit complicated so far and I am definitely considered to be high-risk, but we are hopeful that things go smoothly from here on out."

The group remained in pause for a moment and I added with a chuckle, "It'll certainly be a handful."

The evening continued with conversations on all sorts of other topics. When the dinner drew to a close, we parted ways with additional hugs and kisses and congratulations.

# 38. SOURING

The next day, I joined Carrie for a routine—if I can use that word—visit to the OB. In a small, dark examining room with no window, Carrie was sitting up on the table and a nurse was preparing to draw blood. Dr. Feinman was leaning up against the counter, discussing with us the possibility of having a reduction. The last time we met with him, he was fairly clear on his personal view—that we should keep the triplets. However, this go-around, his demeanor was more matter of fact. He turned to the nurse and asked, "It's a tough situation—what do you think?"

Up to this point, I had waved aside my thoughts that his attitude was uncaring in favor of what I wanted to see—his professional experience. I wanted to respect and trust him deeply, but with his casual attitude this time around, we were growing frustrated. After all, the man who is, by his own estimation at least, one of the foremost high-risk OBs in the country, was deferring to a nurse who only peripherally knew our story.

The discussion went no place helpful and our direct questions were answered mostly with one-liners. Before Carrie had even run through the full list of her questions, he was inching toward the door. He opened it and leaned against it at the same time, firing back rapid responses to our remaining questions.

He slid the door open further and eventually ushered us out and to the front desk to make our next appointment. In a flash, he was gone.

We dropped our rears into the seats of our car and I stopped for a moment to look at Carrie. "Did you feel rushed in there?"

Her eyebrows rose. "Yes. I felt like we were taking up too much of his valuable time."

I sighed. "I don't think we should have to feel like that when we are seeing our doctor. Especially when we have something this difficult going on."

We left the parking lot, actually allowing ourselves to be annoyed with the good doctor for the first time.

# 39. EXPERTISE, BUT NO ADVICE

We walked through the front door of the Long Island Hospital for the first of many times.

The lobby was small, with a very limited and cramped gift shop to the right, a couple of wooden benches in the middle, a small wheelchair parking lot to the left, and an information desk staffed with elderly volunteers.

We caught the eye of one of the volunteers and felt obligated to ask her help in finding our way.

As we approached the desk, we were greeted with an inviting smile. "We have an appointment to meet with Dr. Turno," I said. Dr. Feinman had recommended speaking with one of the key doctors in the NICU—the Neonatal Intensive Care Unit. Here we would learn about the post-birth challenges that could await us. Perhaps the added information would help firm up or tear down our decision.

Her smile turned to confusion. I quickly sensed that queries about the restroom, cafeteria, or locations of overall departments were more her area of expertise. She fumbled with a couple of directories and even made a call or two but to no avail.

"That's all right," I comforted her, "I think we have an idea as to where to go."

We began walking the long hallway toward the elevators, passing an overweight man dressed in a tuxedo seated behind a compact organ, playing Muzak. A mildly amusing and utterly incongruous scene.

At the elevator bank, we encountered a dozen or so people waiting for the next elevator. The crowd was mixed, some holding balloons and brandishing smiles, a couple clenching tissues and holding themselves together, but mostly people with blank stares headed from point A to point B.

The elevator opened, and its large size accommodated the entire crowd.

The doors opened on the third floor, and we shuffled out along with many others, including the balloon holders. A directional sign listed "Labor and Delivery," "Maternity," "NICU," and "PICU." We turned toward the NICU. Following some signs, we weaved our way to a door with a few names marked, including "Turno."

I knocked and the door quickly opened.

We were faced with a woman of average height, short, graying hair, and dressed in street clothes.

"Hi, we are looking for Dr. Turno," I said.

"That's me," the woman responded firmly.

"Hi, I'm Jason Mandel and this is my wife, Carrie. We have an appointment to meet with you."

She shook our hands firmly and swung the door wider. "Sure, sure. Please come on in."

The office was very small. Windowless and more of a closet with bookshelves and a built-in desk running along the wall.

On her request, we shared the history of our pregnancy and explained that Dr. Feinman suggested we come to meet her and get an understanding of the NICU here at the hospital.

She nodded along with our story and waited patiently for us to finish. Her focused body language and silence as we spoke for a long while showed she had no worry we were wasting her precious time. Most other doctors we had met with to this point consistently concerned themselves with the ticks of the clock.

When we finished, the doctor dipped her head to the side a couple of times and sympathized, "You are certainly faced with some difficult decisions and likely a complicated outcome here," she started. "Well, I can tell you a bit about what I have seen in terms of outcomes of triplet births, singleton births, and early deliveries, just to give you a sense for what issues you could be up against.

"With a triplet birth you are facing the obvious first issue, which is a very high likelihood of a premature birth and low birthweight. The three babies would immediately go into the NICU and be evaluated. Based on that evaluation, it is possible—actually likely—that at least one and maybe even all three of your babies will be in separate rooms. We have seven NICU rooms, plus the regular nursery.

"The typical issues premature babies face include possible brain bleeds, which could lead to permanent brain damage ranging anywhere from mild to very severe." She paused for a moment, eyes swinging up to the ceiling as she gathered her thoughts for the next on the list. She tapped her right forefinger onto both her index and middle finger of their left hand, bending them back. "Very often premature babies lack the ability to breathe fully on their own due to lack of full lung development. The lungs are one of the last organs to fully develop. Most certainly before you delivered, if at all possible, your doctors would administer you a steroid shot which helps the babies' lungs develop faster."

Carrie hopped in for a moment. "Yeah. Our niece was born at twenty-five weeks and was in the NICU for quite a while, so we already know some of this. But please keep going, we want to hear it all fresh from you."

She tipped her head. "Oh, I'm sorry."

Carrie straightened up. "No, no. It's OK. She's doing amazing now. Home and healthy."

Exhaling, "Oh that's great to hear." She continued, "They also run risks of a wide variety of issues including jaundice, which we can typically deal with fairly easily, infection, simply because their immune systems are weak and we will be poking them with needles and forcing feeding tubes down into their bellies. They are also at risk for cerebral palsy, visual problems, and developmental disabilities caused by a number of things."

Carrie and I sat in complete silence, listening to a Pandora's box of ailments. Times three. We all sat in silence for a moment, and then the doctor realized she had more to say.

"And as far as a singleton goes, should you decide to reduce, well, we would face most of the same issues. The difference being that with a singleton, it is more likely that you will be able to carry closer to full term. Each week closer substantially improves your baby's odds of surviving and of being healthy. To give you an idea, babies born at twenty-five weeks carry a survival rate of fifty percent. The rate for thirty weeks is close to ninety-eight percent."

I flashed back briefly to the video full of statistics that we watched in a booth not long ago.

"Well," I said slowly. "This is all very difficult to hear, but certainly important."

Carrie followed, "Do you have any advice for us? We're having a very hard time figuring out what we are supposed to do."

Dr. Turno dipped her head, much the same as every other doctor had to whom we had posed this question. "That is a very difficult question. It's certainly not something I can answer for you. I can simply tell you that I have cared for many sets of triplets here and many of them have left here in great shape. But the real truth is, many of them have left here in need of long-term care," she cocked her head to the side, "with permanent disabilities. There are certainly some heartbreaking stories from the NICU—that's just the truth. The odds—purely looking at the numbers—clearly tell you that you have a far greater chance of walking out of this hospital without any problems if you come in with one baby versus three. Now, please don't take that to mean that I am suggesting you have a reduction. I'm just trying to tell you the facts I know—from this side of the world—in the NICU."

I dropped my head to my hand to wipe my forehead, then flopped my hand down onto Carrie's leg.

"Can I answer any questions for you?" asked the doctor.

"I don't know," I said. "We've already heard so much advice from so many different people that I am not sure we have any more questions."

Carrie jumped in with one final question. "What happens if one or two of our babies are healthy enough or get well faster than the other or others? Would you send home one or two of them and keep the third here?"

"That is a good question. We try to send home twins, triplets, and more at the same time, but being in the NICU is very costly and we can only fend off the insurance companies for so long until we simply have to discharge a baby."

We sighed at the response, realizing the further complications.

Dr. Turno broke the silence. "Why don't I show you around our facilities, so you can see what you are dealing with?"

We rose and followed her out of the office and down a long hallway. We came upon a set of large double doors with a sign reading "Neonatal Intensive Care Unit." She grabbed the ID hanging on a string around her neck and pressed it against a black box on the wall next to the doors. A loud click followed and she pushed the doors open.

We walked in behind her. The main area was relatively dark and drab, with a set of windows with the shades drawn from the inside on our right. She led us ahead and turned right around the corner and through a door into an intermediate room between the hallway and one of the NICU nurseries. It was a small space with a sink, a rack of scrub-sets, a table, and shelving with various medical supplies. "You will have to scrub in up to your elbows every time you come into a NICU room. We need to keep the potential for infections as low as possible."

Prompted to look into the nursery, we poked our heads in. There were about ten incubators, each with dozens of wires spilling out and connecting to flat panel monitors overhead. The monitors were chiming, some of them slowly, some of them soft, some loud and urgent. Chime speeds, pitches, and volumes were changing constantly and flashing lights on the monitors came and went. A few parents sat inside near their own babies' incubators—none even turned to flash a glance our way. Rather, one mother kept her hand through an access hole and on the back of a tiny premature baby. Another sat quietly in a rocking chair staring blankly through the plastic into her baby's incubator.

Dr. Turno tapped us and walked out of the room; we followed.

"As I mentioned earlier, we have seven NICU rooms of varying sizes. We generally divide up the babies by their degree of needs and staff each room accordingly. The most severe cases will be in a room with close to one-on-one nurse coverage twenty-four hours a day, and another room for babies nearing the end of their stay at the hospital with closer to five-on-one coverage."

We nodded as we followed her down the hallway. All the while, she would briefly pause to point into another NICU nursery. Lastly, she walked us to the family center, a room with a television and vinyl-cushioned bench seating built into the wall, plus a few chairs. There was a wall full of lockers, which she explained could be used by the families to store belongings while visiting their children. Around the corner there were two computers for convenience and a coffee machine that got a lot of use.

She led us back to her office and wished us luck, offering her card for us to call with any further questions. We thanked her for her time and headed back to the elevators.

"That's a pretty stunning scene in there," I said.

"Yeah. Those babies in there are so tiny—and there are so many of them, too," Carrie responded.

We hustled our way into an elevator with a large crowd, to the main floor, down the long hallway, past Muzak-man and the elderly volunteers, and out the automatic sliding doors.

Our car ride home was very quiet at first. We each reviewed the visuals of the NICU, the motionless babies, and the exhausted parents. I broke the silence. "I keep picturing us trying to go back and forth between three different rooms to be with each of our babies."

"I know. Me too," said Carrie. "I wouldn't want to leave any of my babies alone at all."

"And how do we even deal with having one or two babies sent home while we still have another in the NICU?" I added.

"I have no clue. I'd have to be home with our healthy baby or babies and our sick baby or babies would be all alone at the hospital."

We spent the rest of the ride home each picturing ourselves tag-teaming between rooms. We couldn't even picture, practically speaking, how it would work to have our babies split between home and hospital.

We pulled into the driveway and opened the door to a quiet house, broken only by the sound of Socks' feet as she jumped down from the couch and ran to greet us, tail and rear bouncing side to side. Carrie grabbed the mail as I bent down to rub Socks' belly she had just exposed by rolling onto her back. She tucked her chin to lick my hand while I massaged.

"Oh, the packet came," Carrie said. "The MOST packet."

The letter-sized envelope was filled tightly with a packed folder Carrie slid out from the top. We walked up to the living room and crashed down onto the couch to explore the contents. There was an awful lot of material—a welcome letter, photocopies of relevant articles, coupons for supplies, frequently asked questions lists, and more. We started out reading part of something and shouting out *look at this* back and forth several times. The callouts eventually slowed and we focused more on the real content of the materials.

"Here," I said. I handed Carrie an article on parenting children with cerebral palsy. She passed me a pamphlet on state and federal services for children with mental disability. The information was helpful and it was honest. But it was frightening, especially in light of the extra doctor meetings we'd just had.

# 40. DEADLINE

D-Day arrived. It was time for a final final decision on the pregnancy. We had each spent a lot of time thinking about the triplets and about the reduction option. We both thought of our choice all day, but the pressure built that evening.

"Let's get our parents on the phone, one set at a time, to just talk through all of the issues one more time," I suggested. Carrie agreed.

I grabbed two cordless phones and we each sat on our bed, ready to talk. Carrie dialed her parents first. Carrie's father answered, "Hello."

"Hi, Dad."

"Doo!" exclaimed Matt.

"Hi. Is Mom there? We want to talk to you guys about something."

"Um—sure. I'll give her the phone and I'll go grab another one." His voice had softened, realizing this was a serious call.

"Hi, Doo, how are you?" Carrie's mom, Nancy, asked, softly.

"I'm all right. We just wanted to," a click on the phone indicated Matt picked up, "get a chance to talk to you about the decision we have to make. We set today as our final decision date about whether we are going to reduce. You guys already know that we've met with a lot of doctors to explore this, but the only thing that is clear is that there is no clear answer. We're not calling to ask you to give us the answer, but just to help us talk through the issues, with all of the information we have gathered."

Carrie and I went on for several minutes talking through the various doctors' meetings we had, the statistics we had learned, and the visuals of the NICU at Long Island Hospital. They listened to us in silence, allowing us to share our worries and our wishes, until we ran out of gas.

"You certainly have a lot of things to consider," said Nancy, gently, "and it sounds like you've done all of the homework you could possibly do. Getting to a decision is obviously the hardest part. I don't know how I would be able to make a decision if I were in the same situation."

"I know," said Carrie. "I guess we were just looking to see if you had any thoughts."

"We have a lot of thoughts about this, but it sounds like you've been through them all already," said Matt. "The item that all the doctors seem to agree with is that having triplets leaves you with a very serious chance of one or more of the babies having serious disabilities."

*That's true*, we both thought, nodding to each other.

Matt continued, "I am not saying that you would love a child of yours any less at all if they had a mild or severe disability—not at all. But the risk of disability seems to be the main consideration here—a theme."

"I know, you are right," Carrie responded. "But the alternative of killing two of my babies is so hard to even consider. It seems so hypocritical—that we tried as hard as we did to get pregnant, now we are considering ending two of our babies' lives."

Nancy spoke slowly. "I think you have to think about this situation separately from your attempt to get pregnant. You were successful in getting pregnant—a little too successful—but this is where you are now."

"Yes, but I don't want to play God," whimpered Carrie.

After a long pause, Matt answered, very gingerly, "But you kind of already did." We all stopped and thought for a moment. Silence on the phone line matched the silence in our room as we stared into each other's watery eyes.

Matt continued, "When you went ahead with in vitro, you sort of already did play God. I'm not saying that's bad, it just *is*."

I looked at Carrie and replied to everyone, "Well, you're right about that." We all sat quietly for another minute, then I broke in again. "All right, I think we just need to keep thinking about this and talk some more. We're also going to call my parents and have the same talk."

"OK. I'm sorry we weren't too much help—it's a very hard thing to face. I don't think I've ever faced a decision as serious as this. We love you both." Matt echoed Nancy's comments, then Carrie and I thanked them and we all hung up.

Feeling a bit drained, we took a break for a few minutes to get a drink of water, use the bathroom, and just clear our heads again, before calling my parents.

The phone rang just once, then a cheery "Hello" from my mom.

"Hi, Mom, it's me—and Carrie's on with us also."

"Hi, guys," she said, calming her tone. She knew immediately from my tone and that having us both on the line together meant this would be serious.

"Can you get Dad on as well?" I asked. "We want to talk to you guys and bounce some thoughts off of you."

"Hang on." A click and then both voices were on with us.

"Thanks, guys," I said. "We picked today as our deadline for making a decision about reduction. We thought that we had mostly come to the determination that we were not going to reduce, but we've been to even more doctors and after considering all of the facts that we've been presented with—we're not so sure anymore."

"Jas, Car, you know that we love you both so much," my dad began, "and Mom and I wish that you both didn't have to face a decision like this. We can't make it for you, but we can definitely talk through the issues. I know it is not terribly easy to do it in this situation, but whenever I face difficult decisions in life or at work, I usually try to take the emotion out of it and look at the facts. It sometimes makes the situation easier and clearer."

Carrie looked at me and jumped in. "But how can we remove the emotion from this situation? We're talking about possibly killing two of our unborn babies."

"I know, I know," said my dad very softly, treading carefully. "I understand how emotional this decision is. But just for a moment, let's just look at the facts and the numbers and the potential outcomes that you have spent the past few weeks—on your own—gathering in your meetings with several doctors."

"The numbers start to get confusing after a while," I responded, "but the thing that has struck us most about them is how high the probabilities are for at least one of our three babies having a lifelong disability, potentially very severe. And the numbers are still high for more than one having a disability."

My mom started back quickly. "I know that you are thinking, and it is fully true, that you would love any baby you have, despite disability. But at the same time, you should also consider that loving them is just one thing. If you have one or more babies with lifelong disabilities, you have to understand you could be facing a high degree of special needs. And that need will *never* go away. I have a friend who I used to be very close with—she's had two sons who are disabled. She absolutely loves them both dearly. As her friend, I've watched the toll it's taken. They need her attention *all* the time. And they will never grow out of that need."

We were all silent for a minute. It was clear what they thought was the right decision, without offering direct advice on what to do.

"I understand what you are saying," Carrie stammered, "but I just don't understand how I can kill my babies." Tears began rolling down her face and her words became labored. "We worked so hard to get to the point where we could be pregnant and have children and now it just seems too hypocritical to turn around and take two of their lives."

I leaned over and hugged Carrie tight. "Just give us a minute, guys," I said. Carrie's body shook as she struggled to take breaths between sobs. I held her, rubbing her back, knowing where our decision was heading—and not knowing in what shape *we* would get through this. There were several times over the months before when I held Carrie in just the same way, with sobs pouring out, as we failed to get pregnant. I now found myself in the same physical position, comforting Carrie over our need to intentionally end part of our pregnancy.

I pulled away slightly. "Sorry, guys," I said into the phone.

"We're sorry," said both of my parents. My dad continued, "Please understand that we are not telling you what to do and we will be here for you in any decision that you make."

"I understand." I said. "I understand what you are telling us and why you are telling us. We just need to talk about it some more. We're going to go now, all right? We love you guys."

"Please call us back if you want to talk more or about anything else," my mom said. "We love you both very much."

We each pressed the off button on our cordless extensions and held each other some more. After a long silence, Carrie restarted, barely getting the words out, "So, we have to reduce, I guess."

At this point it had become clearer that reduction was the smart option for us. "I think so. I just get so scared thinking about running back and forth between three different babies in three different NICUs, all with three different problems. And trying to care for three *healthy* babies sounds nearly impossible to me, I couldn't even begin to imagine the same thing with babies with severe disabilities. And I also think, selfishly, about our lives. I know that our lives will change drastically by having a baby and I am ready for that, but our lives will be so unbelievably different—forever—with multiple babies with disabilities. I also know that there is a chance that all of them will be perfectly healthy. The problem is, despite all of the probabilities that we've learned—from Dr. Feinman, from Dr. David, from Dr. Hofmann, they almost don't matter. If we have a baby born with cerebral palsy, or two or three, they have it one hundred percent, not thirty percent. They will either have a disability or not. So, a thirty percent statistic for this or a ten percent figure for that—those numbers ultimately don't help that much."

Carrie listened intently and dropped her head at the end. "I know." A long pause. "We should reduce." She then started but barely finished the last words of the conversation. "I just don't know how I can ever get over this…"

I held her tightly and rocked her back and forth. I worried about the damage a decision like this could do to us—individually and to our relationship.

It would be one.

# 41. ONE MORE TEST

Early the next day, we discussed logistics and quickly agreed on Dr. Hofmann over Dr. David. We had every reason to believe they were both great doctors, coming so highly regarded. We were left only wondering if Dr. Hofmann could perform the FISH analysis that Dr. David had suggested as a fast result for the CVS test. I called and had to leave a message about my question. Surprisingly, it wasn't long at all before Dr. Hofmann returned my call. "How can I help you?" he said.

"Well, first, I again appreciate your consultation with us—it was very helpful—and for getting us in so quickly for the CVS test."

"Sure. No problem at all."

"Carrie and I just wanted to know if you would perform a FISH analysis. We met with Dr. David, who had mentioned it to us. He said it is a lot faster to get the results and getting this taken care of quickly is actually pretty important to us."

In a kind tone, Dr. Hofmann replied, "Sure, I understand. The problem with the FISH analysis is that it is really only ninety percent accurate, so I generally do not do it. Especially for a situation such as you have, where we are basing a reduction decision on the results."

Surprised by his answer, I stammered to get my first few words out. "Really? I...I...well, I am just very surprised to hear that. Not to say that I would expect all of these tests to be a hundred percent accurate, anyway. But I certainly would have expected Dr. David to share that information with us. Well, if that is the case, then I think we would agree—do the full CVS test. Is it all right to go ahead and get on your calendar for the reduction ahead of time, so that we know we can get in on time?"

"Sure you can. The test should take about a week, so schedule it assuming that time frame."

I thanked him for his help, hung up the phone, and reflected on my true feeling of appreciation for a conversation with a doctor who did not feel rushed or of great inconvenience.

A few days later, I walked out of work midday, as I was growing accustomed to doing. The guilt of missing work mixed with the fear that I would in fact not be missed. I popped my head up out of the subway into the blustery winds of that early December day. I stepped over a small snowbank to cross the street as I saw Carrie already waiting for me in front of the hospital. We walked in together, up to the fourth floor, and approached the reception desk.

"Hi, we have a two o'clock appointment with Dr. Hofmann for a CVS test."

"Mandel, right?" she said.

I nodded.

With her eyebrows raised and head cocked, the receptionist said, "You had an appointment for genetic counseling at one o'clock."

A wave of frustration quickly passed over me as I immediately assumed we would need to reschedule and as a result, have to delay the reduction. "We have a two o'clock CVS test. That's all we know about. I don't even know what genetic counseling is."

"All right." She looked at another receptionist and shook her head, clearly frustrated by what I presumed to be repeated scheduling errors. "I think we can still fit you in."

She sent us downstairs to another office for this so-called genetic counseling, where we met our geneticist, a relatively young lady, I would guess twenty-five years old. We sat with her for about a half an hour answering a seemingly endless string of highly repetitive questions, *Is your father still alive? Does he have any genetic diseases that you know of? Does he have any history of heart problems? Any history of this, that, or the other thing? Are his parents still alive? How old were they when they died? What did they die of? Did they have any history of heart problems or this, that, or the other problem? Any known cases of birth defects in your family? Any mental disabilities in your family?*

All the while, the geneticist was drawing boxes, connecting lines, arrows, and dotted lines and making small symbols next to and inside of the boxes.

Finally, at the end, she shared her conclusion. "Well, there doesn't seem to be anything in the family history that points to any particular genetic risks that I can see. In fact, you both actually stand a good chance of not being carriers of similar genetic diseases."

Being a Jew with my heritage traced mainly to Eastern Europe and Russia, I run a real risk of being a carrier of certain "Jewish" genetic diseases. I had been tested for four of the most common ones already, with negative outcomes, but was advised to test for the remaining five diseases—a simple blood test. This was mostly a precaution, advised our geneticist. Since Carrie has a mixed Western European background, that meant it was highly unlikely that she would be a carrier of any of them. Only if *both* of us were carriers would we be at risk of passing it on, with a twenty-five percent chance.

Following the genetic counseling, we were ushered back upstairs, where we checked back in with the receptionist and then sat in the soothing waiting room for just a few minutes until we were called into the office.

The nurse showed us into a small examining room, not much larger than the gurney and ultrasound machine that sat inside. I circled around to the far side as the nurse droned, "Please to get on," in a thick Russian accent as she motioned for Carrie to lie down on the bed. Carrie carefully climbed onto the bed, lay back, reached for my hand, and squeezed. I pulled my focus toward her face to find her furrowed eyes seeking mine. I smiled softly and whispered, "You'll be fine. I love you."

"Please to pull up your shirt," said the Russian in a lab coat. As Carrie pulled up her shirt, the nurse reached for a white towel which she placed half on Carrie's belly and half on her shirt, then wrapped the excess under the shirt. Similarly, she protected Carrie's pants by tucking another towel into her pants and laying the rest flat on top.

"Good afternoon," barreled Dr. Hofmann's seemingly large voice in this small, quiet room. "We are going to be doing a CVS test today, right?"

"That's right," Carrie answered, then stammered, "I'm a little bit nervous."

Dr. Hofmann responded while he snapped on a pair of rubber gloves and reached for his tools, eyes moving back and forth from his task at hand and Carrie. "I understand, but everything should be fine. This is a pretty standard, easy procedure." He smiled for a moment at Carrie and then turned back to his instrument tray, pulling a white plastic film off the top of a white plastic tray somewhat resembling a frozen dinner. "I will talk you through the whole thing. Everything I do will be guided by ultrasound," he said, nodding his head at the monitor.

"Thank you," Carrie responded, sending her still nervous eyes back to me.

Dr. Hofmann pulled a surgical sponge from one section of the tray and dunked it into a dark liquid in another section. "I am going to sterilize the entire area with iodine. This is to protect against any infection getting inside of you and into your uterus." For more than a minute, he rubbed the dark orange-soaked sponge all over Carrie's belly, painting over and over across her. Some small drips rolled down Carrie's sides, staining the bed sheets. I was glad to see his thoroughness in avoiding infections. A minute is a long time to rub over and over the same area. He finally finished rubbing, dropped the sponge back into the tray, and handed it to the nurse, who turned, stepped on a pedal, and dropped it into the trash. The doctor reached for another tray, peeled the top off, and then repeated the entire cleansing process. Now *that's* a thorough job.

He grabbed for a long needle from the instrument table and then turned his focus back to Carrie's face. "This looks worse than it is. I am going to make a *very* small hole in your belly, push this into you, and follow the progress on ultrasound. I will be watching the screen to guide the needle to your uterus, poke through, and take a very small sample of tissue."

The nurse reached across and placed the ultrasound sensor onto Carrie's belly as the doctor readied his needle. Carrie grabbed for my hand and we squeezed tightly.

He talked us through it. "All right. I am going to press the needle into you now, it should only feel like a pinch." He pushed quickly onto her belly and the needle sunk through. All of our eyes turned to the monitor, which showed a mess of rounded objects with one small but growing perfectly straight line—the needle. We all watched as it grew and headed toward the uterus.

"I am getting closer now and just want to be sure everything is positioned properly before I reach for the tissue," he said, then quieted for concentration. "Now I can get some samples."

He began to push and pull the needle in and out by probably only a few millimeters, but looking back to Carrie's belly, it seemed more violent to us at the time. With each motion, the needle pulled up the skin around the incision and then pushed it down.

"That should do it," he said. He pulled up at the needle, and the skin on her belly followed until the tip popped out, snapping her back into position.

He placed a small gauze pad on the needle spot as we all breathed a sigh of relief. "I think we got a good sample there, it should test up fine," said the doc.

After we both thanked him, he shook our hands and was off again.

The whole thing really took only a couple of minutes.

# 42.  A BREAK FOR JINGLE BELLS

The frigid air was bone dry and the car hadn't fully warmed up even though I had let it run for ten minutes. Carrie eased herself into the passenger seat and I dropped down behind the wheel. We were headed to a formal Christmas party at the home of the parents of one of Carrie's good friends. Having been to several parties thrown by the family, we knew to expect formal, classy behavior. Erin's parents, the host and hostess of the party, would surely be moving about, greeting all of the guests. Erin's mom engages you with her smile and caring conversation, genuinely interested in what you have to say. Her dad leads with his humor, sure to elicit laughs with each pocket of holiday revelers he steps into.

The classy behavior typically begins to deteriorate a couple of hours in, as the freely flowing liquor loosens this already jovial group. The music grows louder, and songs more frequently become the top dance hits from Prince, the Police, and Michael Jackson (the early years). The ladies love this stuff.

Carrie turned to me as I backed out of the driveway. "I spoke to Erin yesterday about this party. I warned her that I'd be showing—just so she knows ahead of time."

I smiled. "What did she say?"

"She said that I'm only eleven weeks pregnant and that I'd be able to hide it."

I laughed.

"I know," she giggled back. "I tried to explain to her that I'm showing a little already. Anyway, I tried to tell her, but I don't think she told anyone else."

We made the final turn down a windy, wooded block, with houses hidden at the end of long driveways and behind varied and clean landscaping. We searched for house numbers but that quickly became unnecessary as the lights and activity grew to our left. We reached the first entrance to the circle drive and were directed by a gentleman in a red jacket to proceed further, to the second entrance. As we continued forward, I drove slowly to take in a view of the house. The home was enormous, with a great wingspan spreading outward from a formal entryway in the center. Cars were parked all along the side of the road and in the driveway. I turned left at the second entrance and proceeded to the front door, where Carrie and I were both greeted by two more gentlemen in red jackets. I walked around the car and took Carrie's hand. "You all right?" I asked.

"Yes, I'm good."

She was not lying. Erin is one of Carrie's best friends and I could tell Carrie was nervous, but still absolutely excited to see her.

We opened the front door to the sound of Christmas music and the smell of fine foods. The foyer was grand, with a large mahogany staircase rising toward a balcony on the second floor. To our right an arched opening revealed a formal living area with a couple dozen people chatting away and laughing. A cheery uniformed lady gladly took our coats as Erin appeared through the archway.

"A little?" Erin shouted, with a wide smile across her face. "You said you were showing a little! It's like you are carrying a basketball under your shirt," as she laughed at the situation.

Carrie giggled. "I tried to warn you. I said I might not be able to hide it." Carrie wasn't upset or embarrassed, she was proud to be pregnant.

"Ya *think*?" Erin guffawed.

The party was easy to enjoy. Erin's friends and family congratulated us unendingly, carolers sang and rang bells, superb hors d'oeuvres were passed freely, drinks flowed from at least three different bars, conversation was easy and upbeat, and the chocolate strawberries were the best I'd ever tasted. The difficult part was in explaining the speed at which Carrie's belly had expanded. The real story included the elimination of two fetuses by our choice, a highly personal topic and one less than ideal for a glorious Christmas party. We managed our way through it, largely with less than complete explanations including hyperstimulation, high fluid, and anything else we could think of, but we avoided the truth.

We only stayed a couple of hours, exiting just as the real party started to get underway. I did manage to get a few drinks in me. After all, I came with a designated driver. I must have used the same trite joke half a dozen times, "I'm drinking for two now." It still manages to get a decent laugh.

# 43. WE'RE HAVING MADDIE

We checked in for the CVS tests after a week, but were told to wait longer. Apparently sometimes it just takes longer, we were told. The delay made us ever more anxious. We were both fairly confident the results would come in negative but our concerns grew over the timing of the reduction. The longer we waited to get to the reduction, the more our Christmas trip to Michigan would be at risk. It sounds selfish, but with all that had happened, being around Carrie's family for the holiday was even more important.

The results finally came in and as we expected, they were negative for any genetic abnormalities. The test rewarded us with an additional piece of information that we could celebrate like most normal expecting parents get—our baby was a girl!

From our list of four names, we selected Madelyn Elizabeth, Maddie for short.

# 44. THE WORST DAY IMAGINABLE

A few days after the results came in, we showed up together for our appointment. The day had come for our multiple pregnancy reduction. We walked to the front desk, sweaty palm in sweaty palm. We were greeted and asked to have a seat in the waiting room.

We sat in silence, exchanging glances with each other and looking around the room at the various medical advice and advisory signs. We were anxious to be called but nervous to go in. At the same time we sought to put the procedure behind us and wished it didn't have to be done.

It was not long before we were called in by a nurse. She led us back into an oversized procedure room. There was a gurney in the middle of the room, set with the back tilted up, flanked by an ultrasound machine. There was nearly ten feet of space on either side of the bed to get to the countertops and cabinets, which were the only non-white surfaces in the room.

Patting the bed, our Russian nurse looked at Carrie. "Please go ahead and lay down on the bed. I will be back with Dr. Hofmann in a few minutes." With that, she walked to the exit, pulled a curtain, and closed the door behind her.

Carrie took a breath. "Here we go," she said and slid her rear onto the bed, swinging her legs up. "I'm scared."

"I know. This is not something we should have to deal with." I stroked her hair and leaned in to give her a kiss just as her face started to crunch and tears welled up in her eyes. The emotion flooded over her.

At that moment, Dr. Hofmann walked in with our nurse and pulled back the curtain. "Good morning." Quickly after his greeting, his eyes came up from the chart in front of him to realize the sensitive moment. "I know this is difficult for many people to deal with. I will try to make the physical part of this as smooth as possible."

We both nodded in recognition and he immediately went to work alongside our nurse in preparing the instruments. Carrie pushed her shirt up over her belly. The nurse placed a white towel over Carrie's legs, tucked it into the top of her pants, and pulled down a bit. Carrie's full belly was exposed for the doctor.

He proceeded to sterilize her entire belly the same way he had for the CVS test, with repeated coatings of iodine. As he rubbed, he began to speak. "Well, you both know what this procedure entails in general. Specifically, I will be using a long needle to reach through to babies A and B. I will be guiding the needle's progress by ultrasound, just like in the CVS test." He nodded at the screen to his left.

"The babies may move quite a bit, so I need to be slow and steady. If we can't get through to the right spot because they are moving too much, I will have to temporarily paralyze them, but we prefer not to. Once we reach Baby A, I will insert the needle into its heart and inject a small amount of potassium chloride, which will stop the heart instantly." His harsh reality description of the procedure was not delivered from a lack of sensitivity—it was for clarity. He described the details that we needed to know and understand. We appreciated the direct commentary.

He continued, "Then the next step depends on how it goes. We *have* seen cases where the baby's twin passes concurrently with the first. So we will be watching for activity in both babies on ultrasound. If Baby B does not pass, then we will try to reposition, but may need to pull the needle out entirely in order to reach Baby B. We will then repeat the procedure."

We looked at each other and took a deep breath. Carrie turned back to the doctor. "Please be careful."

He smiled back at her. "I will be, most certainly."

He completed the sterilization and motioned to the nurse to take position. She squeezed some of the blue gel onto Carrie's belly and placed the sensor on top of it. Images jumped to life, all blurry and jumbled to us, but clear as day to the doctor and nurse. They talked to each other about positioning, creating a plan of attack.

"Well, they sure are moving around a lot right now. Doing flips," the doctor said with some concern. We grew even more nervous about the danger of the procedure. Seeing their activity on the screen also made Carrie whimper further. They were very alive.

A plan apparently emerged as the doctor turned back to Carrie. "All right. We are going to get started. You are going to feel a pinch and possibly some pressure as I put the needle into you. Just stay calm and still."

Carrie nodded and her eyes teared. She turned her head away from the monitor and over to me, grasping my eyes in hers. I grabbed tightly onto her hand and Dr. Hofmann prepared the needle positioning.

Carrie released a minute moan as the needle passed through her skin. I peered away from Carrie's eyes and over to the monitor every few seconds. I could see the needle growing on the image as he inserted it further.

"What's happening?" Carrie whispered to me.

"I am just getting the needle into position now," said the doctor, intercepting our conversation.

Carrie and I looked at each other again. Her anxiety was growing the closer it came to the end of one of our babies' lives. She shut her eyes tightly and squeezed my hand.

"All right, I am in position and am going to insert the needle."

He moved the needle downward ever so slightly, all the while with his eyes trained on the screen. He then squeezed the plunger, forcing some of the potassium chloride into its heart. He stopped and watched the screen closely. I turned my attention closely to Carrie, leaning in and bringing my head next to hers.

"The heart has stopped," he said. "We need to wait thirty seconds or so to be sure."

The room remained dead silent for an eternal thirty seconds until he finally confirmed the result. Carrie, working to keep still, let out a very quiet and short whimper. I kissed her head.

"We definitely need to pull out and reposition for Baby B," he said.

We said nothing in response as he pulled the needle out. We kept our heads together.

He again surveyed the ultrasound as the nurse repositioned the sensor to get a better image. He picked his spot and asked her to hold it still, then held the needle over her belly.

"Another pinch," he warned Carrie.

The needle went in and again he followed its progress on the screen. He announced once again that he was in position, inserted the needle into our baby's heart, and pressed the plunger. Silence in the room.

"No heartbeat," he said. "We'll just wait thirty seconds again."

He slowly pulled the needle back and as it cleared the skin, announced, "All right, that's it."

Carrie wept softly for a minute as I held her tightly. My eyes teared, but I did not cry. I don't know why. We were still as the doctor and nurse clanked instruments and disposed of garbage.

He walked around to my side of the bed and leaned in to us. "I know how hard this is, but I think you are giving your baby the best shot at life that you possibly can."

I nodded at him and thanked him. Carrie squeezed out a belabored "Thank you."

"When you feel comfortable, go ahead back into the waiting room and please wait for us to recall you in about a half an hour. We need to recheck the status after a period of time." In other words, in case another miracle of life occurred, we needed to be prepared to re-snuff it out.

We were back in the waiting room, three of us, no longer five of us. We didn't speak much, just sat in linked chairs, tightly holding hands and leaning into each other. Others came and went while we waited, but nobody chose to sit near us—we must have exuded conflicted senses of despair and relief that was to be avoided. We were called back into the examining room a short while later, where the reduction was declared undoubtedly successful. And that was that. Two needle pricks and this insanely confusing and complicated pregnancy should be smoother from here on out.

# 45. CHRISTMAS IN MICHIGAN

Two days of doctor-ordered bed rest came and went just in time for our Saturday morning flight to Michigan. I carried our bags out to the car in the bone-chilling, icy weather, starting the car to let it warm for my precious cargo—wife, baby on board, and Socks. While the car warmed, I walked Socks one more time, set the light timers, and checked the house for any forgotten bags, lights, or running toilets. I placed Socks carefully into the car, in her bag-bed sitting on the back seat. Back inside to summon Carrie. "All ready. Let's set the alarm and go." I held her arm locked in mine to carefully guide her around small ice patches to the front passenger door, where Socks stared at us through the window.

"Get in the back!" I hollered and chuckled. I slowly opened the door. "Stay, stay, stay." I grabbed on to her and opened the door the rest of the way for Carrie to get in.

"I'll just take her," Carrie said. So I gently placed Socks on her lap—what was left of it.

Arriving at the airport always brings some stress, but with a pregnant wife, a dog in a carrying bag, and questionable weather, it was dialed up a notch. We had booked our flight on American Airlines, which had an onboard pet policy that was just slightly more lenient than Northwest's, the key competitor flying non-stops to Detroit. We also decided to leave far too early for the flight, to at least cut out the stress of missing the boarding process. Our only concern was that we would be there so early the airport wouldn't even be open—that no agents would be there yet to check us in. We were sadly mistaken.

We arrived at the American terminal at LaGuardia to giant crowds of people. You had to focus closely to note that there was at least some limited order to the situation. That terminal could bring the Dalai Lama to pushing nuns and shouting profanities. It was also a little bit like 1980s Russia—just get in a line, even if you're not sure what is at the front. The lines were so long, in such a small and crowded space, that we couldn't tell where they led.

"Is this the line to check in?" I asked the person in front of us.

"I think it's the security line, but I'm not sure," the person responded, but just kept standing in the line, hoping that when they got to the front, it would be the right one.

We did our best to keep cool through the process and managed to finally get our boarding passes, through security, and to the gate, though incredibly with only about five minutes to spare before boarding.

After boarding, stowing Socks by my feet, and the typical announcements, we were on our way. About an hour and a half later we landed safely in Michigan. On time for Christmas, and with a healthy mother and single unborn child. We walked to baggage claim and saw Carrie's parents, who spotted us the same instant. Nancy battled past her walking difficulties to rush toward Carrie. They embraced and squeezed tightly.

They held on, but there was no time for me to reach out for Matt. Socks, well aware that her grandparents were right there, violently shook the bag side to side. Matt giggled and reached down for her bag, pulled the handles from me, and ran her outside so he could greet her and walk her.

I turned back and Carrie and her mom were still holding tight. They eventually pulled away, each with a sniffle and short chuckle, mocking themselves for the tear escaping each of their eyes. Carrie's smile, reddened face, bloodshot eyes, and smeared mascara said one thing: "It's good to be home."

The next morning was a traditional start for the family. Coffee aroma filled the air first, soon to be joined by bacon and hash browns snapping on the stove. I sat on the couch, enjoying the hot eye-opening black coffee in my long flannel pajama pants and long-sleeved gray University of Michigan shirt. Outside, flurries of flakes wafted in the breeze, thinly covering the ground with a white blanket.

Carrie and her mom chatted away about the week's plans—pre-Christmas last-minute shopping, a visit to Grandma and Grandpa's, a visit from Aunt Susan, cousin Melissa, and her husband, Mike, that night, and on and on. Trips to Michigan were choreographed with detailed itineraries for each moment on the ground. Even trips that lasted for a full week, like this one.

Matt and I sat on the couch watching ESPN and intermittently discussing sports and the latest technological gadgets. Matt is an engineer and while he's infinitely smarter than me when it comes to anything with electronics or moving parts, I try to keep up and repeat what I've heard from other expert sources—TV, CNET, or newspapers.

After such a challenging period, the world seemed calm and right.

From down the hall in Carrie's bedroom, I heard my ringtone. I hopped up, plopped my coffee on the nearest table, and scampered down the hall. I grabbed my phone and hit talk just before losing it to voicemail. "Hello," I said in a chipper tone.

"Hey, bud. How are you doing?" asked my brother, Adam.

"All good. Flight was fine and we're just hanging out," I returned with cheer.

"Can you call me back from a landline?" he asked. In one sense I wasn't surprised to hear him ask that given the spotty cell service. On the other hand, if he was just checking in to be a good brother, I would instead have expected him to battle through the cut-outs with a few pleasantries before wishing me a good holiday and telling me to pass the same along to Carrie's family.

I hung up the cell and picked up Carrie's pink cordless phone to call him back.

"Hey, it's me," I said.

"Hey. First of all," he spoke slowly and in a calm voice, "everything is fine. Everyone is all right."

Clearly that was not true, I immediately knew.

He continued, "Dad is in the hospital right now." My stomach dropped and a chill ran through me, from the back of my neck and down to my legs.

"He may have had a heart attack—but he's fine right now. He's conscious. He's alert and talking. They've done an angioplasty—put a balloon in his heart to keep everything open and moving fine right now."

"When did it happen? Where are you right now? Where's Mom? Is she OK?" I fired. Carrie had already started down the hall, wondering who called, when she heard this comment from me. She now moved quickly the rest of the way down the hall and with deep concern on her face, mouthed *what happened?* I whispered quickly, "My dad's in the hospital—he may have had a heart attack. He's OK right now." Her eyes expanded, her face dropped, and she sat on the bed. I put up my index finger and then pointed to the phone, *Adam.*

Adam answered, "I'm at the hospital. It happened late last night—Mom drove him to the hospital and we didn't want to call you until we knew what was going on. She's fine, but a little shaken. Dad is awake and being a complete pain in the ass—so perfectly normal."

"Do we have any idea what the situation is now? What's the plan?" I asked.

"They're saying it's not an emergency, but they've scheduled him for open heart surgery tomorrow morning. We'll be here with him. You just stay and we'll keep you informed about everything that happens," Adam said.

My mind raced. Open heart surgery tomorrow morning certainly sounded like an emergency to me. He said it's not an emergency. He's awake and alert. Adam said to stay."

I shook off the confusion. "I gotta go. I'll be on the next flight."

Adam agreed easily, but asked, "What about Carrie? He's going to be in surgery and in the ICU. I don't even know if they let pregnant women in there. And I'm not sure if it's a good idea for her to fly again right now or to be in the hospital even if it's allowed, especially after all that's happened."

After a deep breath, I answered, "I don't know." I pulled the phone from my ear. "He's not sure you should be there, being pregnant, in a hospital and flying again and again."

"Are you kidding? I am going," Carrie whispered aggressively.

I put Carrie off for a moment to hang up on Adam. "Ad, I'm going to figure out the next flight and I'll be there as soon as I can. Please tell Dad and Mom I love them." He obliged. "I love you, too, Ad," I finished and hung up the phone.

By this time, Carrie's parents were in the doorway as well. Carrie had already filled them in while I finished with Adam.

I paused, dazed and trying to figure out the next move. "Car, I need to call the airline and get on a flight. I really don't think you should come."

"Are you kidding me? Of course I am coming!" Carrie said in deep concern.

"I know you want to be there, and I want you there, but it might really not be a good idea for you to keep flying back and forth, to be in the hospital, and Adam's not even sure you're allowed to be in the ICU."

We went back and forth for a few minutes while I grabbed a bag and started to throw some items in for the flight. Carrie's parents jumped in a few times with calming words. Ultimately, we decided that Carrie would stay put. Optimistically, I would just fly there for the surgery, all would be well, and I would fly back for Christmas.

After a quick call to the airline to get on the next available flight, we all headed to the Detroit airport together. When we arrived, Carrie walked me inside and gave me a tight, long hug. All of the racing of the past hour was brought to a warming pause.

"I love you very much," I told Carrie as we broke our embrace.

"I love you. And please tell your dad I love him very much."

# 46. CHRISTMAS IN NEW YORK

I landed at LaGuardia Airport a couple of hours later and took a half-hour cab ride to the Long Island Hospital. After the cab dropped me off, I darted inside, asking for the cardiac unit. It was barely another two minutes of quick-step through the halls and an elevator ride that I found the right hall, asked a nurse, and popped my head into the room. It was the right room—my father was lying in a hospital gurney in a very small room with his typical happy-go-lucky smile on his face as he saw me. I whimpered for a moment as the fear that I would never see my father again was washed away, at least for now.

"How are you?" I begged.

In typical fashion, he responded with a comically dismissively comment and smile. "I'm fine. How are *you* doing?"

"*I* am just fine." I turned to Adam and my mom, leaning in to hug and kiss them both, then turned my attention back to Dad. I squeezed past the machines and in the small space around the bed to get to his head, where I leaned over to give him a kiss.

He didn't look quite right, but certainly didn't look as pale, act as drained, or otherwise exude the sickliness I expected. There was some clear discomfort, with machines attached to him at the finger, an IV in his arm, sticky pads with wires over him, and another tube disappearing up his thigh and into the blue gown.

"How is it going—what's the latest?" I asked, mostly looking at my mom and Adam, well aware that was where I was likely to get more useful and accurate information. They didn't have a chance, though, as my dad jumped in.

"It's not an emergency—that's for sure," he tried to soothe with a smirk.

My mom took over. "He means the doctors don't need to do emergency surgery. They can do it tomorrow."

"That kind of sounds like an emergency to me," I responded.

In a loud voice my dad shot back for comic relief, "That's what I said!" He continued in his mocking, comical tone, "Apparently, if they don't need to operate *right that second*—that instant—then it's not *technically* an emergency. And—you see this tube?" He pointed to the tube running up his leg. "That's for the angioplasty. They did an angiogram first and determined that there was no damage—it wasn't even a heart attack, but just an '*event*.'"

"What the hell does that mean?" I asked.

He chuckled. "I don't know. But apparently it's better."

"Mom—what's going on?" I asked.

"The doctor said that the…" she started but my dad interrupted again.

"Ooh! The doctor!" he said excitedly. "The head of cardiothoracic surgery—guess what his name is. Dr. Hartman!"

I laughed. "You gotta be kidding me. Is that true?"

Giggling, my mom confirmed. "Yes. The doctors that did the angiogram said there is a major blockage, so they did the angioplasty—a balloon in his heart for now, but he needs bypass open-heart surgery. Tomorrow."

The mood quieted. I teared. My dad stopped searching for the next joke. I took a deep breath and then leaned in and kissed my dad on the forehead and whispered, "I love you."

He curled his free hand up to hug around my back. "I love you, too."

I stood as we chatted for a while in the small room. I learned more detail about his condition as we went on. I was angered and frustrated to learn that my dad had been having some pain in his neck and arm for a few weeks and even called his cardiologist to complain about his condition, who was somewhat dismissive of the symptoms. The doctor opted to schedule a stress test for a few weeks out—no longer needed now. My father himself would typically be dismissive of any symptoms, so for him to take the extraordinary step to call his doctor meant it was real. For him to have been put off angered me. I could tell it angered Mom and Dad too, but that wasn't the focus for the moment.

"If you've been feeling this for a while now, what happened today? Was it just worse?"

My dad squinted and looked up at the ceiling as to be thinking. "Um… I'd say it," he looked back down and right at me and emphasized, "was hurting *a lot!*"

My mother took over. "He told me he was short of breath and his chest was very heavy—I asked if we should call an ambulance. He told me to get the keys and drive him—not sure we can wait. So we got in the car and I was racing to the hospital. He was having me go through red lights and around traffic on the shoulder."

I looked to my dad with my eyebrows raised. He shook his head, "Yeah.

It was hurting a lot! We'd come to a red light and I'd say, 'Um...I think you should go through it.'"

"We got here," she continued, "and I ran inside to tell them he was having a heart attack. They actually responded pretty quickly from there until they got him stabilized and knew what was going on."

As we talked more I also found out that a rabbi had come by to talk. Our family is Jewish, but not religious. The rabbi began to discuss the need to understand death. My father kicked him out. Good for you, Dad. My dad always moves calmly forward through difficult situations with a positive attitude. Discussing the adverse outcome was not something he was interested in doing—in particular with someone he's never met before. I sensed from my dad's commentary about the ordeal as that he was actually pretty angered by the comment from the rabbi.

I ducked out for a break to call Carrie with an update, knowing she was anxious for information and deeply conflicted about still being in Michigan. I explained all that I knew and tried to break the solemn exchange with the story about the doctor's name. She was hard-pressed to laugh at all.

Back in the room, after some more talk, stories, jokes, and tired eyes, we prepared to leave for the night. The doctors had told us that the surgery was scheduled for eight a.m. and that we should be there around seven to be sure we could see him off to surgery. My mother wanted to stay the night with him, but there was really no room and my father needed whatever rest he could get in a noisy hospital temporary room.

The three of us took turns expressing our love for my father before filing out the doorway and into the long hallway. We lumbered slowly toward the elevator mostly in silence. At the hospital front door, my mom and I took turns embracing Adam before letting him head to his car and back to the city for his apartment. Mom and I walked to her car as the emotion and exhaustion hit her. She hung her head and whimpered just a touch. For the past twenty-four hours she'd been either racing my father to the hospital, talking with doctors, talking with Adam, figuring out what to tell me, and standing by my dad's side. I hung my arm around her and we kept moving. We reached the car and I grabbed for the keys, letting her sit—for the first time all day with muscles relaxed. She sat helplessly in the seat next to me, drained. It was also the first time all day she'd been away from my dad. She teared and whimpered a bit, but didn't allow a full sob. We talked in the car for a few minutes as I tried to calm her guilt for leaving him at the hospital for the night. Even though I think she knew she had to leave, it appeared to be the hardest thing she'd done in a long time.

By six thirty the next morning, we were all reconvened at the hospital. We joined my dad in his room and the mood was quieter, absent of the slices of humor from the day before. The scheduled time of surgery fast approached.

Despite the quoted eight a.m. start time, we continued to wait. We waited for hours for the surgical team to come take him to the OR.

Eventually, the team arrived, led by a tall, fairly heavy man with a very large face. He had enlarged features and presented with a clown-like wide smile and large wide-open eyes and introduced himself as the anesthesiologist. While we were in no mood for any comic relief, the combination of Dr. Hartman performing the open-heart surgery and the Joker as the gas-man was hard to ignore.

They started to wheel my dad away slowly down the hall and we walked alongside. The team stopped and told us to say goodbye. We each took a surprisingly brief moment with him. I leaned over my dad and told him, "I need you to know that I love you," and I started to tear as I kissed him on the head.

The instant I lifted up and turned to walk away, I cracked into an outright uncontrolled cry. My stomach tensed up and I nearly doubled over as my face contorted. It was brief, but it caught me completely by surprise at how little physical control I had over my body, even for just a few moments. My brother grabbed me around both shoulders and walked with me toward the waiting room. For the first time in my life, I believed there was a good chance I would never see my father again.

The waiting room was unimpressive. There were some old newspapers lying about. The couches were wooden-framed blue-cushioned love seats. There were plastic chairs and wooden end tables with pamphlets for a variety of ailments and grieving support groups. Coffee cups and half-eaten donuts sat next to concerned family members quietly reading books and newspapers or watching the muted television up in the corner. Some groupings would hold quiet conversations for a little while, then sit silently again.

An elderly man sat near the door at a desk with an old rotary phone and a lamp. Every so often, the phone would ring. The ring was loud and rattled nerves with every ding as the hammer swung quickly back and forth between two metal bells inside the casing. The man would answer, "Waiting room." The room somehow grew even more silent than it already was with all eyes trained on him.

"Family of Casey?" he would query to the room. A few people would hop up and walk quickly over to him and take the phone. "Thank you," they'd say, before hanging up the phone and walking out.

My mom, brother, sister-in-law, and I sat in the room for hours, taking turns with brief trips to the vending machine or cafeteria. We talked occasionally about a variety of things, but not much about Dad. It seemed too hard to do that.

Right around five o'clock, the elderly man stood up and announced in a soft voice to the room, "When the phone rings, pick it up. Good night."

Then he walked out.

Adam and I looked at each other quizzically for a moment, then shrugged. Apparently the nice gentleman must have been a volunteer and now those of us left would have to fend for ourselves.

I called Carrie a few times during our wait to update her on essentially nothing.

Over the course of the next couple of hours, the room grew emptier. The people manning the phones would get called away for their family member and others would take over. Eventually the phone rang and the stand-in operator called out, "Mandel."

We all jumped up and my brother trotted over to the desk and took the phone. "Yes. OK, thanks."

He hung up and turned to us. "He's out of surgery and the doctor will be here to talk to us in a minute." We all breathed a cautious sigh of relief. If he was out of surgery, he must be alive, right?

A short Asian man in scrubs and perfect English showed up asking for us. He walked into the waiting room and then motioned us to the closet area to provide marginal privacy. He lifted a blank piece of paper to the wall and began to draw on it with a BIC pen, explaining what they had done. His explanation was confusing and the drawing meant nothing to us, but it was clear when he said they ended up doing a quadruple bypass, not just one as planned. A quadruple bypass. This seemed more severe to us, but we were all really just looking to get past the details and get to the key answer— "How's my dad?"

My brother asked a few questions about the drawing while the rest of us stood mostly silent until he hit on the important question. "So, are you saying it went well and that he's OK?"

"Yes," he said, perhaps finally understanding that he had not yet conveyed the most basic fact before diving into the medical particulars. "Yes, he's fine and he's being moved to the ICU right now. You can go to the fourth floor, through the doors to the ICU, and ask for him,"

We very briefly thanked him before breezing past him toward the elevators. Waiting for the elevator, I rubbed my mom's back and gave her a kiss on the head. She flashed a smile filled with trepidation and anxiousness.

I quickly dialed my cell for Carrie and without any great detail relayed that he was out of surgery, he did well, and we were going to see him right now.

The large "Intensive Care Unit" sign was bolted into the wall next to the oversized double metal doors with a warning "Restricted Visiting Hours. One visitor per patient." We all pushed through the doors, which opened automatically after the first shove. My brother led the group toward the nurses' station. "We're looking for Barry Mandel. Just out of surgery."

The nurse rose and walked around the desk to lead us down the hall to the last room on the right. On the way, we met up with Dr. Hartman, who began talking and walking with us. "He did great. While we were in there, we saw additional blockages and bypassed I think a total of four arteries."

We all arrived at the room and Dr. Hartman led us in. I had expected to see my dad lying there unconscious with an IV in his arm and some sensors attached in a mostly quiet room. Rather, his face was colorless white, and his tongue was wrapped and taped outside of his mouth to the side of his face. There were dozens of tubes and wires running out from underneath the blanket—presumably all attached at different locations. Dr. Hartman walked over to my dad and leaned in right to his face calling out in a surprisingly loud but calm voice, "Barry! Barry! You're all right! You're in the ICU. Everything went fine! Your family is here!" His eyes twitched slightly, an acknowledgment that he'd heard the mysterious loud voice, but not any nod, wink, or other sign of understanding.

Dr. Hartman explained to us he'd likely be in the ICU for a day to watch him very closely, then be moved to a room. It would be best if we didn't stick around much for the night, rather coming back early in the morning would be good. He left and we all hung around for a few minutes while the nurses began to put my dad back to a marginally more comfortable position— untying his tongue and placing it back in his mouth, for example. One at a time, we took a moment to tell him how proud we were of him, how much we loved him, and that we'd be back to see him early tomorrow. He gave us minimal response. We walked out of his room as directed, down the hall to the large metal doors, and through them to a small waiting area with a couch where we paused for a moment. We exchanged still cautious but more relieved glances and small smiles. In all honesty, he looked pretty awful—but alive—and the doctor was pleased. It took a moment to soak in the situation.

"He said he's all right. He's going to look even better tomorrow morning," I said.

Everyone smiled and agreed. With little left to say or do, we headed out of the hospital for the night.

Early the next morning, I awoke to the sound of my mother rumbling around in her room. I walked down the hallway and poked my head in the open door. She was already dressed. It was only six a.m. and still dark out but she was understandably anxious. I said nothing other than "I'll be ready in ten minutes."

We arrived at the ICU expecting a slightly better version of last night's dad.

As we turned into his room at the end of the ICU, he was elevated in the bed, almost sitting up. He looked up from a newspaper and said in a chipper voice, "Hi!"

We were both taken aback by the overnight restoration in his coloring and consciousness. The night before, he was merely a human body in survival mode from a traumatic event. That next morning, he was Dad.

We both broke into wide smiles and responded quickly with "Good morning" and "I love you" and "How are you feeling?"

He told us about his night and that apparently he came out of the fog from the surgery only minutes after we left, so said the nurse on staff. He was awake much of the night due to the discomfort and was more sore than in outright pain.

Not long after, my brother and his wife arrived and were as pleasantly surprised as we were to see his renewed condition. For the day and into that night, we took turns visiting with Dad, leaving the room for examinations, patronizing the cafeteria and making phone calls in the hallway to other family and friends with the good news.

It was clear all the while that although my dad was past the surgery and trying to act himself, he remained in some real pain and discomfort. His chest ached, his energy was thin, and he hated the tubes and wires running in and out of him.

Later that day, they moved my dad out of the ICU and into a large room filled with patients separated by a series of curtains drawn along tracks in the ceiling. By the end of the day, he was thoroughly exhausted and wishing for a private room.

As the evening extended, he begged me to get back on a plane for Michigan and return to be with Carrie and her family. His request was fully genuine. I ultimately agreed and booked a flight for the next morning. I would make it back in time for Christmas in Michigan with Carrie.

# 47. A SPECIAL GENERALIST

Back in New York after Christmas, we were glad for several blessings. The reduction was difficult but successful. The timing worked for getting to Michigan for the holiday. My father's heart attack—er... heart "event"—was caught early enough and surgery was successful. I was able to return to celebrate the holiday with my wife. And now our New Year was poised to start on a positive note.

While I was at work during the small space between Christmas and New Year's, Carrie called my office line. "J. I'm bleeding a little."

"Bleeding? Like spotting or bleeding or what?" I fired back quickly in surprise.

"I mean—it's kind of a lot," Carrie said nervously.

"Shit. Call the doc and I'll meet you there."

Carrie arranged an emergency appointment with one of the partners at our OB. I raced down and grabbed a car to head to the doctor's office. We met there at close to the same time and the nurse got us in quickly.

Dr. Dingus performed a Doppler. I don't recall his real name, but this seems appropriate. He rubbed a device over Carrie's belly and we could all *hear* the heartbeat. "Everything seems to be OK. The heartbeat is normal and you're not having any contractions. The bleeding could be residual from the reduction," he said.

We took the diagnosis somewhat unwillingly and left the office.

"He didn't even do an ultrasound," Carrie said to me as we stepped into the elevator.

"I thought the same thing, but I don't know how to tell them how to do their jobs," I said with frustration.

Just a day later, I was again sitting at my desk and the black phone rang.

"I'm bleeding. A lot. I'm really bleeding," she blurted.

The words tore through me, certain this was the miscarriage we both anticipated but prayed to avoid. "Call the doctor and call me back. Tell me where to meet you."

We hung up and I sat in my office, dumbfounded. I was in the middle of still trying to get caught up on work and trying to refocus myself. All I could do was stare at the phone's caller ID, waiting for instructions.

Half a ring in and my hand ripped the receiver from the base, "Hello," I answered.

"Hi. He said that it's probably just from the reduction and that we shouldn't worry too much, just to watch it."

I waited a moment to hear more—there was no more. "That's bullshit. We're going to the hospital. Are you still bleeding right now?"

She wasn't denying my *bullshit* call. "It's on and off, but it was a lot a little while ago. I'm still bleeding a little now."

"Watch it? How long do we let you bleed? Forget that asshole. Stay there. I'm coming home. I'll take you to the hospital."

Hearing no disagreement, I hung up and dashed out.

It took me more than an hour to get to Carrie, where I embraced her firmly yet gingerly. I gently helped her into the car and drove away.

As I pulled up to the ER parking lot, an overweight, slow-moving security guard waddled to my window asking in a disbelieving tone, "Do you have an emergency?"

"Yes, my wife is pregnant and bleeding right now. Can you get her a wheelchair?" I lanced my words with aggression to slay his skepticism. His eyes perked open and he called out behind him for a wheelchair. In short order, a nurse arrived and helped Carrie out of the car and into the chair. They wheeled her away as I called out that I'd be there in a moment.

"Can I park here for now?" I asked. With no words he pressed the button, raising the long wooden arm and allowing me into the special emergency lot.

I ran into the hospital and quickly found Carrie in triage talking to the nurse, who wrote a clear and large "BRB" for *bright red blood* on a piece of paper and waved us through the main door, ahead of a roomful of barely patient patients.

We were quickly ushered into a room with a bed, which Carrie moved onto, propped to nearly an upright position. Within minutes, a doctor walked in to ask some questions—the most pertinent of which was "Are you still bleeding?"

"No, I don't believe so right this moment. I was bleeding a lot of bright red blood about an hour or two ago, but that's stopped since."

"All right," he said and the tension eased a touch. He performed some basic exams—looking in her ears, eyes, nose, and throat. While he examined her, a nurse walked in with some vials and tubes on a tray. The doctor finished and said, "We're going to get some blood from you and we'll be back to do a further exam," and then disappeared.

"Hi, guys," said the nurse. She was very friendly and asked questions while she prepared the vials to take blood. "Is this your first?"

"Yes. It's our first," Carrie replied. "And it's been a crazy ride already."

"You've had other problems with the pregnancy?" she asked.

We each smirked and let out simultaneous "Ha."

"You can say that," Carrie answered. "We've had our share of problems with the pregnancy and before that, we went through all of the steps to get pregnant—all the way to IVF."

"Oh, I know the drill. I had two kids. Then I spent two years on Clomid trying to get pregnant again. I finally gave up and then got pregnant with twins." She chatted back and forth with us about the emotional and physical trials of our efforts while tapping Carrie's vein for several vials of blood. Snap—she yanked off the tourniquet from Carrie's arm. "I'll be back soon."

About a half hour later, a different nurse stopped in and introduced herself as the new nurse on shift. She asked if we needed anything, but we didn't bother to ask how long to see a doctor.

Another long two hours later, the nurse came back into the room, looking at her clipboard. "All right," she said very slowly, while she lifted up a couple of pages and read some notes. "You—are free to go."

Carrie and I looked at each other and giggled a touch. I let Carrie respond. "We haven't seen anybody yet. Saw a doctor for a minute when we got here and a nurse to take some blood a couple of hours ago."

"Are you," she stumbled through the papers on the clipboard, "Janet Weiss?"

Carrie turned her head slowly to the right and swung it back to the left while letting out a simple "Nope."

"Um. I'll be back in a couple minutes," and she left the room.

We mused back and forth about the silliness of the evening. We arrived at the hospital. Carrie was whisked away in a wheelchair, swept past a packed house in triage and into a private room in the ER. Then left for dead.

About half an hour later, our nurse returned. She walked in briskly with no clipboard this time and quickly surveyed the room, taking note we were alone. She looked back at the doorway she just came through and leaned back, looking down the hall. "Did they just leave?"

Once again, we giggled to each other. This time I took the honor, responding in good humor, "Did *who* just leave? Nobody has been here since you discharged us a half hour ago."

She huffed and walked back out.

Finally, ten minutes later, she walked back in, flanked by a doctor and an apparent student doctor who would go on to say nothing the whole time.

"Good evening," said the doctor. "Sorry for the delays, it has been a busy one for sure. So, you were having some real bleeding earlier this evening—any more since you've been here?"

"No," Carrie responded.

He pulled up a tall stool next to the bed and dragged an ultrasound machine on wheels over toward the bed. "Pull up your shirt for me, please? I want to see what's going on." He squirted cold gel on Carrie's belly and touched the ultrasound wand to her. The screen lit up in green shapes on a black background. Within a moment or two, he identified a heartbeat and calmed us initially by pointing it out. But then his scans of her belly slowed and he leaned closer to the screen. "I'm sorry, can you tell me your pregnancy history?"

"It's a long one, but I'll give you the high points," Carrie started. "I am fifteen weeks pregnant. We used IVF to get pregnant, putting in two embryos. They both took and they both split, so we had two sets of identical twins." He glanced away from the screen for a moment and made eye contact with us one at a time, then back to the screen. "At around seven weeks, we found out that one of the babies no longer had a heartbeat. We were advised that our best chance for a successful and healthy pregnancy would be to reduce, which we did. At twelve weeks, we reduced the twins, leaving one baby." She paused as the room was silent. "And that probably covers it."

The room hung silent for several minutes more as he repeatedly swept the wand over Carrie's belly and stared closely at the images. He tilted his head to the side several times, squinted, pushed his face closer to the screen, then backed away. This went on and on.

Keeping his eyes on the screen, he finally broke the silence with slow and deliberate speech. "I follow your story, but I'm struggling to reconcile it with what I am seeing."

He took a breath and continued, "Obviously because of the reduced twins, there is a lot of distraction in the ultrasound that I'm trying to work with, but something doesn't match up with what you are telling me."

We looked at each other and shook our heads in concert, preparing for the next phase of news.

He put the wand down and swiveled the stool back around to look at us. "This kind of complex pregnancy requires a dedicated trained high-risk OB/GYN, so I'm not so sure I can properly understand what is going on here. The twin fetus that you are telling me died back toward the very beginning of the pregnancy on its own," he paused for a breath before continuing slowly, "is actually larger than the surviving fetus." He paused again. "And you said the surviving twins were reduced at twelve weeks. But the twin that died first, at seven weeks, is also bigger than the reduced twins. It just doesn't make any sense."

Bells went off in my head and I thought I might instantly understand what was happening.

I said, "When we were deciding on whether or not to have a reduction, we learned a lot about something called twin to twin transfusion, where identical twins can share their blood flow through arteries in the umbilical cord and placenta. Can something like that happen with a twin that's not alive? Can our surviving baby be pumping blood into its deceased twin which is letting it grow?"

His eyebrows rose and he pulled his head back. He tilted his head to the side. "I really don't know." He swallowed. "As I said, I think you need a high-risk OB that deals with complicated pregnancies. I guess that sounds plausible, but I really don't know. The other thing is that the enlarged deceased twin is acephalic." Before we could ask, he leaned in to deliver the difficult description. "It doesn't have a head."

We both gasped. I dropped my hand onto Carrie's shoulder and gripped tightly, but kept my eyes on the doctor. Tears welled in my eyes.

The doctor wrapped up, "There is something going on here that you need to explore for sure. But for right now, I don't see anything *emergent* that requires attention tonight. Your bleeding has stopped and your baby has a heartbeat. I suggest you go home and set up an appointment with a high-risk OB as soon as you can."

I nodded and thanked him. He walked out and I leaned over Carrie to hug her. I felt her whimper underneath me. I tried to console her, but this string of bad news was seriously beginning to wear on me.

The nurse came to have us sign the discharge papers and offered a horrendous attempt at a comforting salutation. "If not this time, you'll be successful another time."

Late that night, we returned home, as anxious as we'd been the entire pregnancy. Since Dr. Feinman had already blown off the bleeding, we thought about who else may be able to help. We called Dr. Blum's office instead. While their job was technically done already—getting Carrie pregnant—we figured they could do us a favor to take a look. Upon getting the answering service, we were informed Dr. Jansen would call us back shortly.

*Shit,* we both thought. He was the newest and least experienced member of the practice, not to mention hard to understand, with his Slavic accent.

The phone rang shortly afterward. "This is Dr. Jansen. Someone called for me?"

"Yes, Dr. Jansen," I said with an appreciative tone. "We just returned from the ER where we went because Carrie was bleeding. She isn't bleeding anymore, but in the ER, they told us of a potential complication with the deceased twin. I know this isn't your exact area of expertise, but our OB can't see us for a few days," a white lie, "and we are very anxious to see someone."

He hesitated for a moment, but recovered. "Yes. It is no problem. Of course I can see you. Please come to the office around nine thirty tomorrow morning."

We were beat from another long hospital experience and emotional thumping, though still neither one of us slept well, thinking about the partial information we learned that evening.

First thing in the morning, we were in the car headed to the city. We arrived in the waiting room, busy as usual, and checked in. Oddly, we were called quite quickly and found ourselves in the exam room with Dr. Jansen in record time.

"Good morning," I said immediately. "Thank you so much for agreeing to see us this morning."

He responded with a soft smile and calm voice. I assumed the partners of the practice had moved on to teaching bedside manner. "It is no problem at all. Please tell me, what did you learn in the ER last night?"

He prepared to scan Carrie's belly as Carrie answered, "They said they saw the twins that we reduced—and that they were getting smaller. But he also said that Maddie's twin, who died at seven weeks, was larger than her. And he called it," she slowed her speech and raised the pitch to the tone of a question, "acephalic? She has no head."

"I see," he said as he scanned. "Well, I clearly see Mandy's heartbeat."

Carrie and I looked at each other and silently mouthed, "Mandy?"

"And I see sort of a clump of tissue in Mandy's sac, which I believe is the deceased twin," he continued. "I don't exactly see what you are describing or what the doctors in the ER told you. But then, I don't want to make a diagnosis about this, because it really isn't my specialty." He pulled the wand off of Carrie's belly, replaced it in the holster, and looked at us. "From what I see, everything is progressing as it should, but again, I want you to see your OB as soon as you can to get confirmation."

"Of course," I said. "We have an appointment set up for Monday already, but we didn't want to wait that long to get some information. Thank you very much for agreeing to see us."

Monday morning, we arrived at Dr. Feinman's office for the "emergency" appointment. We were already perturbed that the most immediate appointment we could get after reporting bright red bleeding was three days later.

The short, cocky doctor entered our exam room. "Hello," he said with a smile on his face. "How are you feeling?" he asked Carrie, as he began preparing the portable ultrasound.

"Well, after we called your office and we were told not to worry, we worried. So we went to the ER to get checked out."

He shook his head and rolled his eyes. "Oh man. You guys should never go to the ER. They're all generalists and have no idea what they are looking at, especially for a multiple pregnancy."

I could not let his comment go and said firmly back, "Well, we called your office, but the doctor on call simply told us not to worry and to make an appointment to come in on Monday."

He laughed off my apparently idiotic interaction. "Well, if you really needed to be seen, you just have to tell him that." He turned to Carrie and started the ultrasound. "Now let's see."

As he scanned, the tiny screen appeared to our untrained eyes as just a mess of green splashes and pixels. He pointed to parts of the screen. "Here's the heartbeat."

Carrie continued her answer from his earlier question. "In the ER, they told us what we said didn't make sense based on what they were seeing. He told us that Maddie's twin, which died at seven weeks, was as large or larger than Maddie—that it must still be growing. We asked if that could be a form of twin to twin transfusion with a deceased twin and they said they had no idea."

He laughed off the crazy diagnosis from the ER. "And that's why you come to us. I see Maddie here and she looks just right. So everything is fine." He holstered the ultrasound wand and pushed the machine back to the wall.

I interrupted, "I understand that you see Maddie's heartbeat, but do you see the twin?"

He grudgingly pulled the machine back toward us and placed the wand back on Carrie. "Here is Maddie's heartbeat."

I could make out nothing on the screen, but appeased and asked, "OK, but do you see her twin?"

"Everything else in the uterus looks fine," he said, pointing to a few spots and not saying much. He reholstered the wand and pushed the machine back again. He looked specifically at Carrie. "You are fine and Maddie is fine. Next time you have a concern, just avoid the ER and call us," as he stood up and disappeared out the door.

We left the office, forced to accept all was well. We remained skeptical, but no longer had any evidence to allow that feeling to drive further action.

# 48. A SPECIAL SPECIALIST

Weeks went by with no new abnormalities. No bleeding and no pains out of the ordinary. After eating dinner, we sat calmly watching a *Friends* rerun when Carrie asked calmly, "J? Feel this."

I scooted closer and put my hand as she directed, onto her belly. I quieted and then whispered, "What am I feeling for?"

"It feels like my belly keeps tightening up. Tightening up really hard."

At that moment, I felt her belly clench. I pulled back. "Are you doing that?" I asked.

"No. That keeps happening. It keeps squeezing. Tight as a rock."

I could feel the strength of the flex all over her belly until it loosened. I softly poked at her with my finger. "Feels normal now." My finger could depress her skin on her oval belly. A few minutes later, the clench repeated and again I could feel it. As I tried poking again, it was as though I was pressing on a bone through the skin. But it was a dome—a bone that covered her fully belly.

"We have to call," I said.

"No, not again. They're either going to make us go to the hospital or tell us it's nothing."

"Well, whatever it is, we have to call." I grabbed the phone, dialed, and left a message with the answering service. About a half hour later, the phone rang. It was Dr. Nadler on the other end.

"Good evening, Dr. Nadler. Thanks for the call back. Let me put Carrie on."

"Hi, Dr. Nadler. I keep experiencing real tightening in my belly."

I clicked into the call by picking up the kitchen extension.

"That's all right. You're getting further along in the pregnancy and it's normal. It's just the baby moving around in there."

I jumped in. "It's Jason again. I felt it. Her whole belly tenses up. I don't

179

feel any movement or any parts—the whole thing is solid."

"I'm sure it's just the baby moving. Early on, people can mistake it. It's just the baby changing positions."

Reluctantly, I again accepted an answer that left me unsatisfied. The tightening continued but over time slowed and disappeared. I guessed he was right.

A few days later, Carrie tapped my shoulder in bed early in the morning. "You awake?"

"I am," I responded quietly—just then waking up with my face still in the pillow.

"The tightening is happening again," she whispered.

My mind quickly snapped awake and I turned over. I put my hand on her belly, felt, and asked, "It's tight right now, isn't it?"

"Yes. And it keeps happening," she said.

I reached into my nightstand for a notepad and pen. "We are going to note down every time you feel it. I want to keep track and if it keeps happening, we're going to call."

"It's happening."

I marked the time.

"It's happening."

I marked the time.

"It's happening."

I marked the time.

"It's happening."

I marked the time.

"It's happening."

I marked the time.

"It's happening."

I marked the time. "That's six times in an hour," I said. "And every single one of them feels like it must be a contraction—I don't feel Maddie moving at all."

"I know. Me neither," Carrie said reluctantly.

"I'm calling—and we're going in."

Carrie got up to get herself ready, while I dialed for the answering service. Dr. Nadler called us back shortly afterward. He quickly realized there was no stopping us. He directed us to the hospital and said he'd notify them that we were coming. He directed us not to go to the ER, but instead to go to the obstetrics area.

When we got to the hospital, we made our way to obstetrics and were received by a nurse at the station up front. She quickly directed us into the examining area—a room with six or seven beds and curtains and with several ultrasounds and other monitoring machines. Carrie was directed to sit on a bed and lift her shirt over her belly. Instead of examining her with the ultrasound, they wrapped two elastic bands that looked much like ace bandages around her body and attached circular monitoring devices to each. The devices were connected by cord to two separate machines. The nurse directed Carrie to lie back and adjusted one of them slowly by dragging it around her belly until suddenly we could hear a heartbeat. She tightened the strap in place.

"OK, honey," said the nurse. "We're going to monitor you for a bit first. This one," she pointed to one of the devices, "will monitor your baby's heartbeat and this one," she pointed to the other, "will monitor for any contractions." With that, the nurse rose and walked away.

"They're already kind of going away," Carrie said to me, almost disappointed that they might not catch it.

"Surprise. Isn't that the way it always works?" I said and laughed.

We waited for a while until Carrie said, "I think I feel one."

I looked at the contraction monitor, which was slowly and steadily spitting out a stream of paper marked with a dark black line near the *zero*. As I watched the paper come out, I could see the line beginning to rise from zero. "I see it. It's showing something," I told her. She let a small sigh of relief that she wasn't crazy and craned her head to see the paper I was holding up as it came out.

I turned to the nurse behind me. "I think she's having one," I said.

The nurse turned her attention to us and looked at the paper. "Yes, I see it. She is. Doesn't look too bad. The doctor just wants to monitor you for a while."

After a few more contractions over the course of an hour or so, a nurse walked into the room and told us, "Time for an ultrasound." She helped remove the monitors from Carrie and get her into a wheelchair. We rolled to another area of obstetrics with a waiting room filled with people that we passed right by and into the back. There were four doors marked numerically. We rolled through the open doorway marked number "3" into a room only large enough for the exam table, two stools on either side, and a large, new, and highly sophisticated-looking ultrasound machine.

The nurse locked the wheels and said, "All right, let me help you up on to the exam table." Carrie slid onto the table and lay back with her back and head tilted slightly upward.

"Good morning," said a nurse dressed in green scrubs with a black long-sleeved shirt underneath as she walked in. "I am going to take a look and then Dr. Pine will come in afterwards."

She looked into Carrie's file. "So I see you are having contractions. You are…eighteen weeks?" she asked with a tone of skepticism as she looked up from the file and at Carrie's belly.

"Yes."

She dimmed the lights, slid herself onto the stool, and pulled the ultrasound closer to her. She pointed up at a TV in the corner of the room. "You can watch right up there."

As she placed the wand on Carrie's belly, the ultrasound screen jumped to life, as did the screen near the ceiling.

"Now, please refresh me on your full history. I saw it briefly in the file, but go ahead and let me have it."

As I took a deep breath to begin speaking, the ultrasound tech was already hard at work taking freeze-frame pictures and body part measurements.

Instead, Carrie took over. "Well. We used IVF to get pregnant, putting in two embryos. Both took and both split. One of the babies was found not to have a heartbeat at seven weeks. Then we were advised that we should strongly consider a reduction to improve the odds for a successful and healthy pregnancy. So we went ahead with a reduction of the two live twins, leaving only the one baby whose twin had died at seven weeks. Since then, I've had some problems—I went to the ER for bleeding, which stopped on its own. And more recently, I've been feeling these contractions that ultimately brought us here today." She looked at me. "That cover it?"

"I think so," I responded. "We've gotten pretty good at getting to the key points."

The room was left silent for several minutes as the tech took more pictures, drawing circles and lines to record measurements. This continued for a while with the only sound filling the room being clicking buttons and the hum of 3x3 pictures rolling out of the machine.

"I'm trying to follow what is going on here and what you are telling me doesn't quite match up with what I am seeing." She again asked for the dates of the pregnancy that each event occurred. As Carrie repeated all of the key events and gestational dates, my shoulders sank and I took deep breaths as my frustration grew.

After Carrie repeated the history, the tech was left wrinkling her nose and tilting her head. "I'm still having trouble reconciling everything with the images."

Something about the way she repeated that same comment triggered my heartbeat to jump and shivers to climb up my spine. "What *are* you seeing?" I asked a bit louder than the room's norm thus far. "Because we *were* in the ER at this hospital a few weeks ago and another tech was telling us something similar. Telling us that our story doesn't match the ultrasound. We went to our OB and he scanned Carrie and blew it off, so we moved on. But it sounds like you may be seeing the same thing."

The tech looked up at me and then at Carrie, gaining some confidence in her thoughts, which she still hadn't shared with us.

"I'll be right back. I'm going to go get Dr. Pine," she said also with more anticipation. She ripped the pictures off of the machine and quick-stepped out of the room.

"I think we're about to find something out," I said.

Carrie just breathed deep and squeezed on my hand.

The tech returned to the room followed by a middle-aged black lady in a long white lab coat. "Good morning. I'm Dr. Pine," she introduced herself as she took the commanding position at the ultrasound and the tech stood by Carrie's feet under the TV, looking up at the show.

"Good morning," we responded.

While she steadied herself on the stool and prepared the machine, she said, "Jennifer gave me the update and I'm going to take a look at a few things. Just relax and we'll figure out what's going on in here. While I'm looking," she stopped and looked at Carrie, "and I'm sorry but I know you've done this over and over, please tell me your history."

Carrie began the history run-down again while Dr. Pine put the ultrasound through the paces. She pressed buttons, adjusted knobs, and spun the trackball. She retook several measurements, froze the screen, and rotated the image. She switched into 3D showing live moving pictures of what looked like clay models. She switched to a blood flow view that we'd also never seen, showing streams of red and blue moving in rivers in several directions. She turned on the sound, filling the room with Maddie's heartbeat, then tuned the sound to a deeper, more muffled sound of flow, rather than just beats. "Hwaaaaaaw, hwaaaaaaaw, hwaaaaaaaaw," the machine bellowed.

She opened up some form of EKG on the bottom of the screen with lines jumping up above a baseline and dipping below with each sound of flow.

"Sorry for some repeated questions. When was the first fetus found to no longer have a heartbeat?"

Carrie answered.

"When did you have the reduction?"

Carrie answered.

"You for certain reduced the live set of twins?"

Carrie stuttered, but answered.

As she asked the questions, she continued to use all the features of the ultrasound machine, dazzling us with the images, figures, and graphs displayed.

Dr. Pine stood for a moment as she watched the screen, set with the blood flow visible in color, a live EKG monitor onscreen, and the muffled sound of blood flowing and slowing. Flowing and slowing.

I looked from the screen to Dr. Pine's face. She watched the screen closely and then turned to the ultrasound tech. As she opened her mouth to speak, she unintentionally grinned. "Are you seeing what I am seeing?" she asked.

The tech looked at her with a stunned, wide-eyed face. "Yes."

Dr. Pine regained her composure and wiped the unintended look of discovery away. She spoke slowly, "You have an acardiac twin. The healthy fetus—Maddie—is pumping blood through a vessel in the umbilical cord into the deceased twin, allowing it to grow, but over time that is putting increased strain on Maddie's heart. Maddie is doing double duty."

I responded quickly. "So is that the same thing as twin to twin transfusion, but one live fetus and one deceased fetus?" I asked anxiously.

"That is just about right. It's basically the same thing," she responded.

Carrie and I looked at each other. Her eyes were welled up with tears. My emotions were mixed and thoughts were flying through my head. Images quickly flashed in my head of the ER visit, the trip to our fertility specialists, and the dismissal by our high-risk OB. I was angry with Dr. Feinman for holding himself out as the multiples king. I pushed the anger aside for the moment. "And is it also acephalic?"

She ticked her head back an inch in surprise and answered, "Yes."

"That's what the ER doctor said weeks ago," I said quietly, shaking my head.

Dr. Pine took a deep breath, turned off the ultrasound, and cleaned off Carrie's belly with a few paper towels. "Let's get you cleaned up and out of here so we can go talk for a little while. I'll meet you in just a few minutes." She turned and nodded to the tech to help us.

The tech quickly but carefully helped Carrie off the table and into the wheelchair waiting outside of the room. She quickly wheeled Carrie away and I followed. As I walked briskly behind and off to the side of the wheelchair, I reached out and grabbed onto Carrie's shoulder. She reached her opposite arm up to her shoulder and covered my hand.

Very shortly we were in another part of the pregnancy wing, back into the room where Carrie was tested for contractions earlier. We were directed into a side of the room and the tech pulled the curtain around us. "Dr. Pine will be right over here."

We both sat next to each other on the hospital bed and weren't alone long enough to discuss the latest news as Dr. Pine then pulled the curtain and walked in. She dragged over a chair and sat eye to eye with us.

She began slowly. "Your baby has an acardiac twin. It is a condition called TRAP sequence or twin reversed arterial perfusion. It is basically the same thing as twin to twin transfusion. One of the twins is acephalic and acardiac, which means that it doesn't have a head *and* it doesn't have a heart."

I had my arm around Carrie and pulled her tighter as the news flowed.

Dr. Pine continued, "This is an extremely rare condition—it's the first time that I have ever seen it with my own eyes." The comment helped justify her grin in the exam room as a condition that piqued her academic curiosity.

She continued as we kept silent. "There are really only two doctors I'm aware of in the country who can help you with this condition. One is in Florida and the other in Arizona. Dr. Rodriguez in Florida is really the pioneer for this type of surgery and more experienced as a result. So really, it's Dr. Rodriguez that you will need to see. He has a procedure called a cordial ligation, where he goes in through a small hole and laparoscopically ties off the cord connecting the acardiac twin with Maddie. This stops the blood flow and greatly reduces the strain on Maddie's heart. Without the surgery," she paused, "Maddie's heart will fail."

We both just continued nodding, prompting her to continue.

She kept going. "With your permission, I can send him all of your information to confirm the diagnosis and to tell us if you are a candidate for the surgery."

We broke the silence, with Carrie beating me to it. "Yes, of course. You have our permission."

I followed up. "Do you have any sense for the risks of the surgery or probabilities of success?"

She nodded understandingly. "I know you are going to have a lot of questions, but I can't answer them properly. What I am going to do is to share the information with him and have him get back to us as soon as possible." She paused, then said, "I know this is hard. This is very difficult information to take in. It is an extremely rare complication of an extremely rare type of pregnancy. Let's just wait to hear back to decide what to do next." She stood up, smiled at us, and walked through the curtain.

I stared at Carrie and she stared back, both of us set to speak, but no words flowed. I was stuck for a moment on the rarity of our situation. Two embryos both took and then both split. One fetus died and we reduced the other set of twins with a goal toward a successful healthy pregnancy only to be struck by another extremely rare condition. One percent odds times one percent odds makes for lightning-strike odds.

Finally I spoke. "I *can't believe* this. I can't believe the odds of another major condition like this and I can't believe," my tone grew angrier, "that we basically knew about this weeks ago and our *high-risk* OB blew it off completely. The ER doctors—unspecialized—handed our *expert high-risk* OB a complex diagnosis on a silver platter and he *blew us off!*" I shouted in a whisper.

"I know, I know," Carrie said, trying to calm me. "We just need to focus on what we have to deal with now."

As she said that, the curtain parted again and Dr. Nadler walked in; we had no idea he was even there. "Hi, guys, how are you?" he asked in a sympathetic tone. Even with Carrie's comments to me to focus us on the issue at hand, we were both unhappy to see anyone from that office.

"Hello," I said coldly.

He continued with his sympathetic tone. "I had a chance to review your situation with Dr. Pine. You have a condition called TRAP sequence. The healthy fetus"—I took note of his use of the word "fetus" instead of

"Maddie"—"is pumping blood for both itself as well as its twin, even though the twin is deceased and has no chance of survival. This is a dangerous situation for the healthy fetus."

Having just heard this information, we nodded politely.

He continued, "Dr. Pine is going to get you connected with Dr. Rodriguez in Florida to further assess the condition."

He stopped and an awkward silence ensued as he awaited any response or questions. We had plenty more questions, but not for him.

He raised his eyebrows slightly, noting the awkward silence, then broke it. "I'd like you to come in to see me. Can you come to the office on Thursday?"

I looked at Carrie and she nodded. I figured I would just chalk it up to yet another day where I disappeared from work for several hours. "Sure. We'll be there," I said.

He left the room. I raised the left side of my top lip and tilted my eyebrows. "What was that?" I whispered.

"I have no idea," she whispered back. "And what does he want to see us for?"

A few minutes later, Dr. Pine returned. "I just spoke with Katie Jane in Dr. Rodriguez's office. She handles all of his surgery candidates. She is going to send over a list of images and measurements they need, so I'm going to need you to come over to our office on Northern Boulevard so we can get everything we need, all right?" We nodded.

She gave us the directions and told us to head over there and she'd see us there in about an hour.

On the walk to the car and in the brief car ride to her office, we first marveled at the rarity of our situation and then fumed about the missed diagnosis. We exchanged angry blows at Dr. Feinman. Did the missed diagnosis cost us valuable time? How could the "Multiples King" not have seen this, especially when given much more than a hint? How could he even see anything on that small monochrome ultrasound at their office when compared against the state-of-the-art machine we had just witnessed?

The hospital was only a couple of blocks from Northern Boulevard, a major thoroughfare with two lanes in each direction and a center turning lane. Cars whipped by in large volume and gaps in traffic were short, requiring a heavy foot to turn left across the oncoming lanes. Slowing down to look at building addresses was a dangerous feat as tailing traffic typically rides to within inches of your bumper before yanking the wheel to change lanes and pass you. Carrie searched for the building numbers until she finally shouted, "There!"

I barely slowed down and made a fast turn into the office lot. We drove ahead down a very narrow one-lane path toward the back of the building and carefully maneuvered the SUV around the full lot that appeared to have been built for mid-sized cars. We found a spot on the lower level and made our way to the elevator at the center of the garage in the basement of the building. Carrie pressed "2" and we rose slowly. The doors opened and we saw entrances to two waiting rooms on opposite sides of the short hallway. We walked toward the sign with Dr. Pine's name alongside seven others.

The entrance opened up into a large rectangular waiting room with receptionists sitting behind sliding glass windows on either end. Near where we walked in, there were signs for a practice of plastic surgeons. We headed to the other end.

Carrie approached the open window. "Hi, we're here to see Dr. Pine. She sent us over from North…"

"Yes, we're expecting you. Come on through," said the receptionist as she motioned to a light wooden door to our right.

We walked over to it and heard a click. I pushed the door open and let Carrie walk through. We were met on the other side by a nurse. "Come right this way," she said.

We were guided past a couple of empty examining rooms. I peeked inside each room to find the same state-of-the-art ultrasound machines we just witnessed at the hospital. The nurse directed us into a room.

While we waited, I snooped over the ultrasound machine. The keyboard was built solid, with strong plastic and a double handle to pull firmly around the room. The trackball was large, like a Golden Tee arcade game. There were half a dozen groupings of keys including a standard keyboard, a number set, function keys, specialized measurement keys, and others with purposes I didn't understand.

"Hello," said Dr. Pine walking in, and smirking as though she caught a toddler quizzically peering over a telephone for the first time.

"I have the list of images and measurements that Dr. Rodriguez needs, so I'm going to ask you to lie down for me. This is going to take a little while—they need a lot of data."

Carrie complied, lying on her back and lifting her shirt.

Dr. Pine spent a minute entering data into the machine, including Carrie's full name, date of birth, date of last period, and others. While she was finishing up, Dr. Jain walked in.

"Hello again," she said in her pleasant Indian accent.

We were relieved to see her. When we met during our many consultations, Dr. Jain was so very level-headed, intelligent, and still caring.

"I am also going to take a look at the condition if that is all right with you."

"Of course," Carrie responded quickly.

Once Dr. Pine completed the basic data entry, Dr. Jain took the reins. She slipped onto the stool by the ultrasound, grabbed one of the handles to pull it closer, and reached for one of the two white bottles sitting upside down in a double cupholder. She waved it over Carrie's belly, squirting the blue goo.

Carrie made a soft moan. I asked, "You all right?"

She giggled. "Yes, fine. It's just warm. I was expecting it to be cold like usual."

Dr. Jain smiled and said, "Yes, these warmers are nice—it feels much better than the cold bottles." She pressed the wand against Carrie and the screen jumped to life. She spent a few minutes getting her bearings of the situation and then the two doctors spoke back and forth for a few minutes. They didn't lower their voices to keep us from hearing, but we didn't understand much of what they were saying.

Dr. Jain stopped and replaced the wand. "I just wanted to spend a few minutes looking as well. I agree with the diagnosis that Dr. Pine has given you and Dr. Rodriguez is the worldwide expert on this type of surgery—he pioneered it."

"Thank you," Carrie answered.

Dr. Jain nodded and walked out, while Dr. Pine took back the controls and spent twenty minutes taking the required measurements and pictures.

Finally, she finished up and reminded us, "You are going to get a call from Katie Jane. She works in Dr. Rodriguez's office and handles all of the pre-surgical discussions. She will already have all of the records she needs, so just ask her any questions you have. I wish you both the best of luck."

As she began to walk out, I stopped her. "Dr. Pine. Can I ask you something else?" She turned back and nodded. "Can you explain how you fit into this hospital? What I mean is, we are patients of Dr. Feinman and Dr. Nadler, but I think," I looked at Carrie and nodded questioningly, "we have both lost total confidence in them."

Carrie followed immediately. "Yes, absolutely. This could have been caught a few weeks ago."

I tag-teamed, adding, "I get it that this is a very rare diagnosis, but the generalist ER doctor basically found it and we handed it to Dr. Feinman on a silver platter. He didn't do much more than brush us off. I don't feel comfortable with them anymore."

"Well," she started with an understanding but uncomfortable look, "our practice is dedicated solely to high-risk pregnancies and we are happy to help out with Dr. Feinman and send him our findings."

I could tell she was holding back, but I pressed more directly. "But how does it work if we wanted to switch offices? Are you taking more patients?"

Dr. Pine took a deep breath and started with the first few words flowing slowly as she carefully picked each next word. "It is not really done that patients switch doctors in the middle of a pregnancy, to another doctor…with privileges at the same hospital. We all work together here and don't," she paused and searched for the right phrase, "take patients from other doctors."

I began to understand the sensitivities at work but pressed further nonetheless. "But if a patient *requests* it, rather than a doctor offering it up— can that be done? I'll be clearer. *We want to switch.*"

She stammered for a moment and almost started again to explain the taboo, but clearly understood the gravity of this error. "The only way we could do this is if you request through Dr. Feinman to switch to this office. We can't make that request for you."

I smiled softly and even took some delight in the thought. "No problem. I can *absolutely* take care of that."

She returned quickly, "But I think it would be best to wait until after we deal with Florida. This is a sensitive time and there's no reason to do something silly like lose access to files while in transit."

I nodded. "Very true. We'll wait until we are back. Thank you for all of your help, Dr. Pine," I finished in a deeply sincere tone.

"Yes, thank you so much," followed Carrie similarly.

She left the room and Carrie and I looked at one another with oddly relieved expressions. We had just received the most troubling news of the pregnancy so far, yet we were pleased to find an office with true experts, high technology, patient focus, and a caring nature, and to leave behind one that felt more like a factory.

# 49. "JUST START OVER"

A few days later, and just two days before our scheduled trip to Florida, I snuck out of work early to get out to our appointment with Dr. Nadler. We still weren't entirely sure what the purpose of the appointment was, but in any case, I met Carrie at the train station. I stepped off the Long Island Railroad train car, walked up the stairs, and jogged across the street into a strip-mall parking lot where I saw our black SUV waiting. We drove the short trip to the office and squeezed into a small parking spot in the basement.

We were not in the waiting room for more than a few minutes before we were summoned to Dr. Nadler's office, where we were directed to two chairs facing a large oak desk attached to the wall with an oversized shelving unit covered in medical books, family pictures, and doctor-themed trinkets. On the wall behind his large leather chair hung his diplomas, laced with Latin text.

"Hi, guys," we heard from behind us as Dr. Nadler walked in and closed the door. He walked past us, around the edge of the desk, and sat down, generating a soft *koosh* from the chair.

"I asked you both here so that we could discuss the diagnosis and what you have ahead of you now. You have had a very difficult go of it already with this pregnancy, but you have something great going for you. You are very young. You have years of childbearing years ahead of you."

I think Carrie and I both swallowed hard as we could sense the direction he was headed.

He continued, "A doctor like Dr. Rodriguez, while excellent at what he does, will want to do the surgery because it is what he does. I'm certain he *does* believe he can fix the problem. Whereas, *I* am the doctor people see when they come back. I have to help patients deal with the outcomes of surgeries like this, including very premature births and several other complications that arise."

His word choice and tone made it sound like we were going to South America with a bag of cash for an illegal surgery.

He stopped for a long pause and we said nothing. He continued, "With your age and these complications, I think you should be considering very seriously terminating the pregnancy." A short pause. "I can do it for you in the office, it doesn't have to be a hospital visit."

We were speechless. We didn't say much for what felt like minutes, but I finally responded with something simple like "Thank you. We'll think about what you said."

With that, the meeting was over. We rose and took turns shaking hands and then left.

We rode the elevator down to the car in silence. We got in the car in silence. Pulled out of the lot in silence. I headed back for the train station, but then turned off the road into an empty parking lot. "We need to talk to someone," I said. "*What the hell was that?* He called us back for an appointment to tell us to abort the pregnancy?"

"I just can't take much more of this," whimpered Carrie, dropping her head. I rubbed her back.

"I know," I said. "This is unreal. Who can we call to talk to about this? Let's call some people to figure out what we can." We hadn't even viewed the trip to Florida as a choice. It was simply what needed to be done to fix the problem. The alternative "fix," to terminate the pregnancy, hadn't even entered our minds. Still, while neither of us thought there was much of a choice to be made, I pulled out my cell phone. "Let's call Dr. Hofmann. See what he says about this."

Carrie nodded listlessly.

I dialed and immediately connected with the receptionist.

"Hi. Good afternoon," I started. "Can we speak to or leave a message for a call back from Dr. Hofmann? My wife is a patient of his."

"I'm sorry, but Dr. Hofmann is at a conference in Florida right now. Can I leave a message for him?"

I sighed. "All right. Can you please have him call me on my cell phone?" I left my number and hung up.

"Should I call Dr. Pine or Dr. Jain?"

"Sure," Carrie said.

I dialed their office and got the receptionist. "Hello, can I speak with or leave a message for Dr. Pine or Dr. Jain please?"

"Dr. Pine is off this week and Dr. Jain is at a conference in Florida. Can someone else help out?"

I furrowed my brow and stuttered to respond, "In Florida?"

"Yes, that's right," she said.

"All right. No problem. No message," I said.

"What the heck is going on with this Florida conference?" I said to Carrie.

We sat in silence, unsure of what to do next. I opened my mouth to draw in a breath to speak when my cell phone rang. I looked down to see a blocked number. I pressed the green button and said hello.

A woman's voice responded with a strong background of murmurs from a crowd of people near her. "Hello, this is Dr. Steel. I work with Dr. Hofmann. Is this Jason?"

"Yes, it is. This is Jason and I am with my wife, Carrie, right now." I twisted the phone and moved it between us as we both craned our necks to position our ears nearby.

"I got a message that you called for Dr. Hofmann. We are both in Florida at a conference right now and he won't be able to call you back for a little while."

I replied, "Well, thank you for calling us back. We were just trying to get some advice and some thoughts from Dr. Hofmann about our situation. It's a little bit complicated..."

She cut me off. "Yes, I know. I know about your situation. Dr. Jain is down here at the conference as well and we've discussed it."

The hair on the back of my neck stood as Carrie and I glanced at each other and we connected the dots. Before I could respond, she continued, "The surgery is no certainty in terms of success, but Dr. Rodriguez is the right doctor for this condition."

"Right, that's what we are told," I said. "We just had a meeting with our other OB who told us he thought we should terminate, so we just wanted to talk to someone and get another view."

Dr. Steel replied, "You can legally terminate up to twenty-four weeks, so you might as well try the surgery and hope for the best."

The doctor's matter-of-fact tone caught me by surprise, especially in context of a risky surgery and potential complications that would drive us to a late-term abortion.

I answered back slowly, "All right. Well, that makes sense." I didn't feel there was more to get out of this conversation. "Thank you so much for calling me back so quickly."

"No problem," she said. "Good luck to you."

I chose not to return to work, but rather to go home so we could seek some advice from our families. We spoke to Carrie's parents on the phone for a while, then my parents. Later on, my mom and my sister-in-law, Alyse, came over to talk through everything.

After a gut-wrenching roller-coaster day, we decided later in the evening not to terminate—back to where we were before the day's appointment. We would make the trip to Florida and do our best to keep our healthy baby. My mom insisted on accompanying us to Florida, an offer we were happy to accept. Carrie's parents also decided they would make plans to meet us in Florida. The days ahead were likely, even in the best-case scenario, to be taxing emotionally and physically. We could use the extra hands, ears, and hearts.

I went back to work just for a day. I was mostly useless at my desk, able to think only about the surgery ahead. I was worried not only about the risks to our baby that sat ahead, but concerned for Carrie. To this point, her body had been through an awful lot with the treatments, needles, procedures, and checkups to get pregnant, plus the many challenges of a multiple pregnancy so far. That only accounted for the physical strain—the mental strain was at least as grueling, if not more.

With the trip to Florida, I would be missing a few days of work, not just disappearing from the office for a few hours at a time. I decided to discuss the situation with my boss. While I was not at all concerned that he would challenge me on the time off or the severity of the issue, I thought about a balance of information to share. Too much information was not necessary and not enough would leave him wondering about the reality.

I walked across the floor, around a set of gray cubicles about head height toward his office. It was not quite a corner office, but was at least the end of the row of offices with a window view across Vesey Street toward a hotel. It was unimpressive, but better than my office with no window. As I approached, I could see his door open, but heard him finishing a conversation. I wandered around a few times until I heard the final good-bye and click.

I peeked my head around the corner and into his office, gently tapping on the large oak door hanging open. "Jon, do you have a moment?"

He snapped his head up. "Sure, come on in."

Jon and I had not gelled as a close partnership, but I sensed he had a fair degree of respect for me as a developing member of the team. His physical stature was nothing to impress, with a modest height and less than medium build.

I closed the door behind me and sat in one of the two uncomfortable visitor chairs. "I haven't explained a lot about what has been going on with me, having taken a few days here and there and leaving the office for a few hours at a time, but I wanted to share at least a little color with you about what's been happening. My wife is pregnant."

He smiled broadly and began to open his mouth to offer a congratulations, which I prevented by continuing, "But it has been a very complicated pregnancy so far. Very complicated." His broad smile retracted into a manufactured look of concern.

I continued, "We actually need to go down to Florida tomorrow so she can undergo a complicated surgery. This doctor in Florida is the only one in the country who performs it, actually."

His concerned look turned to fear as he opted to jump in to avoid getting any further information. "Oh, you guys go do whatever is necessary. Don't worry about the office at all. Just take the time that you need."

His fearful response was all I needed, and I shared nothing further. "Thank you for your understanding, Jon. I really appreciate it."

I rose, opened the door, and walked out.

# 50. FLORIDA IS USUALLY FOR VACATION

The next evening, my mom, Carrie, and I were in Florida. Carrie's parents were set to fly down the following day and be there for the surgery.

We followed the directions closely to the Holiday Inn Express nearest the hospital, which sat on a major thoroughfare, across the street from a large shopping center. After checking in, we drove around back, pulling head-in to a spot facing room 124. To the back and left of our car, I noticed in the dark a quiet pond with a bench—perhaps a nice place to relax at some point during this ordeal.

We keyed our way into the room to find a perfectly adequate space. Two double beds, a bathroom, a TV, and a mini fridge. "Looks fine to me," I said. Carrie agreed and we walked out to check on my mom, a few rooms away.

"All right by you, Mom?"

"Sure. Perfect."

We spent a few minutes pulling our bags from the rental car and rolling them into our respective rooms. Afterward, we drove across the street to have a bite at Bennigan's, where we introduced my mother to Death by Chocolate for dessert. That wonderful choice put us under and we were all ready for an early bedtime, especially with a big day ahead.

The next morning, we woke early and had a quick bite from the limited continental breakfast at the hotel. We gathered into the car with directions in hand to make way toward St. Ann's Women's Hospital. The drive took about ten minutes with some confusion along the way and about which lot to park in at the hospital complex. The grounds had a very Florida feel—palm trees providing a shady entrance and geckos scurrying away from our feet as we walked to the building.

The automatic double doors parted for us, exposing a quiet interior with no immediate signs of life. I then noticed a guard way down the hall at a podium, so we headed there for direction. The fifty-year-old graying female security guard dressed in full uniform directed us farther down the hall, a couple of turns and to a waiting room for pre-admission.

Upon arrival, we found life—the room was already mostly filled with patients sitting in chairs, filling out forms, doing crosswords, or watching the faintly audible thirteen-inch tube TV hanging below the ceiling in the far corner of the room. My mom settled into an open seat and spread her purse and sweater across two other adjacent seats while Carrie and I found the check-in window.

"Hello," I said. "We have an appointment with Dr. Rodriguez this morning."

We were greeted in return, directed to mark ourselves on the sign-in sheet, and given a clipboard full of paperwork to complete.

We sat in the seats my mom had reserved and Carrie began filling out the forms. As she did that, my eyes wandered around the room. There was a full variety of ages and races, some pregnant couples and some elderly men and women. The waiting room itself was warm from the sun beating through the glass and only modest size. We sat on plastic chairs that for the most part did not match each other.

Carrie eventually finished the forms, which I turned in along with her driver's license and insurance card for a quick photocopy. We then waited essentially in silence for almost an hour.

"Carrie Mandel," a nurse with a clipboard finally called out.

Carrie and I rose. "We'll see you in a bit," I said to my mom. We were led back to a small room in which we immediately noticed one of the advanced ultrasounds from Dr. Jain and company's offices. The room was small, just large enough to fit the examining table and ultrasound. Carrie sat on the edge of the examining table and I perched on the stool in the corner on the far side of the room. It was only a minute or two before a fairly tall, thin woman with brown hair dropping onto the shoulders of her white coat walked in.

"Good morning," she said. We responded in kind, but the small talk was kept to a minimum. "Go ahead and lie down and pull up your shirt for me."

Carrie assumed the standard position, lifted her shirt, and our ultrasound technician squeezed the blue goo onto Carrie. The tech began the exam with her wand drifting over Carrie's belly and staring at the shapes and colors on the screen. She dragged the wand across her belly in each direction to get her bearings. Unlike many of our previous first-time ultrasound scans, she did not appear disoriented and did not ask any questions. As she figured the positioning inside of Carrie, she took several measurements, then turned on the sound. Carrie and I smiled softly at each other as we heard the heartbeat. Our technician remained focused on the task. She measured and listened, then flipped another switch and red and blue colors jumped around on the screen. Real-time graphs appeared at the bottom while the technician held still to watch. She turned on the three-dimensional feature and gazed at all angles around Maddie and her siblings. All the while, the machine hummed as photo printouts emerged from below the keyboard. The pictures remained attached as they rolled out, much like a run of winning tickets in Skee-Ball. Several times during the lengthy, thorough scan, I looked at Carrie, who returned the unspoken thought—*What is she seeing?* On the one hand, the lengthy scans reminded me of multiple recent scans where the doctors were at best confused by what they were seeing. However, her demeanor never indicated any uncertainty over what appeared on the screen.

Eventually, she stopped and tore the long train of photos from the machine and lightly folded them over a few times before fitting them into our medical folder. "I'm just going to step out to discuss with Dr. Rodriguez. We'll be back shortly." She grabbed a towel and simply covered Carrie's belly. "Just hang out like this for right now in case we need more pictures."

As she walked out of the room, I softly commented, "That was one heck of a scan."

"I know. She was thorough—that's for sure."

We sat calmly and filled the room with minor small talk about dinner and the hotel and the flight down to Florida. We were both nervous that Dr. Rodriguez would find something different than what we knew.

The technician returned in short order. "I need to take a few more pictures."

We sat in silence once more as she scanned and measured and printed for another five minutes or so. Toward the end of the scan, Carrie broke in. "This seems pretty thorough. Does this cover me for my twenty-week scan?"

"Oh, absolutely," she answered. "This is far more detailed than you'd get at a standard twenty-weeker." She paused, then said, "And that's all I need. I will be back again in a few minutes." She tore the new photos from the machine and again covered Carrie.

In a few short minutes, the tech returned flanked by a dark-haired man with a dark complexion, dressed in dark slacks and a blue button-down collared shirt. "Good day, I am Dr. Rodriguez," he said in a strong, deep voice with a distinct Latino accent.

We both greeted him as he reached for the ultrasound. He removed the towel from Carrie and scanned. He switched the screen into the blue and red colors, moved the wand slowly to get perfectly into position, and with a press of a button, froze the screen. "There it is. That's the diagnosis right there."

He pointed to the blood flow speckled lines and then a section of the chart on the bottom showing a dip below the zero-line where the chart turned red.

"That's the diagnosis—TRAP sequence. Reverse blood flow in the acardiac twin—through the umbilical cord being pumped by your baby."

We sat silent for a moment, soaking in the authoritative nature of the diagnosis, and the simple straightforward reconfirmation of what we already understood to be the case.

He continued by turning his attention away from the machine and to us directly. "Tell me more about the procedures you've already had—the CVS and the reduction."

Carrie began to explain we had the CVS to gather more information about our children before making a decision as severe as a reduction. She went on to explain the complicated position of our children during the reduction, which as a result required two needle sticks.

He was not pleased, asking quizzically to describe the reduction again, and why two sticks were needed.

After a loud exhale through his nose and a fresh breath in he said, "Having three sticks already into the uterus definitely makes this procedure riskier."

He paused just long enough for Carrie and me to separately and silently fear he would not help us.

He glanced back at the screen once more and continued, "The three sticks and the difficult positioning of Maddie's sac makes this complicated, but I will do the surgery."

Half of my body was relieved he would perform for us and the other half was paralyzed by the reality that he would. It was a strange moment. I don't believe either of us realized this appointment was an evaluation for our candidacy. We thought that had already happened with the medical info our doctors had sent ahead previously. I asked, "Is the surgery more or less complicated by the fact that it's an acardiac twin, and not straight TTTS?"

"It actually makes it a bit riskier, but I hope not to have to touch Maddie's sac at all. I am going to have Dr. Anand come join us so I can show him everything. He works with me, learning this procedure."

The authoritative Dr. Rodriguez didn't wait for any approval from us and in a moment, a shorter doctor with an uncomfortable smile, submissive slumped shoulders, and hairy hands walked in. He meekly greeted us with a hello and Dr. Rodriguez briefed him on the details, pointing him through the unfrozen images on the screen.

After the teaching session, Dr. Rodriguez turned to us and offered his farewell. "Dr. Anand is going to take some more information from you and the nurse will give you instructions for tomorrow morning. See you in the morning," and with that he was gone.

Our eyes turned to the subordinate doctor, who fumbled for his pen and medical chart. "Can you tell me any medications you are on, allergies, surgeries you've had and conditions you have?"

We looked at each other and both smirked, knowing the list was fairly long. Carrie shared her hypothyroidism and current prescription, nodule that was detected on her thyroid, her allergy to Pyridium, a drug most doctors seemed not to know, her rare blood condition that other than being rare has no known adverse effects, her recurrent kidney stones and lithotripsy procedures to eradicate them, her polycystic ovarian syndrome which ultimately led us down the winding path that brought us to this very room and the procedures during her pregnancy. The list was long and as usual, Carrie was overly descriptive and included minor issues that some others might have omitted, intentionally or not.

Carrie finished and looked to me, raising her eyebrows and tilting her head, silently asking if she missed anything. Dr. Anand snapped his first normal smirk of amusement. "Is that all?" he asked with unexpected sarcastic humor.

"I think that's it," Carrie offered and chuckled.

He began to close the chart when Carrie interrupted, "Oh, and I have a heart murmur."

Another glimpse of a sense of humor from Dr. Anand came with his mocking response, "Is there anything else?!" amused by the last-minute recollection of a pertinent medical condition when considering the upcoming surgical procedure.

Carrie laughed. "Yes, I think so. It's a benign functional flow heart murmur."

Dr. Anand reopened the record, made a notation, and flipped it back closed. He smiled at us softly and quiet filled the room for a shade too long. He broke it with, "We'll see you here tomorrow morning at eight a.m. Try to relax tonight and have a nice evening." He turned to leave and halted abruptly. "And no eating after midnight. See you in the morning."

We smiled back at him as he turned and left.

I leaned in and lay across Carrie, wrapping my arms around her.

# 51. PREP

The travel alarm blared to life with its incessant beeping and I lurched to silence it. I turned back and Carrie's eyes were open without squinting into the bright room as the blackout curtains failed at their job. "You've been up for a while?" I asked.

"Yes."

"What have you been thinking?" Of course I knew generally the topic, but not the details.

"It could go either way." Silence. She connected eyes with me. "We may or may not be pregnant after today."

All of the start and stop, rush and wait with the symptoms, the interrupted scrambles for a diagnosis, and it all came down to today. The simple thought that it could just be over today was halting. We could go back to the airport and return to New York as just a couple again, not an expecting couple.

"You are right," I eventually responded. Enough times we've heard from others *It'll be all right*, and I wasn't about to blow smoke. "We can pray for a good day today, but you are right. Today could be a bad day. Just know I'm with you and I love you."

We embraced and held tight for a solid minute.

"All right," I interrupted and pulled back in a more positive, energetic manner. "We've got someplace to go. Let's get up and get ready. And hey— your parents should be here soon."

Matt and Nancy were supposed to have arrived from Detroit before our alarm went off.

She smiled back. "Yes—hopefully the flight was no problem."

We dressed, brushed our teeth, packed up a bag for the hospital, and then there was a knock at the door. Carrie answered it and was immediately in her mom's arms for a relieving hug. Then to her dad. After brief greetings and the appearance of my mother, we locked up and filed into the rental cars to follow each other to the hospital for the cord ligation—the formal name for the surgery.

I pulled out of the hotel slowly, allowing Matt and Nancy to keep behind. As we pulled into traffic and reached cruising speed, I pulled my right hand off the wheel and dropped it atop Carrie's shaking hand on her knee. I pulled a glance from the road to her eyes, reddened and moist with worry. My best comfort was to give a quick soft smile and small kiss into the air.

We parked the cars and all walked together into the hospital very quietly.

"Carrie Mandel," Carrie said to the desk attendant in the surgery office.

The woman bounced the eraser end of her pencil down a list of names until finding the spot to flip it around and mark a dot. She reached to the side and grabbed a beeper to hand to us—as though we were awaiting a table at Applebee's.

The five of us sat in the waiting room waiting for the beep, speaking about meaningless items—Death by Chocolate, the flight down, the hotel room—anything to escape the coming event for a few more minutes.

Without a long wait, the beeper summoned us back to the desk. I hurried to check in and was told we would have to begin the surgery prep and only I could accompany Carrie. Carrie took turns with long hugs from my mother and from each of her parents, who all wished luck, but avoided telling us "everything will be fine." I assured them I would come back out to post on developments when I could.

For the next two hours, we bounced back and forth between blood work, medical history, Carrie escaping to the bathroom for nervous poops, IV prep, and more medical history. At one point, when Carrie was completing a medical history to the anesthesiologist, I interjected to remind her of the heart problem. "Carrie has a benign functional flow heart murmur," I offered.

He glanced for a moment then tilted his head down to make a notation, saying, "Are you a doctor?"

We both giggled, as our command of the medical terms, if not their explanations as well, had improved dramatically through these various trials.

"You are all ready now," our nurse finally said. "We are going to move you to another room and when the doctors are ready, probably in less than an hour, we'll bring you into surgery, all right?"

We turned the corner and through an open doorway went into what appeared to be a recovery room with several beds aligned with their heads along the wall, protruding out into the room with a couple of the curtains drawn along ceiling tracks closed around their respective beds. Facing the beds were several nurse's desks along the opposite wall and a fair amount of bustle with coming, going, and conversation. The room was bland, with white walls, scratched and faded in several spots. The sound of construction—pounding, sawing, and jackhammering—was unmistakable behind our new nurse's explanations. "Hi there, honey, my name is Star," she said in an awkwardly chipper tone. "We won't be in here for too long, but you need to just try to relax as much as you can—it will help with the surgery. You will be medicated and sedated but will also have to be awake and conscious enough for the doctors."

Between the fear of pain, the surgery's potential results, and the relentless hammering outside, Carrie faded to a sob. I placed my hand over her forehead and tears began to stream out the sides of her eyes and toward her ears.

"Oh, honey, you are going to be all right. They are great doctors. Let me give you something to help you relax." Star stole away to her desk near the foot of the bed and rustled up two pills and a small baggie. "Here you go, sweetie. Take these—it will calm your nerves—and put this on." She handed the baggie to me and I pulled out a set of cheap plastic headphones printed with "St. Ann's Women's Hospital," attached to a small pill-bottle-sized device that I discovered to have a dial on the side to adjust the preferred FM radio station—not a bad idea given the loud noises.

Carrie took the pills and I set her up with a calm radio station. I fluffed the pillow under her head and pulled the blanket higher. Carrie blinked her eyes slowly and stared at me for a minute as I draped my hand over her forehead and began to softly stroke back her blonde hair. For the next twenty minutes, I kept sliding my fingers over her head as she gradually calmed and actually drifted to sleep, much to my surprise.

Star approached me. "They're just about ready. We have to do one more ultrasound before she goes in."

"All right," I said. "Is there any way she can see her parents one more time before?"

A big smile across Star's face. "Sure thing. Go ahead and get them—they can watch the ultrasound."

Knowing Carrie would need to be awake soon, I gently palmed the side of her face and leaned in to wake her without a start. "Car. They're almost ready to start. I am going to get our parents so they can say hi again."

As I walked out into the waiting room, I discovered my mom staring down at her phone, and Matt and Nancy inattentively watching the television. "Hey, guys. Carrie's going in a few minutes—you can come in to say hi one more time."

The three of them quickly shuffled to their feet, grabbing purses and newspapers. I led them down the hall and into the pre-operative room. We walked briskly to the far end of the room and discovered Carrie in bed with her gown already pulled over her belly and Dr. Anand working the wand. Carrie didn't look much like herself with puffy, red, watery eyes, a long face, and a weak, exhausted smile. Nancy rushed to her and wrapped her forearm around the far side of her head, leaning down to plant a soft upside-down forehead kiss. We circled around the screen as Carrie realized, "Mom, this is the first time you've seen her like this."

As we stared at the screen, an image of a curled fetus came into view, but only momentarily. In an instant it was gone, and then found again, flipping and kicking. "She's active right now," said Dr. Anand. "We will have to work carefully and may have to adjust the sedation, but we'll try to avoid that." He pulled the wand off her belly and rolled the ultrasound away.

"We are ready now. Go ahead and say your 'see you laters' and Star will bring you in."

The four of us took turns bending over the bed for tight hugs and reassuring kisses. I went last, whispering into her ear, "Just try to relax as much as you can. You are an amazingly strong woman and I love you more than anything. I will be there to see you as soon as you are done."

# 52. SURGERY

Carrie was wheeled into an ice-cold operating room. She followed instructions and swung her legs around to get off of the gurney and sit, turn, and lie down on the freezing cold operating table. As they prepared the instruments and monitors and sanitized her belly, she drearily dragged her eyes from one action to the other like a misty three-ring circus. The relaxants were helping to dull the sharpness of the actions around her, but her fear of not being in control still remained somewhat. The nurses prepared a site and splashed a small needle into her belly, numbing the area. The large needles and scopes came out next, with a deeper injection, drifting further inside— to the uterus. As the doctors lowered the instruments into her, they watched a screen above with a view inside. While the numbing helped at the surface, Carrie felt discomfort and pressure inside. The pain was not quite sharp nor dull and the relaxants continued to obscure the broader senses.

She drifted off for some period of time and was woken by Star, still in the OR and still in the same position. "Everything went very well, Carrie. If you look up at the monitor," Star said, leaning down to place her head near Carrie's and pointing upward, "you can see what we did."

Carrie, holding Star's hand and seeing an arm in the image, interrupted, mustering some words, "Is that the healthy baby?"

In a dour voice, Star lowered her eyes and responded, "No, sweetie."

Carrie's eyes cleared more and the image appeared more clearly. Clear enough to see red lesions covering the very white arms and body of the acardiac twin. She squeezed her eyes shut and immediately knew that would be an image that she could never unsee.

She didn't open her eyes again for Star to point out the incredible successful actions that had been taken inside of Carrie's belly through a tiny needle hole. What she saw was more than enough to handle.

As the participants in the room clinked and cleaned up, a new bed was rolled up next to the operating table. "Now we need you to scoot over and onto this bed," Star said.

At the first attempt to activate her muscles to reposition her body, a heavy cramp kicked in. She froze in position and silence. It eased for just a moment for her to exclaim a cry of pain when it returned again with great intensity. The cramps were clenching her uterus uncontrollably and Carrie began to roll back and forth. "It's cramping," was all she could get out, focusing the whole of her breath on the clenching muscles.

The doctor scrambled for a needle, extracted some liquid from a clear glass bottle, flicked the side, shot some fluid out to clear the air, then jabbed it into her arm. After a few moments, the clenching pain receded. With much discomfort, Carrie wiggled and scooted to get herself from the operating table to the fresh bed sheets.

After Carrie was wheeled away from us and into the cold operating room, I experienced the opposite end of the spectrum. I had taken a walk to the cafeteria. The room was dark. There were straw wrappers, sugar crystals, and sugar packets lying around the coffee station. The mixture of smells in the room coalesced to a pungent collision of coffee, pizza, fried chicken, fries, burgers, and soups. I grabbed a green tray, still wet from a rag wipe, and surveyed my options. At the moment, I was the only patron and there was only one worker, refilling the large silver catering dish with more pasta. I motioned to the pizza and she motioned back with her index finger for *one moment.*

She walked around the back to the pizza station and doled out two slices onto a flimsy plate and pushed it out to me. Seeing it up close now, I figured the pool of grease would be difficult to sop up with the paper-thin napkins. But it was on my tray and staying. I grabbed a soda and placed my tray on the track leading to the register, where my pizza server and the pasta-refiller paused her other duties to come around and ring up my order.

I plunked my tray down at a table with my mom and Carrie's parents. About halfway through the first slice, the doctor came out. "Mr. Mandel."

My eyebrows jumped first, pulling the rest of my face up to meet the doctor's eyes. "Yes." It had only been maybe twenty minutes since Carrie disappeared. I hadn't even sopped up the oil on my second piece, checked my BlackBerry emails and voicemails, or read the paper. My stomach fluttered with fear that fast news is bad news.

"Everything went very well."

My breath returned.

"There was no need to touch Maddie's sac, which is of course something we were concerned about. So really, it all went well."

"That's great," as I exhaled.

"After the procedure, Carrie had a couple of big contractions. We immediately gave her terbutaline and that calmed them down quite a bit. Come with me. You can see her now."

I turned to my mom and Carrie's parents, who had overheard everything. I began to speak when they all shouted in unison, "Go."

I hustled out to the recovery room to go find Carrie. I was hoping to see her resting comfortably.

"J," she pleaded as I came around the curtain. "I'm hurting. I keep cramping."

Her hands were palming her belly, avoiding a fresh bandage off to the right side. A strap around her belly was hooked to a monitor, streaming out paper with black printed lines. I softly placed my hand on her forehead and kissed her lips. I looked at the paper coming out of the machine showing repeated rolling hills well above the zero-line.

I turned to Dr. Anand and asked about the contractions.

"They are strong and regular right now. This is not entirely unusual, but we will have to watch closely and continue medications to control them. The surgery went well, but the next twenty-four hours are still very important."

We thanked the doctor, who then left us in the busy room.

I made all efforts to comfort Carrie and only wanted to take her pain away and stop the contractions. For the next half hour, she continued to squirm with each contraction and shuffle positions in the bed, desperately seeking to find the elusive comfortable spot.

It wasn't terribly long before a nurse walked to the bed. "All right. We are going to move you to your room now." An aide walked in and very efficiently clicked to release the wheels, unplugged Carrie from the monitor, laid the wires on the bed alongside, and pulled the bed and rolling IV stand from the stall. I followed as Carrie was wheeled out of the room and down the hall. We passed by the waiting room, where I poked my head in to post our parents of the move. They quickly grabbed their things and followed.

We rolled into a large private room, with wood grain accents on the walls, a TV, a credenza with flowers, a leather couch, and a set of tall windows. I turned back to our parents and imparted my surprise with a quick lift of my eyebrows. Nice accommodations compared to the other areas we'd seen so far.

As the handler situated Carrie, hooking her wires back up to a new monitor, she groaned again. "J, I'm really hurting."

At that moment, a new nurse walked through the door, welcoming us all and introducing herself as the nurse on shift for the next few hours.

"How are we feeling?" she asked Carrie.

Seeing her discomfort, I answered for her. "She is still in an awful lot of pain and keeps having the rolling contractions. Is there anything more we can do for her?"

After a brief look at the chart's standing orders, she looked up at Carrie.

"All right. I can give you something to take the pain down a notch. It may make you a little drowsy and loopy."

Carrie nodded and I answered verbally, "That would be great, thank you."

I watched as the nurse drew liquid from a vial into the syringe and then injected it into the IV line hooked to Carrie's arm.

I turned to our parents and shared the doctor's comments. "It went very well and was successful. But the next twenty-four hours are still pretty critical. Carrie is having a lot of contractions and they're going to try to control them as much as possible with meds."

They all nodded, visibly concerned about Carrie's current condition.

We sat around and spoke intermittently for the next half hour as the drugs kicked in. Carrie began a pattern of dozing off and waking suddenly. Her body would shake for a second, pulling her out of her sleep to apologize to all of us for sleeping.

I implored upon her, "Carrie, it's fine. Just relax and let yourself get some sleep. You don't need to entertain us."

She again drifted away and woke to apologize again.

The sun was falling and my mother suggested they all get going and leave the two of us in quiet. As I hugged everyone, Carrie woke again. "I'm sorry. You can stay."

"No, no," my mom said. "We are going to leave you alone. We are going to get some dinner with Aunt Cheryl. Just rest."

Carrie was visibly exhausted and anxious at the same time, frustrated she could not be a better host.

"Go ahead, guys," I said. "Enjoy dinner. We also have some stuff in our fridge at the hotel if you need. Some yogurt and other stuff. Feel free to have anything you want from in there for tonight or in the morning."

"And there's beer. There's beer in our fridge," Carrie jumped in, seeking again to better host our parents.

I turned to her with a smile and a chuckle. "Carrie, we don't have any beer at the hotel. Just rest."

She shook her head, trying to force off the confusion brought by the medication, and then chuckled a bit herself. "I don't know why I said that. I know we don't have beer at the hotel."

They each took a quick turn kissing Carrie goodnight and then I shuffled them to the doorway.

"I love you," Carrie squeezed out as she slowly drifted back to sleep again.

As they walked out, I hoped the drugs would settle Carrie and the night would be smooth.

Unfortunately, I knew better.

For the next couple of hours, Carrie startled awake every ten minutes or so, moaning with the pain of another set of contractions. Each time, I would repeatedly rush to her bedside and she would grab my hand and place it on her belly. "Do you feel that?" she would ask. I could feel every one of the contractions, with her belly firm like an overinflated basketball. "Yes, I do," I would reply, with my eyes on the paper spitting out of the monitor. At the end of each contraction, I could unfurl the stretch of waxy printout and see the progression of contractions charted out in mounds rising from the flatline zero level. More and more through the night, Carrie had difficulty falling back to sleep between the contractions despite her extreme exhaustion, only adding to her understandable irritability.

After some time had passed, the staff nurse and Dr. Anand came to check on us. As he asked how Carrie was feeling, he tore off the rolling printout to review. Carrie's complaints matched what the doctor saw on paper and he suggested we move to try something else.

"I would like to move on to a terbutaline pump. This is not going to make you any more comfortable, but," he said, motioning to her belly, "will hopefully keep your baby safely inside. The terbutaline is fairly strong, but also will probably make you jittery. I know that is not what you want, but I think it is our best option at the moment." Terbutaline was used to halt preterm labor but was determined years later to be unsafe for the baby.

Carrie visibly and audibly sighed, seeing no relief for herself, but rather immediately said, "Yes, let's do that, then."

"All right," Dr. Anand responded. "We are going to run a new IV into your thigh and connect a pump that will provide small doses every hour, but will drop a larger dose every four hours, starting with the first one now."

We thanked both of them and they filed out of the room. I draped my hand onto Carrie's forehead and stroked her hair back. "I'll be right here with you. This doesn't sound like it will be fun, but if it will slow the contractions, I guess that's best."

"I know," she said and forced a smile up at me. I dropped down to kiss her for a moment and the nurse walked back in.

"I just need to bother you for a minute to run the new line and hook up the pump. Then I'll let you be," said the nurse. She had rolled into the room another IV stand, with a beige box hanging from it. She had Carrie roll slightly and succeeded with the prick and new IV on the first shot. When she finished, her attention turned to the pump itself, which required programming. She pecked away at keys, generating short, high-pitched pulses while her eyes darted back and forth from the chart to the pump. Eventually she finished and left us alone once more. Carrie tried to rest quietly.

Less than ten minutes later, "J—come here," Carrie rushed.

I hopped up from the cushy lounge chair to her side. Her eyebrows were furled, lips pursed, and she dropped short breaths out through her nose.

"I feel like crap. All awake and… I don't know, just uncomfortable. It's like a hyper, can't relax, intense feeling."

I took her hand in mine and rubbed it slowly. "I'm sorry, baby. I think this is just what they warned about. How is your belly?"

"I don't know. OK right now, I guess." As she finished the sentence, her face tightened further and her free hand covered her belly. "Here it is again," she squeaked out through clenched teeth.

I could see the monitor reading tick higher and the softness in Carrie's belly disappear.

Over the next few hours, Carrie drifted between the jittery uneasy feeling with contractions and a more subdued state, generally dictated by the timing of the intermittent machine-controlled injections. During one of the downtimes that allowed Carrie a twenty-minute nap, I shrunk into the lounge chair and typed. I fired away with my thumbs on my work-issued BlackBerry, explaining in modest detail how the surgery had gone and the current conditions. It never quite occurred to me at the time why, but I felt a need to share. While typically a private person, on this night I wrote. I didn't blog my experience, contribute to a chat room, or post it on Facebook. I had no Facebook account (and still do not). Instead, I typed out a lengthy email with the day's events and my worries about losing the pregnancy soon.

When I was done, I really wasn't sure who to send it to. I chose a handful of close friends and even added some work colleagues. Perhaps sending to colleagues was more of a need to prove that I was not on a beach or in a bar somewhere, but rather working through some heavy medical and emotional situations that obviously trumped anything they might be going through or have ever gone through. We all have our incredible stories, so this thought process was presumptuous, but it was also around three a.m. and the cobwebs were forming between my ears. I may have also been thinking in there somewhere that if I laid this all out, nobody would ask any questions when I got back.

I don't recall getting many responses from the email blast after that night. I presume most of my friends simply did not know what to say and my colleagues less so. Carrie and I were the first of our friends to marry and the first to try to have a child. Even basic pregnancy details would likely have left them dumbfounded, let alone intrauterine surgery for TRAP sequence to separate an acephalic twin from our surviving baby.

After a few more interim doses from the terbutaline pump, Carrie begged for it to be taken out before the big fourth-hour dose. I tracked down the nurses with speed and got them to get the approval from the doc, switching instead to a muscle relaxer. The night drew on and the contractions continued but they waned gradually. Between the smaller and smaller peaks on the printout, Carrie began falling asleep easier and I eventually started to doze off as well.

The Florida sun sliced through the edges of the window shade, poking me to wake. Carrie was sleeping soundly. I quietly shoved aside the hospital blanket and rose from the pleather chair to head around the bed to the printer. I pulled on the long string of paper to see a series of shrinking hills.

As I held the papers approvingly, the pair of doctors walked into the room. Nobody sleeps in a hospital, or so one would think from the way the staff goes about their duties.

"Good morning," Dr. Rodriguez said behind my back from the doorway. It was no yell, but there was also no restraint or whisper in his voice.

I spun around quickly, greeting the two doctors while dropping the papers like the cat with the canary.

He inquired about how Carrie had been since the difficulties into the night.

"Better. I think she's finally been getting some sleep and the contractions have calmed." Carrie's eyes fluttered open to a blurry grouping discussing her well-being.

"Yes, it got better finally," Carrie said. I edged my head back on my shoulders, surprised at Carrie's coherence after a lack of sufficient sleep and multiple heavy drugs.

"Well, it seems as such. We're going to work through some instructions with you and then let you go soon." He looked at me and back at Carrie to ensure focus. "Bed rest. Strict bed rest is key as we discussed. You're not flying back for a few days, right?"

We confirmed with nods. It was part of the requirement to qualify for the surgery—willingness to limit any strenuous movement for a few days including travel.

"When you do travel back to New York, please try to take it slow and easy. And then right back to bed rest." They continued with further instructions, but this was really the one that mattered.

Hours later, Carrie was discharged from the hospital and rolled in a wheelchair out the front door to the car my mom had waiting for us. We carefully helped Carrie into the car and headed for the hotel. Carrie didn't speak much during the ride, hand on her belly, staring out into the sunlight.

We arrived and carefully transitioned Carrie from the car into the bed in our hotel room. I worked to place and move and prop pillows for her maximum comfort.

"I'm good. Thanks, Jas. I'm comfortable."

I turned on the TV on low volume and we both sat, exhausted despite the limited physical effort so far for the day. I stared out the window to find the peaceful pond only to see a large eighteen-wheeler with a racecar painted on the side had parked in front of it. Great. Confined to the hotel room and even our view of the glorified sump out the window was blocked by traffic.

The next few days passed with little activity and little incident.

# 53. LET'S GO HOME

Travel day finally arrived.

Carrie's parents left early in the morning for their Detroit flight and we headed out a bit later.

Carrie walked slowly with us through the airport. After checking our bags, I held her arm as we headed to the elevator bound for the departures level. A green light lit with a soft ding and the elevator door opened. A man standing next to us pulled aside and motioned for Carrie to go ahead. She walked in, as I held her hand and followed. My mom walked in behind and then the gentleman.

He looked at Carrie again and motioned to her belly. "You're not going to give birth right here, are ya?" and chuckled.

Carrie fake-chuckled back. "No." It never ceases to amaze about the comments some people believe are appropriate to make. Carrie held her composure well, but squeezed my hand in annoyance. In all fairness and thanks to this crazy pregnancy, Carrie was twenty weeks but looked full term.

We made our way gradually through the airport, reaching the gate with plenty of extra time, and sat patiently until called to board. The clientele all around us at the JetBlue gate was notably older than us.

"We will now start the preboarding process. Anyone in need of extra time during the boarding process please come forward."

A caravan of wheelchairs rolled through the crowd and toward the Jetway. I was used to seeing maybe one or two wheelchairs in my past travel, so this caught us all by surprise and we couldn't help but giggle at the scene. In fact, the preboarding process seemed to board half of the aircraft.

After a long few days in Florida that were very serious and emotionally challenging, the comic relief of what we were witness to was actually welcomed. And there was more to come.

The rest of the plane boarded and we pulled away from the gate, taxied, and blasted off right about on time. We weren't in the air long before the seatbelt sign was shut off and an older lady across the aisle from us rose carefully to head for the small bathroom.

I sat staring out the window until I noticed a faint smell. I squinted my eyes as I turned my head toward the center of the plane and sniffed again. "Do you smell something?" I asked Carrie. She has an acute sense of smell and if she didn't smell anything then I knew it was in my head.

"Smoke," she said right away, but not alarmed. "That's smoke. But it's cigarette smoke."

Moments later we noticed two flight attendants knocking at the bathroom door and calling out for the occupant to open the door and come out. Soon after, the door opened and the flight attendants were angrily but calmly speaking to the older lady. The smoke smell quickly became far more noticeable. We were too far away to hear much on the airplane, but it was obvious she was being scolded for her illegal behavior. They sent her back to her seat and as she walked away from them, the two attendants shared a look of disbelief.

Only minutes later, the same lady was pressing her service call button above her head and one of the two showed up seat-side to see what now.

As much as we cared to snoop, the loud plane made overhearing the conversation difficult, but the lady was clearly motioning to the overhead bin. Then she spoke up enough for us to hear, in an incredibly raspy voice much like Rip Torn, "I need it for my emphysema!"

Frustrated, the attendant opened the bin and pulled out a metal tank to place on the ground next to her seat. The passenger with emphysema needed her oxygen after sneaking a cigarette in the bathroom of the plane.

Carrie turned to me and laughed. "What the hell is going on?" I dropped my head in hard to control laughter, trying not to be overly obvious who we were both making fun of.

The lady held the oxygen mask to her face and pulled it away several times to release heavy, wet, tarry coughs. Moments later they were followed up by loud and prolonged belly burps.

Now with a far louder voice, but still deep and coarse, she turned to the unlucky passenger next to her and offered, "I have a lot of gas!" The explanation surely was comforting to her seatmate but Carrie and I together turned away to cover our uncontrolled laughs.

The two of us laughing idiots looked around and we each one after the other made brief eye contact with one of the flight attendants, who smirked and quickly looked away as well to avoid breaking up into a full cackle.

The comedic plane ride eventually came to an end and we were excited to finally get back to our home. When the seat belt sign dinged off, the two of us remained seated, waiting for the door to open and provide an opportunity to move. The overhead bins were being opened and an older man flying with his wife reached for her cane for the trip down the Jetway, when it tumbled out onto Carrie's head.

"Ow!" Carrie shouted. She wasn't trying to be mad or rude, but simply reacted to the sudden slam on her head. The man barely apologized and took the device back from Carrie for his wife.

"We better get off this plane before anything else happens," I quipped to Carrie.

"Let's go!" she agreed.

Finally down the aisle and stepping off the plane, we walked past the gate-checked luggage and a lineup of wheelchairs with attendants that ran the full length of the Jetway.

We were finally back in New York and soon back to our house and our own bed.

# 54. CAN'T DO BED REST ALONE

Back in New York and with the surgery over, it was time to formally switch doctors. Following the instructions given to me by our new preferred office, I faxed a letter to Dr. Feinman requesting files to immediately be transferred. I followed up with a call to his office, asking the secretary to leave a very clear message. "If there are any questions, call ME, not Carrie."

The last thing I wanted was for Dr. Feinman to call and get Carrie on the phone—and make her feel bad for wanting to switch.

He did call me later that day.

"I received your request to transfer," he said.

"Yes. Please have the records sent over," I said plainly.

"Can I ask why? Is there some reason for this?" he asked somewhat meekly. I sensed he already had a clue.

"Because you missed this." That was all I said, and allowed the line to lay silent. I had an urge to expand but landed on being direct and to the point with no confusion and without diluting the focus.

"OK," he said and the conversation was over.

At home, Carrie and I waited for our candidates to arrive. We had decided that strict bed rest while I was commuting to work would mean that Carrie needed help. Help with preparing her meals, doing laundry, handling some cleaning, walking Socks, and anything else that would otherwise require standing and walking. We were both nervous to meet the caretakers. We weren't looking for nurses, but people who were qualified just enough for the simple tasks needed, and therefore costing way less than skilled help.

The doorbell rang and I walked down to answer. A man stood at the front door, and I could see past him to a car parked on our street in front of the house. It appeared to have someone in it.

"Hello, good morning," I greeted.

"Hello, how are you?" the man answered kindly in a modest Latin accent. He could tell by my puzzled look that I wasn't prepared to let him in without understanding the situation. The help we had scheduled for interviews all happened to be women.

"Can I help you?" I asked, still on my side of the threshold.

"Oh yes. I'm so sorry. My sisters are Mary and Olga." He motioned to the car. "They have an appointment to meet with you about the job."

I again looked past and could now make out one woman in the front seat with her head down in her hands apparently sobbing. It was unsettling and awkward, but I invited him in. At very least it had become clear they were here for the same reason we were expecting company.

I invited him up to the bedroom, where we decided the interviews would take place. After all, Carrie was on bed rest and that room would be Carrie's spot for most of the time going forward.

"I am Stephan," he introduced himself to me and then to Carrie, shaking our hands. Carrie looked up at me with furrowed brows. *Why is there a man here?* she asked of me with just her eyes. *I have no idea*, I responded with only my shoulders.

He continued, "My sisters are very interested in helping out. In this job."

I tilted my head and had to ask finally, "Is there some reason they aren't here with us now?"

Surprised we might ask such a thing, he answered, "Oh, don't worry about that. Mary is in the car outside. But she is very nervous and doesn't speak much English." Carrie and I locked eyes.

He started asking us questions about the job, the pay, how long it would likely last, how many hours per week, and more. We answered them one by one, hesitantly.

"I'm not very sure this is going to fit right, since it's a short-term job. We're looking for something a little bit longer," he suggested.

Snatching the opening, I groaned back, "Well, that's too bad. Maybe this just isn't the right fit for both of us. So sorry about that."

He seemed surprised I took to his hint of uncertainty by closing the book, but Carrie smiled at me approvingly. I helped usher him back out to the door and wished him luck.

"What was that?" I came upstairs spouting as their car drove away. "Is he their pimp or something?"

"I was so confused when you came up here with a guy," she blurted back and dropped her head into her hands laughing. "That was so weird."

"She was in the car crying! The car was right out front and I could see her in the front seat!" I shared.

"No fucking way!"

"Way!"

We laughed together for a minute until we came to realize that our slate of candidates could all be quite interesting.

We waited well past the time for the second appointment with nobody coming to the door. Eventually the phone rang. It was Lupe—our second candidate. She apologized to me for failing to show, but that she had just taken a job. Wonderful.

Eventually our third appointment actually did arrive, and this time, it was our candidate—live and in person. "Hello, I'm Zaria," she greeted me as I opened the door for her. She seemed nice right off the bat and able to communicate clearly. We walked up to Carrie in the bedroom and the chat kicked right off with ease. Zaria was bubbly and excited and kept telling us how hard she was willing to work. "I can make you food and bring you anything you need. If you run out of things for me to do, I can clean the house. If you have a cleaning girl, you should just fire her. I can do that job while I'm here with you all day. Usually my whole family gets together at one of our houses and we clean all day—we all love it."

*Who is this? Mary Poppins?*

She continued, "When I do caretaking, I'm usually with the elderly, so this will be a breeze for me. I've been doing this for fifteen years. Here's my license and green card," she offered to us. We hadn't actually thought to ask, but we inspected them and appreciated the offer of identification and information.

After enough time had passed, I helped her out of the house. "We really thank you for coming by. We just need to discuss it, but I'm pretty confident we'll be reaching out to you very soon." I thanked her sincerely and saw her off.

We hired Zaria ten minutes later.

Several days after returning home to New York, we arrived for our follow-up appointment with Dr. Pine. The appointment went smoothly and we were told the blood flow looked good and was limited only to Maddie. "Stick to strict bed rest," Carrie was instructed. "Just up for the bathroom and showering and you should be back in a reclined position in bed—not sitting up."

We hit twenty-one weeks that day—another important milestone.

Success of the surgery felt great to us. The past few months had been challenging. We faced new and disturbing information followed by huge and difficult decisions on a seemingly regular basis. Carrie was restricted to her bed, but the time ahead seemed like it could be relatively smooth sailing. For the following week, I would go to work each day, knowing Carrie was taken care of by Zaria. I would come home and have a picnic dinner in bed with my beautiful pregnant wife, watching *Jeopardy*, *Wheel of Fortune*, and other shows for the night. It didn't really occur to me just how much different it was for her. All day and all night sitting in the same room save for bathroom runs, just feet away. No sun, no wind, no people. Well, not no people. Occasionally some friends or family would stop by for a chat. It finally did dawn on me when we woke on Sunday and Carrie asked if I thought it would be all right just to make it downstairs to spend some time on the couch in the living room for the day. We agreed to go for it carefully.

As we got down to the living room and I helped Carrie get settled, I could see tears. She whimpered a few times and I came to her side. I asked what was wrong, if she was hurting. "No," she squeezed out. "I don't know. I just haven't seen our living room for a week. All I've seen is our bedroom and bathroom."

I had not realized how difficult it could be handling strict bed rest. Despite movies, TV shows, books, and the Internet—I had not considered how restrictive life in one room could feel, even for a short period of time.

# 55. REALLY?

Carrie's parents arrived in New York for another brief trip so see their daughter. They stayed at our house as usual and this time accompanied Carrie to a checkup. As she was still on strict bed rest, doctor visits were on the list of good excuses to stand and move.

I remained at work for this visit, leaving Carrie's parents to keep her company. It was a bonding opportunity in any case. The purpose of the checkup was nothing more than a continuation of the necessary routine of tests and follow-ups. Before being called in for the ultrasound, the attendant at the window passed Carrie a small bottle. It was the glucose screening test for gestational diabetes. Carrie knew what to expect, having done the research in advance for this test, as with most of the other standard tests. The liquid was sweet and designed to see how the body processes this blast of sugar.

Soon after, Carrie was called in and she motioned for her parents to follow. This would be their second chance at a real live ultrasound of their granddaughter.

"How are we feeling?" asked Dr. Laura Stern-Martin, one of the partners in the practice. By this point, we had met all of the doctors at one appointment or another, and they shared it was weekly standard practice for the full team to have group meetings and discuss all of their patients. No matter who we saw, they knew our full story inside and out.

"Big," Carrie said. "It seems like I'm really big."

"Well, you are pregnant," she replied with a smile. "But yes, you are, compared to a normal pregnancy. But we both know yours has been anything but that. So let's take a look inside your belly."

Carrie lay back on the bed and the show began. The images were confusing but growing clearer over time and experience.

"There is the head and there are the legs," she directed Carrie's parents. After a few landmarks, the doctor stopped the guided tour and began a series of measurements.

She pressed a button and the screen switched from a black background with floating images to a more space-age view of the inside—it was the 3D imagery. Carrie and her parents could see body parts far more clearly this way. Another press of a button and the machine hummed out a screenshot that she handed to Carrie.

"Here's your baby! Things look good, but you definitely do have a lot of amniotic fluid. More than normal. So you're not imagining that you're feeling big." The doctor raised the idea of trying to drain some of the fluid, but suggested instead that we watch it closely for now.

The checkup was over, except for waiting an extra twenty minutes for a blood draw to get results from the glucose test.

Several days later, after Matt and Nancy had flown back to Michigan, I left work to meet Carrie again for our next follow-up appointment. I sat in the husband chair in the examining room while Carrie partially lay back on the exam table and the nurse took vitals.

Outside of the office, we could hear Dr. Stern-Martin saying sweet good nights to her kids. It was a pleasure to hear her speak to her family and at the same time treat us so well when she had her own children who wanted to see her.

"Have you been under stress today?" the nurse asked, bringing our attention back into the room.

Surprised to hear any question at all, Carrie responded, "Um... no. Nothing different from usual. Why?"

"Well, your blood pressure is a little high. LSM will be here in a moment." We picked up that everyone in the office called this doctor by her initials.

After finishing up with the kids, LSM joined us in the room. "Hi, guys!" she said, but was interrupted by the nurse. The interruption was not rude, it was focused and professional. She had discovered something during vitals that was above normal and raised it to the doctor quickly and clearly.

After looking at all of the vitals, LSM directed Carrie to lie fully down and on her left side. The position could help ease the elevated high blood pressure.

"I don't really like the BP where it is, so just rest for a bit. There's something else I have to talk to you about, but I'm a little nervous to. Can you remain calm as we talk?"

Not sure what was about to come, "Yes," Carrie responded.

"The readings came back from the glucose test and you have gestational diabetes."

Carrie let out a small groan. "Don't we need to run the second test?" As usual, Carrie had done her homework and the test typically has a second leg with longer waits between the fluid and blood draws.

Impressed, LSM continued, "Yes, that is right. But in your case, the levels were really so high that we're certain of it just with the first test."

Carrie's face pouted and I rubbed her head but felt the frustration of yet another risk to contend with.

"There is actually a GD class going on tonight down the hall if you can stay for it. All we need to do is manage with proper diet and you'll be fine. After you have Maddie, in all likelihood the diabetes will go away and you'll be fine. But we just need you following a strict regimen of diet and testing. They can explain everything."

Without any hesitation, we agreed to stay tonight for the class and learn right away, rather than wait and come back another time.

A while later, the class was getting started and LSM had Carrie get up from lying on her side. We walked down the hall into a reasonably sized conference room with a long wooden table and chairs occupied by other patients tightly spaced around. For the next hour we learned about diet—primarily good and bad food combinations. Eat carbs together with protein and starch, count your carbs, eat evenly throughout the day. Cold cereal maybe isn't the best way to start a day. Fruits as a snack are fine, but best paired with a protein like nuts. We learned to prick fingers and test blood for sugar levels. We learned how to check for ketones with pee sticks. In the end, it was explained that if properly managed with diet and regular testing, it shouldn't cause a problem. Easier said than done. We were now facing yet another risk factor not only for the pregnancy but also for Mom's health as an individual.

After the class, LSM greeted us back into the examining room for a follow-up blood pressure test. The class was somewhat overwhelming, long and filled with information to recall and certainly didn't do much to help Carrie's nerves calm. LSM flopped the wrap around Carrie's arm, velcroed, and pumped the black ball. The sleeve tightened around her bicep and the mercury in the gauge on the wall bounced higher. We trained our eyes on the meter as the quiet hiss of air releasing from the pump dominated the room.

LSM twisted the dial faster and the arm band deflated quickly. "It's still too high," the doctor said.

Carrie and I huffed a breath in frustration.

"Just lie down again and relax for me. Hang out in here. Don't get yourself all worked up talking about this medical stuff. Talk about some pleasant thoughts or places you've been. I'll come back in a little bit and we'll try again." She smiled, tilted her head seeing our confirmation, and walked out.

Preeclampsia is very dangerous. High blood pressure brought on by pregnancy can be dangerous for both mom and baby alike. We both knew it from our research, but we weren't about to discuss it. Nor were we going to discuss gestational diabetes.

"Barbados," I said. At the moment, my family was there. "The pictures look amazing. Seems like a great place to go with Maddie." Sun and beaches.

Perfect things to think about when trying to relax your mind. Carrie didn't respond verbally, trying to remain calm, but nodded and eked a small smile.

"The warm sun on our skin. I love how that feels," I continued, trying to put Carrie on that beach. To let her mind feel the Vitamin D sinking into her body. I continued softly painting a picture for half an hour while we sat and rested. Carrie's breathing had slowed noticeably over the time and her facial muscles were relaxed, eyebrows calmed, lips loose and eyelids heavy.

Tiptoeing back in, LSM offered a soft "Hello."

We smiled back as she reached for the black band once more. Carrie maneuvered, allowing her arm to be wrapped.

LSM pumped pumped pumped and the mercury danced.

The hiss again commandeered the airwaves as we awaited the verdict.

"Much better," LSM shared.

We both breathed a sigh of relief.

"Why don't you guys go home and get some rest. You've had a lot going on."

We agreed, thanked her, and gathered up to leave.

Driving home in the quiet, I looked over and saw Carrie's head dipped down as she fought back small sobs.

"Hey. It's all right," I tried.

She shook her head slowly. "I know. I guess. It just feels like a lot. Overwhelming. Why do I keep having everything go wrong?" she said quietly.

Rather than paint a rosy *all will be well* picture, I sympathized. "I don't know. It doesn't seem fair and we're having a hard time catching a break. We just have to keep rolling with it somehow. It's all going to be worth it."

We took turns dialing up our parents to share the latest round of news. Sometimes it wasn't advice we needed, but just to share. Talking about it out aloud, especially with loved ones we could trust, was at least cathartic.

We dialed Carrie's parents in Michigan and then mine in Barbados. At some point along the way, the caller ID coming from us must have become a source of fear for our parents. Perhaps they'd beg or pray real quick before picking up that there was just a pleasant chat ahead and not some new development. This time, it must have been abundantly clear to my parents that we were calling with bad news, reaching out to Barbados.

We spent the ride home talking to them on the speaker phone and ended the second call as we pulled into our driveway. I turned off the car and we sat for a moment in pure silence. The sounds of the doctor's office, the beeps from the glucose meters, the class discussion, the speaker phone, and the car engine were all gone. It was peaceful. We sat with long breaths for a moment and turned to lock eyes. Together we took deep breaths, closed our eyes, exhaled, and then broke the silence with our doors. We were both beat and it was high time for the comfort of our bed.

# 56. LIFE GOES ON

So, we went onward. What's one more thing to deal with? We both knew there were many tests and much unknown still ahead. So what do you do? You do whatever is next.

Back to work for me. I woke early, kissed Carrie gently as she slept, and made the regular trek into the city.

While I was eating lunch at my desk, the phone rang with our home number in the monochrome display. For a moment I felt what my parents had likely been feeling—a twinge of fear.

"Hey, sweetie," I answered.

"Hi. How are you doing?" she answered calmly. There must be no medical emergency, I figured.

"Fine. Just finishing up lunch. Working. Nothing special," I responded.

"Zaria," she said. It was an odd tone. Accusatory. Something was going on.

"Yeah? What about her?" I asked, very curious.

"She just left my room. She's been in here for half an hour," Carrie said in a half-whisper.

"What? What the heck for?"

"She showed up this morning, walked Socks, and then came in to tell me that she has to go to court. For child support," she explained and I listened intently. "She came back a little while and came upstairs crying. She went through this whole thing explaining about her ex-husband and her kid and that he doesn't ever pay his child support but the court hasn't made it happen. I don't know. I mean, I feel bad for her and I listened and I offered what sympathy and advice I could, but what the hell?"

"Oh no. We got a drama girl?" I asked.

"I don't know, maybe. This is the first time she's really talked to me about anything real. And normally, I'd like to think I'm a good listener, but…" She paused to collect her words. "But I'm on fucking bed rest and supposed to stay as calm as possible to keep my blood pressure down and here she is popping into my room for first time really, crying and telling me her sob story."

"Holy crap," I jumped in.

"I hate to sound insensitive. I do feel bad about her situation. Her ex-husband is a deadbeat and she's fending for herself and her boy," she said.

I thought to myself about how to broach the subject with Zaria. How to explain that she needed to keep her woes to herself—that Carrie needed to remain as calm as possible to ward off high blood pressure and to avoid the mini rounds of contractions that seemed to come and go. *Next time*, I decided. She'd obviously had a rough day dealing with difficult personal and family issues, so I'd let it slide unless it happened again.

Defense. I had been feeling more and more a need to build a cocoon around Carrie to protect her from stress, people saying dumb shit, and even doctors we didn't fully trust. This was just a woman who'd been coming to our house daily for a few weeks that for the first time shared something rough in her life. But my reaction was to yell at her—that Carrie and Maddie were physically vulnerable right now.

Days later, I came home early from work to bring Carrie to another checkup. The office moved up our appointment by a few days after we informed them of the intermittent rounds of contractions Carrie was still enduring. The doctors took a look and found things to be fairly stable. The contractions could continue, but we should watch to see their frequency and intensity. Carrie had been diligently keeping a notebook of all food and drink intake and all glucose level readings and as such, the day's tests showed the diabetes in good control.

"Should we just stop at the diner for a bite? We'll get you home to the bed right afterward," I suggested.

Carrie jumped all over the opportunity at a meal out, even if it was just the diner.

We parked and I helped guide Carrie out of the car and up the stairs. Most of our adventures out in the past few weeks were really just for doctor visits. Walking into a diner, I was far more in tune to the strangers around us. Carrie's belly was still very large from the strange pregnancy and at least must look like twins or more to anyone else.

"Two of us, please," I asked at the front.

We were ushered through the crowded diner, Carrie ahead of me. She managed to get a few steps ahead as a waiter with a tray full of goods walked out in front of me and I held up. I continued to follow several steps behind, when I heard a comment.

Two women seated where Carrie had just walked by looked at her and then each other.

"Try to cover up a little more," one of them said toward Carrie, quietly enough for her not to hear, but loud enough for her friend to enjoy.

Carrie was wearing a shirt that was being pushed out by her belly and from an angle below, such as sitting at a table, one could see some underbelly skin. It was not Carrie's intention to "show skin," but neither of us had been to a maternity shop in a month given all of the developments. In that time, Carrie continued to grow and it was hard to find perfectly fitting clothes. We also did not plan on venturing out into public. The woman making the snide comment knew none of this and only saw a pregnant lady and a slice of her belly.

The comment came long enough after Carrie passed but right as I was passing. I spun around and flashed back to their table, bending down to eye level. "My wife has had a rough enough go of it so far that she doesn't need some shitty comment about her looks because she keeps outgrowing her clothes. Maybe you should say it loud enough for her to defend herself or otherwise shut up and keep it to yourself."

The stunned woman's open mouth twitched a few times as her mind skipped around to find a response. None came and I stood and walked onward. Out of the side of my eyes, I could see raised eyebrows at booths in the vicinity as I walked past to find my wife.

I found her seated with the sun flooding in on her back. It was cold outside, but a sunny day and the tall windows allowed Carrie an opportunity to soak it up. I sat with her and we picked up the menus. She apparently hadn't seen or heard the ruckus behind her on the journey through.

"What took you so long? I was waiting at the table for a minute. I thought you were right behind me," she asked.

"You didn't see or hear that?" I asked back.

She shook her head. I wasn't sure if I should share the event. I didn't want her to feel bad about her look or clothes—she shouldn't.

"Well, someone at a table along the way said something stupid," I said and went on to explain the run-in.

"Oh my God. You really said that back to her?" she asked.

"She deserved it," I replied.

Carrie broke out into an adorable chuckle. "Aw, you defended me," she said.

I smiled broadly and confirmed that I had.

"What can I get you, dear?" Our waitress arrived quickly after being seated. She took our orders and before leaving said, "You look like you're just about ready for that baby to come out."

Perhaps the complexity of our pregnancy often made us both

uncomfortable to handle comments from strangers and Carrie responded, "Yes, still some time left we hope. It's been a little bit of a difficult pregnancy." Carrie was trying to shield herself from any follow-ups. Presenting some discomfort about the pregnancy typically would end the conversation.

"Well, I'm sure it will be all right," our waitress said and turned to go.

"I hate that," I said to Carrie once we were alone again. "I know she's just trying to be nice, but I hate hearing that from people who know nothing, 'It'll be all right.' What the hell does she know? About us or anyone else. Why say that?"

"I know, I know," Carrie said in agreement, but also hoping to just tamp down the situation to enjoy our meal together. She was right—I was just being defensive.

Back at work for the day, I shuffled through my emails for anything I may have missed. I spent time getting around with my colleagues and as much time on the trading floor as possible. With my absences building up, I wanted to take advantage of my facetime as much as possible while I was there.

Back at my desk, I retrieved a voicemail from Carrie. "Nothing urgent. Just give me a call back."

I dialed and she quickly answered, "Hey. Oh man. I don't want to bother you, but I just have to tell you something. Have to tell someone," she said in a half-giggle.

I told her to go on. "Well, Zaria came into our room again today. Nothing bad, no stress. She was just talking to me about all kinds of stuff."

"Oh boy. Here we go," I said.

"Yeah, exactly. So apparently she has a broken eye. One of her eyes doesn't work," she said. "She was asking me for advice."

"Advice?!" I asked, surprised. "What the hell kind of advice can you give for a dead eye?"

"I have no idea. She said she's thinking of having it replaced with a glass eye. Something about the eye that can start to rot or something. I don't know. I'm not sure she knows."

"What? She doesn't know? What kind of doctor does she have?" I asked back.

"I don't know. I asked her about the glass eye so I could understand better. I asked if she looks to the side without turning her head if both eyes go or just the good eye and the bad one stays staring straight ahead."

"Yeah?" I asked.

"She just said 'huh' and shrugged her shoulders. She said she hadn't thought about that! And she didn't really seem concerned."

"What the hell? We try to find out everything we can about a car we're thinking of leasing—she hasn't thought about what questions to ask before getting her eyeball replaced?!"

Carrie laughed back into the phone and I joined her.

"This is who I left to take care of you?" I said, jokingly incredulous.

# 57. A CHANGE OF SCENERY

For the next couple of weeks, Carrie was back and forth to the doctor for regular checkups. The high-risk OB practice wanted Carrie there every few days, her only reprieve from otherwise remaining horizontal at home. The exams were detailed looks inside at Maddie, at the fluid levels, and at all else in the uterus.

"I don't love how stubbornly high your fluids are—and they're up again. I want to put you on a medication that can help reduce a bit," Dr. LSM said to Carrie. With complete trust, Carrie agreed and they easily moved onto the next topic—the fetal fibronectin test. The fibronectin protein helps to bind the fetal sac to the uterine lining and if its presence is found in this test, it indicates the protein may be leaking, an early warning sign of preterm labor. A negative result means labor likely isn't on the way.

"We've been discussing using this test for you. Some of the others are worried about your on-and-off contractions, and if we get a false positive— which does happen sometimes—that it could add stress and exacerbate the contractions. I'm more in favor of doing the test. It could prove to be calming and helpful to know if it's false, but I need you to be confident and promise me that you will stay calm if it's positive. If it is positive, it could be a false reading and if not, we're here for you and we'll make sure you and Maddie get the best care possible. We'll also be able to start steroid shots. If we're worried Maddie could be on her way out, we need to get her lung development sped up. We'd rather let Maddie's lungs develop at their normal pace, but if we know she's coming early, we'll want to speed her up."

"I'm good. I'll be OK. I want to know if we should be doing something for Maddie. I am good with the test," Carrie answered confidently.

Carrie was twenty-six weeks pregnant and the test was done.

To our delight, it came back negative! No protein should mean the glue was holding and Maddie was hanging on inside for now. The result was calming, but also exciting. Carrie was going to keep Maddie cooking inside for at least another two weeks. Everything was a race against time. Keep her inside as long as possible. For all of the medical advances in the world, inside the womb was still the safest and most physically nurturing place for our baby. The lungs are the last to develop and giving Maddie a chance outside meant keeping her inside long enough for her lungs to mature. Thinking about her lung growth allowed us to breathe easy for the moment.

As I was hanging up on a call at my desk, my other line rang with our home in the display.

"Hey, babe," I said into the line.

"She's nuts," Carrie started.

"What? Who? Zaria again?"

"Yup. She brought her kid today. He's been here the whole day. He's walking Socks and just hanging out. I don't know what to say. I guess it's not really a problem, but what the hell?"

"She's something special," I responded.

"And when she came up here to talk, she was being totally over the top. I don't know how real it is. She said she's used to taking care of older people and their homes and then she called them her 'masters.' She said she always works hard to help her masters and visits them at the hospital if they have to go in. She talked about how loyal she is. She said when I go to have the baby, she will come to see me and bring me anything I might need."

"What did you tell her?" I asked back quickly.

"I said that was really nice but not necessary. That you would be there and other family to help. She said she has a hard time letting go of her masters." Carrie drifted into a louder whisper as she finished with, "I think I'm her master right now!"

"Well, that sure is creepy," I responded slowly. "She can't be bringing her kid with her. I don't know. Maybe I'll call her. I'll explain that you really need to be as restful as possible and can't be concerned about a child on your property, walking your dog outside and shit." I paused. "She won't be with us for very much longer anyway. Just hang in there."

The next day we met to see Dr. Jain for another checkup.

"Your fluid is way down," Dr. Jain said and Carrie and I smiled.

"It's really down," she said while continuing to watch the ultrasound screen. Our smiles left. "You're at about eight centimeters now, down from twenty. Eight is at the very low end of normal." She continued looking around inside of Carrie for a while. She pushed the paddle around on Carrie's belly, twisted it and angled it over and over again with the room remaining silent. She would stop and lean in to look closer at the screen. Suddenly she stopped and replaced the device. "Why don't you get cleaned up and then come into my office," she said quietly and walked out.

We didn't really speak, but hurried to get back to normal and go find out what she was trying to see. Walking down the hall toward her office, I reached down and grabbed Carrie's hand, where I felt thin trembles.

We walked in and sat down, Dr. Jain already seated and ready for us.

"I'm concerned about a couple of things," she said in her clear, direct, and professional manner. "First is the fluid level. We wanted to bring it down, but it came down very fast and far. It makes me concerned you could be losing fluid—could be leaking fluid. We need to watch it very closely. And second, I couldn't quite tell, which is why I was trying so hard to see at different angles, but I thought I saw a placental abruption. The placenta may be separating from the uterus. It's a dangerous condition, but again, I couldn't tell for sure. Both of these could be serious issues that require very close attention. I may want to do an amnio with a blue dye so we can see if you are actually leaking. I believe you need to be admitted to the hospital. It would be for the long haul now. I'd like you to go over to admitting at the hospital and I will see you later."

I turned to Carrie. "OK, let's go. I'll bring your bag."

"No," said Dr. Jain. "You can't go home. You need to go to the hospital right from here," she said with a pick-up in urgency.

"No, that's fine," I said. "It's in the car. We keep her bag with us."

"Oh good. I'll see you there in a little bit. I'm going to call over. They'll be expecting you."

We drove over to the hospital, not far away. The car ride gave us just long enough to quickly call both sets of parents to inform them the hospital stay was beginning. No long conversations and we had no answers for the questions they asked.

I dropped Carrie right in front where she walked into admitting while I left to park the car across the way, in a large garage. I ran back as fast as I could and found Carrie seated with an admitting administrator.

"Because this wasn't planned. It's an emergency," I sat to hear Carrie explaining. The person checking us into the computer couldn't understand why paperwork hadn't been mailed to us in advance and why we didn't have it filled out and ready.

It took a while, but we managed to get through the process and then Carrie was taken by wheelchair down the hall and up a floor in the elevator, all the while as I tracked alongside. We arrived at Labor and Delivery, where the reception was far more prepared. "Hi, Carrie," said a nurse we had never seen before. "I just want to get you set up with an NST right now."

The non-stress test would monitor for any contractions and Maddie's heartbeat while Carrie rested and while the doctors decided on next steps. Carrie rested back in a bed, tilted up slightly for comfort, while I sat in a chair up near her head.

"There's one," Carrie said, as a contraction started. Nothing terribly unusual, but a small tightening of her belly. In due time, the tightening released and all was back to normal. I could see the mound registered on the NST printout.

Dr. Surly came around the corner to grab at the printout. "Looks like a small contraction," she grumbled near us. We didn't respond, not knowing if she was talking to us or asking a question.

"Well?" she said again, picking her head up and connecting eyes with Carrie. "Was it small? Do you get them a lot?"

"I ..um…yes. It wasn't very big. I get them … irregularly, I guess," Carrie tried to answer. We had never met this doctor before and she never bothered introducing herself, though we later found out she worked with another practice that had rights at the hospital. Since we never had a proper introduction, we never even knew her name. So Dr. Surly is what we chose for her.

"And this doesn't look very low," she stated again, this time pointing to something inside of Carrie's chart hanging open cradled in the other hand.

We remained silent, unsure if or what to answer.

"Your fluid was an eight. That's not bad," she said and we waited again. "Your contractions are low and irregular and fluid is on the low end of normal. I'm not sure why you're here."

I spoke up with a simple statement. "Because our doctor sent us here."

Our consultation ended with the abrupt turn and departure of Dr. Surly.

"What the hell is wrong with her?" I asked Carrie quietly.

"No idea. I didn't even know if or when she was asking me something."

Before our banter went on for long, Dr. Jain pulled the curtain and appeared. We both breathed a sigh of relief to see her professional and caring face.

"Hi, Carrie, how are you?" she asked.

"I'm fine, thanks. Just resting."

"Hello," said Dr. Surly as she walked back into our area. Dr. Jain walked over to the machine to pull up the printouts and appeared to be already dismissing the grumpy doc's presence. "I'm not sure why she's here," Surly said while Dr. Jain tore off the paper and studied the lines.

"May we?" said our doc, motioning to move outside of the curtains and have a word.

Dr. Jain started off firmly but quietly so we couldn't hear. We could hear. "My patient has a possible placental abruption. She *had* an AFI of more than twenty-five just two days ago and now it's eight, so I'm concerned we could be looking at leaking fluid. And look at this." The speaking stopped and we could hear the waxy printout ruffling for a moment and then silence.

The quiet broke with Dr. Jain pulling the curtain to walk back in toward us. Dr. Surly was no longer in sight.

"There are a few things we're concerned about right now," she began in a far softer tone. "They may all prove to be nothing, but all taken together and with your history, we don't want to take any chances. The readout shows just a fairly mild contraction, but at the same time, Maddie's heartbeat slowed a bit."

Carrie and I took deep breaths at the same time.

"That could indicate some stress, so we're going to go ahead with a steroid shot now. I want to help her get developed as much as possible as quickly as possible if we end up needing to take her sooner rather than later."

The words sunk through us quickly. This could be it. The steroid shot is reserved for high risk of imminent preterm labor. As with so many developments throughout the past several months, we understood and moved quickly to acceptance.

Just moments later, Dr. Jain asked Carrie to roll onto her side to allow for the large needle to have access to her rear.

A sharp breath in from Carrie as the needle pushed into her backside. After so many shots, it was obvious this one was hurting more than normal. She held her face tightly with closed eyes and kept the air frozen in her lungs as the plunger depressed, forcing the serum into her. The wince worsened over the few seconds until the needle was withdrawn. Carrie exhaled heavily and opened her eyes widely. "That stuuuung," she whispered to me.

I pressed her hair back from her forehead and offered a positive spin. "Well, she's getting what she needs now. Let's get those little lungs going."

We rested together for a little while waiting for the next move. One of the nurses we'd seen around came over and clicked up the side bars and depressed the pedal underneath to free the brakes. "Let's get going. I'm taking you to a room now and you can just rest for a while, all right?" she said in a sympathetic tone.

I walked alongside the bed as it rolled down the hallway, through double doors, and around again until we reached a nurses' station outside a hallway full of hospital rooms. Our driver received instructions and turned Carrie to wheel her in through one of the open doors. The room was small from what we could see, with curtains drawn on both sides and Carrie now placed in the middle. Based on the initial voices, Carrie was the third patient.

"This is the Swing Unit," our nurse explained. Also called the antepartum unit, she continued, the rooms were for pregnant women having some form of trouble before childbirth. "I'm going to leave you here now. Your Swing Unit nurse will be along soon to introduce herself. Good luck, guys." We thanked her.

The entire room was small and our space had enough room just for Carrie's bed, a small utility nightstand with drawers, and a small chair, which I plunked down into. Privacy gone.

# 58. SWING LOW

The afternoon wore on into night without any critical medical development, but plenty of vitals. Welcome to the hospital—the nurse comes by to take vitals on an incredibly regular basis. Every couple of hours we'd be visited for temperature, blood pressure, pulse-ox, and the special prize for gestational diabetes—a finger prick. Carrie lay in the bed resting as I sat at her side in a wood-framed chair with maroon pleather cushions. A grab at the armrests and forcing back converts the chair into a lounge, perfectly uncomfortable for sleeping.

We were both resting, bored but still on edge about the unknown. Waiting around usually comes with a feeling of anticipation, of wanting the thing to happen. In this case, we were waiting around, hoping *nothing* would happen.

I stepped out into the hallway and pressed autodial on my Nokia cell phone. "Hi, Zaria," I greeted. "Zaria, there has been a change. We all knew at some point this was coming. Carrie was admitted to the hospital today and they're expecting to have her stay until the baby is born." I stopped and she offered her sincere best wishes and asked what she could do to help.

"Thank you so much, but there's not much to do now. I think we mostly just wait around now, but just here instead of there. We really thank you for all of the help you've given us and wish you the very best of luck, but I don't think we need your help anymore. We all knew at some point this would end." This was the first time I had ever fired anyone, but it was really more of a known eventuality. She took it well and thanked me.

I chatted with the nurses at the station for a few minutes to get the lay of the land. They explained that so long as things were going all right, Carrie would fall into a bit of a routine. Someone would come to collect her probably twice a day to go down and have an ultrasound and a non-stress test (NST) performed. They also apologized about how full the unit was right now, which was why Carrie is jammed in with two others. I got the sense that there was a form of seniority that took place—where expecting mothers that had been on the Swing Unit for longest end up in single rooms. I gathered some more intel and then turned to head back into the room.

"Hey, baby. I took care of Zaria. So that's done." I continued by filling her in on what I'd learned. I ended the download telling her the annoying but understandable news. "They don't really want me sleeping here with you tonight, since there are two other patients in with you."

Carrie pouted her lips at me but nodded. "You should get going soon anyway. Socks has been alone for a while and you need to get some sleep too."

I kissed Carrie and for the first time in my life, left my wife alone in the hospital.

# 59. FLOW STATES

The next morning, I returned early, shunning work for yet another day. I found the unit already buzzing with activity and Carrie was wide awake.

"Hey, good morning," as I leaned in for a kiss.

"Good morning," Carrie said in a tired, soft voice.

"Did you get any sleep?" I asked, just as a nurse walked in to wrap Carrie's arm for vitals.

"A little here and there. But it seems this isn't much of a place for sleeping," she said and nodded with a smirk to the lady performing the blood pressure test. Apparently they'd already become friends.

Beginning with a whisper, I leaned in to hear, "My roommates are loons."

"Oh boy. What the hell happened?" I asked.

"Well, this one," she said, pointing to the curtain over her right side, "she's a patient of Dr. Feinman. He was here already this morning. She's having triplets. And she complains about absolutely everything. And all night, all she did was chew on ice. Like, loud!"

I chuckled and dropped my head. "Oh, good for you. What about that one?" I whispered, motioning the other direction.

"That one is *nuts*," she said with a twist of her head. "She doesn't really have to be here. They're trying to get her to give herself a shot. She just needs to be able to do it once a day and she can *go home!* But she's too much of a wimp."

"You've got yourself sandwiched between some real winners," I said.

"And nobody sleeps around here. They leave the lights on all the time. Nurses come and go and they don't even try to be quiet. It's always go go go around here," Carrie said and then dropped her head back onto the pillow.

With that, a nurse walked in and prompted us, "Time for your NST."

She helped Carrie into the wheelchair she had brought and pushed onward out of the room and down the hall as I followed.

We were headed to the Maternal Fetal Medicine Department for a sonogram and non-stress test. The MFM unit, as we came to know it, was the area we'd been a few times before already. There was one room with several beds and curtains along the walls with machines for NSTs and then out into another hallway were several small dark rooms for doing the sonograms with the high-tech machines.

"Hi, I'm Julianne and I'm just going to get you hooked up for your NST," the nurse said to Carrie as we arrived. She helped Carrie into a bed and began wrapping the elastic around Carrie's belly to gauge any contractions and slid the Doppler around to search for a heartbeat. When she found it, she tucked the device underneath the elastic to hold it in place and turned down the volume. We could watch the printout ribbon sliding through with a zero reading for contractions and bouncing lines for Maddie's heart.

"You're just going to lie here for a while and we'll monitor you," Julianne said.

Perhaps an hour passed with little action on the machine—it seemed Maddie was behaving. Eventually Julianne came over to help Carrie out of the contraption and prepare her to head down the hallway for her sonogram. We passed by Dr. Pine, who waved hello to us and turned to follow us in for the exam.

"Good morning. How are we feeling?" she asked.

"Feeling all right," Carrie responded.

"Well, let's see where things stand now and if we can learn anything further," Dr. Pine said as she prepared the machine and Carrie's belly. Another nurse walked into the room and stood by Carrie's belly. She assisted the doctor in preparing the room.

The exam began and we sat in silence while the doctor concentrated, changed views, took measurements, and studied the shapes. "Your fluid looks a little better. Back up to a ten," she said.

We were relieved by the first piece of information. While it was beyond us how the fluid could go back up, it seemed to indicate it couldn't possibly be leaking.

The mouse floated around the screen while our doctor rolled the trackball and settled on a red line on the screen and clicked. "Wha-wah. Wha-wah. Wha-wha." We could hear Maddie's heartbeat as the volume was turned up and we watched the visual representation of her tiny pumping heart in the form of a bouncing line moving across the screen. Peaks and valleys crossed the screen and then disappeared and began again from left to right.

"It looks like intermittent flow," she said to the nurse in the room, who nodded in agreement. The doctor wound up the sonogram, turned off the TV, and faced us.

"So here's the update. Your fluid is back up a little which is great to see. There are two things we need to watch closely. I still can't tell exactly what's going on back behind the placenta. It looks like there could be a hemorrhage behind it and could be tearing away, but I can't actually see. So we are going to continue to keep a very close eye there. Also, I'm seeing some intermittent flow. When Maddie's heart pumps, the blood rushes forward in her arteries, including in the connection to the placenta. The blood slows towards the end of the push and then rushes forward again when the heart beats. Even though the blood slows between pumps, it normally continues to move forward. But it looks like Maddie is having occasions where the blood stops moving at the end of the push, right before the next pump. This adds some stress and makes it a little harder for her to get the same amount of oxygen and nutrients."

We nodded along to the detailed explanation. She was doing an excellent job of explaining a complicated medical situation and the reason it was of concern.

She continued, "It's called intermittent absent end-diastolic velocity. It could advance into absent-end diastolic velocity, which is when it is happening persistently. That just means more strain. What we really don't want to see is the flow reverse. Reverse end-diastolic velocity, where at the end of the pump, the blood not only stops, but reverses for a split second before the heart pumps again."

I swallowed the lump in my throat.

"Does that all make sense to you?" she asked.

"Yes," we both answered at the same time. "Is there anything we can do and anything it means or causes?" I asked.

"No. There's not much we can do for the condition, but we do have to watch it closely. It does cause intrauterine growth retardation, or IUGR." My eyes must have opened wide since she followed up quickly. "That means her growth is being stunted. She's not getting all of what she needs to keep growing at a normal pace. She could grow slower. And if it turns reversed, then the strain gets more severe and that's when we could start making decisions about taking her. But we are *not* there yet," she said slowly and clearly.

She knew it was enough bad news that finishing off with a more comforting conclusion was the least she could do for us.

Carrie was helped back into a wheelchair and we headed back up to the Swing Unit, where we sat and talked for a while about this blood flow news. There wasn't much we could do about it but wait and hope and pray the flow was good enough for Maddie to get bigger and stronger.

# 60. LIFE IN THE UNIT

I showed up early the next morning, a Saturday, giving me a couple more days to help Carrie get into a routine before finally returning to work again.

"Good morning," I said, walking in and planting a kiss. "Another awesome night?" I said sarcastically.

"Oh yeah," she said back, rolling her eyes in humor. Whispering, "I got a new one over there. The one who couldn't give herself a shot is gone. Don't know what they did with her. But this new one. Oh my God, J."

"Oh boy. Let's have it," I said.

"She can't even get up." Her whispering turned quieter, and I pulled my head closer. "She pooped in the bed pan!"

I yanked my head back. "Oh shit!"

"Yeah, exactly," she quipped. "It was gross. It stunk. And it took a while for the nurse to come take it. So gross, J."

"We've got to find a way to get you into a different room. And fast," I said, looking around as though I might find some help nearby.

At that moment, Dr. Feinman walked in and breezed right past into the curtain to Carrie's right. I think he saw us and chose to skip by. We didn't feel the least bit awkward, but he sure did.

I looked at Carrie and smirked as he began to speak to his triplet patient just feet away but unseeable.

"This kind of thing happens all the time. It can get very crowded in there and hard to see all that's happening," he started from the apparent middle of a prior conversation. We were left to catch up.

"What's he talking about?" I whispered to Carrie, hoping she knew the details. She just shrugged her shoulders and touched her index finger over her lips to silence me.

The patient moaned and continued chewing on her ice chips and the doctor explained. "This is no problem at all. I've handled plenty of quadruplet births."

My eyes jumped wider and I turned to Carrie, whose mouth was agape.

The patient continued to moan and chew while he explained a variety of measurements and details and expected timing, but we had already heard the important part of the story. Our former and super-famous top-in-the-world, high-risk OB had misdiagnosed a quadruplet pregnancy as a triplet pregnancy. He missed a baby! A whole baby!

"Holy shitsky!" Carrie whisper-yelled in my ear.

"Ya-huh!" I intelligently whispered in return.

There were few fully formed sentences that we were able to put together, aghast at this development. Yet, somehow the patient on the other side of the curtain seemed calm. Moaning and chewing, but unsurprised and unfazed.

"We've gotta write a book about this someday," Carrie whispered in my ear.

We sat around and chatted for a while, passing the time doing some research on the Internet, using our home laptop that I'd brought for her. We researched AEDV and the other blood flow variants, we researched IUGR, we researched what we could expect to have to deal with in a NICU after Maddie was born, and more.

Carrie's breakfast arrived—cereal and milk. "I don't quite get it," she said. "A nutritional specialist stopped by to explain that I've been signed up for special meals for gestational diabetes. Cereal with milk is all carbs and no protein. I don't get it."

"Hello, Carrie," said a voice from the doorway. We acknowledged and invited the woman in. She was carrying a clipboard and some folders. She walked close to the bed and leaned in so we could have a touch of privacy. "I understand that you're pregnant, but you have suffered a loss in-utero. I am here to help provide some support if you need it, and at very least provide you with some information."

We continued to acknowledge and let her continue. "I know this can be a difficult time to grieve while you are still so focused on your baby growing inside. We have support groups that can help with the grieving process, either now while you're still pregnant or later on after you give birth." She passed over a folder with several leaflets inside describing such groups.

I turned to Carrie to let her speak. "Thank you, but I think we really just want to put all of our focus and effort for right now on Maddie," as she rubbed her own belly.

"I can completely understand that. Just know we are here to help if you want to reach out. I also wanted to discuss some planning with you. I want to let you know your options with regard to the babies that you've lost. If you can't focus on this beforehand, you have up to a month to decide what you would like done with the remains, if anything. We can help handle cremation or burial. We work closely with some local funeral homes who will handle the little ones and provide for them to be buried at no charge. We also work closely with Pinelawn Cemetery that has an entire section dedicated to the little ones."

We had not really focused on this issue at all, tied up with so much else to think about, so we stammered with our questions. "We were told there would be a lot of reabsorption of the deceased babies. Will we have remains to bury? It sounds like a strange question, I know," I asked.

"No, no. It's not strange at all. And you are right. There will definitely be some reabsorption, but there will be remains to be collected. And again, you do not need to do anything at all with them if you choose not to. This is about your grieving process. And as for the remains, you are permitted to see them, but I would really advise against that, especially for babies that have passed in-utero."

We tried to speak quietly to create our own ring of privacy but without question our roommates could hear. Perhaps this morning, we were the odd ones.

"How does it work—can we bury them all together? There are three deceased babies," Carrie asked.

"I believe so. But you would just need to discuss with Pinelawn on their rules," she said. We remained quiet and she finished up. "We can help to arrange for services at the burial site when it's an appropriate time, or you can just visit on your own. The most important thing to realize is that we are here for you to help you with your grieving process. We understand you're incredibly busy with something else right now and nothing needs to be dealt with right away, but we want you to have the information."

The kind and soft-spoken woman stood straight up and asked, "Is there anything else I might be able to help out with at *this* time?"

We told her we would think about other thoughts and next steps, thanked her, and she was on her way.

"That was intense," I said to Carrie.

"I know. I totally wasn't expecting that right now. I really hadn't even thought of any of this." She paused. "I don't think I want to see them and I think I'd like them to be buried together at Pinelawn."

I had started shaking my head about not witnessing the remains and waited for her to finish. "Yes, I agree. I have the info and I can get in touch directly with Pinelawn to figure out more. I'll handle all of this. Don't worry much about it. Do you want to look into a counseling group?" I asked, expecting she would not.

"Oh, no," she answered right away. "I mean, I don't know what I'll want later on, but right now, we should both focus one hundred percent on Maddie."

The routine feel of the hospital set in quickly. I would drive to the town by the hospital in the morning before work and park at a friend's mom's house near the train station where only residents were allowed to park. I would go to work for the day and come back to the same place to grab my car and go spend some time with Carrie. She would tell me about her day and how the NSTs went, if she hadn't already called me at work with some news. News came and went. There was always a good day with better heart function, flow, and activity and days when things seemed weaker. Maddie's AEDV was generally intermittent, but it was there and her growth measurements were trending higher, but at a slower than normal pace.

About a week in, I was greeted at the hospital after work one day with a big smile. "Hey! Come here," Carrie said as I appeared in the doorway.

"Yeah, what?" I asked, excitedly.

She looked both ways and then whispered, "I'm getting out of here! They're moving me to a single down the hall. A room opened up!"

It sure was great to see Carrie in such a good mood. Sometimes it's the small things in life. She was still carrying Maddie in a dangerous pregnancy, stuck in a bed in a hospital alone nearly all of the time. Yet she grinned ear to ear on this day.

"Oh, sweet!" I tossed back. "When?"

"Sometime tonight I get to go."

"Awesome. On a separate topic, I need your help. I spoke to Pinelawn Cemetery and they sent me a form." I waved it in the air. "This is actually a little complicated—for us."

"Yeah? Why?" Carrie asked.

"Well, a couple of things. First, there's the name. We know Maddie's twin was Maya Brynn, but we don't know if the other twins were boys or girls. We never really named them, just picked boy names before we knew much. So we have to decide what we want to do about that. Then there's the date. The form asks for a date and since we don't really have a birth or death date, I don't know what to put."

"Um. OK. Those are both good questions," Carrie said, scrunching her eyes and looking up at the ceiling. "Well, instead of 'Maya,' can we say something about all three of them?"

"I don't know, maybe. Like 'Maddie's Siblings'?" I pondered aloud.

"I don't love using Maddie's name on their stone," she said.

"Good point," I responded and we kicked around some ideas until Carrie thought of a good suggestion.

"How about 'Our Three Angels.' That could work, no?" she asked.

I liked it and wrote it on the form. "Now, the date is pretty complicated too. Maybe we could just put '2004.'"

Carrie thought for a moment and then shook her head. "The problem is that the first baby died in 2003, the reduction on the twins was in 2003, but then the cord ligation was in 2004. So which is the death date for the first baby that died, at seven weeks or at the surgery?"

"Oh, shit. That's right. Not only don't we have a date, we don't even have a year!" I said back and dropped my mouth open. "Maybe they'll let us do it just without a date?" I asked, rhetorically.

"I guess we could try. Maybe just 'Our Three Angels' and 'Mandel,' with nothing else," she suggested.

I leaned to write on the form. "I'll try it."

We waited around for a while, gathering up the belongings Carrie had started to accumulate from living in this triple and placing them all on the bed, ready to go. After a couple of hours—things generally don't move fast in a hospital unless you're bleeding—one of the regular Swing Unit nurses walked in. "It's time!" she said.

Carrie had quickly grown popular with the staff. She didn't whine, never asked for things unless she absolutely needed to, spoke politely and with respect, waited patiently for everything, and perhaps most importantly, sent me out to the nurses with leftovers anytime we had them. We fast grew accustomed to ordering food in from local restaurants rather than eating the hospital food. The meals did not become more regularly compliant with her diabetes needs anyway. So we figured, let's get some Italian, Chinese, diner, and enjoy!

"Come on, let's get you out of here," our lovely nurse said with a big smile as she unlocked the wheels and pulled on the bed out the door. I leaned on top of the nightstand on wheels and followed along, pushing the nightstand as we went. She ushered us just a few doors down and into a room that might have been even slightly larger than the last one, but with no roommates. The space felt significantly larger, without the visual obstructions of the curtains and with the large window framing a view of other sections of the hospital from our sixth-floor perch.

"This is the life!" I said, half serious and half sarcastic.

"I know, right?" Carrie responded similarly.

They pushed the bed up against the window wall lengthwise so she would be able to stare out into the open while lying on her side.

The room was really nothing special. Like the rest of the ward, it was a little outdated and run-down. The window shades were green slats of aluminum, reminding me of elementary school. The walls were white yet drab. All that said, there was nobody's business to be in and nobody to be in our business. Plus a bathroom.

We settled in, properly arranging the nightstand and chair as well. "Hey, maybe I can stay here now, right?" I asked Carrie.

"I think so. You better ask one of the nurses," she redirected me.

"OK, I'll go ask. But I think I need to go home tonight. Socks is there and I didn't make a plan for her to be walked tonight or in the morning and I don't have anything."

"Of course, that's fine," she said, smiling while setting back up some of her personal items. The computer sat on the windowsill, available for a grab at any moment. We arranged the TV remote, a large white device connected by a long and solid thick cord to the wall, along the bed and wrapped around the metal bed rails to keep it available and from falling.

"I could really use a little snack," I said, as we finished the redecorating.

"Oh, grab an apple!" she said excitedly. "They give me at least one with every meal and I toss them in that drawer." She pointed to the rolling nightstand.

I opened the drawer to find about a dozen red apples. "Ha! Perfect! Why don't you eat them?"

"Well, they don't serve them to me right. With the diabetes I'm supposed to have some protein with a sugar like fruit. But that's not what I get."

"Amazing. It's a hospital. Whatever," I said and snapped into the apple.

We hung around for a while, chatted, and watched TV until it grew late. "Your parents should be in by tomorrow night around dinner time, based on when they're leaving," I said. Matt and Nancy were getting on the road for the long drive to New York to celebrate Easter with us in the hospital that approaching weekend. "I'll come here right from work around the same time and then it's the weekend!" The market closes on Good Friday, giving me a nice three-day weekend. The timing for getting into a single was quite fortuitous.

I helped draw the blinds and prep the room for bed. I kissed Carrie, wished her a good and restful night, and headed home on the Long Island Expressway.

I woke to my alarm on Friday morning, wanting to get all three of us over to the hospital bright and early, but only after gathering a few things. Matt and Nancy made it to New York in time for dinner together in Carrie's new spacious studio. The embraces were long and teary and lovely to watch.

With the privacy of a single, there would surely be some gifts I could bring to brighten the room. I walked around the house and grabbed a few small photo frames of us, our families, and Socks.

"What are you doing?" Nancy asked me.

"Shopping for Carrie," I responded and she laughed. I wandered around, shopping in our own home, and found a bag of almonds and some peanut butter. They would pair perfectly with the apples to make for a healthy nutritionally balanced snack. I found some DVDs to bring—Carrie could watch them on our laptop. I found a small dolphin statuette I gave to her in college, acknowledging her favorite animal. I found other trinkets and card games and a notebook and pens to fill the shopping bag hanging on my arm like a bargain-hunter at TJ Maxx. Or TJ Junk, as Carrie and her mom would call it. I gathered some fresh clothes, a comfortable pillow from home, and a small soft throw blanket, threw all of it into a larger duffel bag, and prepared myself to head over. We stopped at a flower store on the way and grabbed something colorful and fresh to liven her room.

"Hi, babe!" I said as I turned the corner into her new single. The room was flooded with sunlight. Carrie was wide awake, sitting up in bed eating breakfast. She turned to us with a large smile.

"Hi! Good morning," she said in the most chipper tone I'd heard since we lived at home.

"You sure look good this morning!" I said, as I handed over the flowers.

"Aw, thank you," she said slowly and sincerely. "The sun! The sun and the privacy. It makes such a huge difference."

"I know. I wasn't even sure you'd be up yet. And here I turn into the room and it's like being at the beach with how bright it is." She hugged her parents and I swung the duffel bag off my shoulder and onto the bed.

"What's this?" Carrie asked. She unzipped and began pulling out the items. Carrie thanked me for each one and placed it where it belonged. The trinkets and picture frames went on the windowsill. The nuts and peanut butter when into the bottom drawer with the trove of apples. "Yay! Now I'm all set up!"

Carrie was 28.5 weeks pregnant and for the most part since being admitted was more or less stable. Every day Maddie stayed inside was a day to be grateful for.

Out of the blue, it dawned on me and I asked, "Hey, whatever happened to Zaria?"

"What do you mean?" she asked back.

"Well, remember she called you her master and that she can't ever leave her masters and that she always goes to visit and bring anything they need?" I reminded her.

"Oh, yeah. I guess there goes that." She shrugged. "Never heard from her."

"Maybe she's getting her eye replaced," I said and we all chuckled. I grabbed for a deck of cards that I'd brought and shuffled. "Play?" I asked.

"Sure," Carrie said. I finished shuffling and before dealing grabbed for my sunglasses. "What are you doing?" she asked me.

"It is seriously bright in here. And I'm facing the window. It's like being outside." I finished shuffling and dealt out a hand of gin.

Two raps at the door and we looked over to find Dr. Jain. I noted a look of confusion and surprise on her face. I quickly figured out the reason. The hardworking doctor was making her rounds at the hospital, visiting her patients who were carrying risky pregnancies. She had to dole out bad news on an incredibly regular basis and perform risky and sometimes urgent procedures. She had to make difficult judgment calls that could determine the paths of mother and children. She knew our case intimately and came to check on Carrie's current state. Here she found a flood of sunlight painting a bouquet of flowers, several four-by-six frames of family members and our dog, a computer, games, trinkets, Carrie's parents keeping us company, and Carrie and I smiling widely engaged in a card game while I leaned back in the chair with my feet up on Carrie's bed and head turned back toward the door to reveal my Risky Business sunglasses.

"Hi, Dr. Jain," we said at the same time.

Dr. Jain is an incredible doctor and incredibly serious. Today, she cracked a smile. "How are we doing today?" she asked as she slowly made her way into the room. Nancy thanked Dr. Jain for all of her work and guidance. Both sets of parents probably felt they knew our doctors since we updated them on details all the time.

We discussed all of the latest measurements and readings and Dr. Jain suggested that things seemed stable, but still very risky and we should just continue our routine of testing and sonograms. Everyone in the room seemed equally pleased with the update and the good doctor turned to walk out of the room with the smirk still hanging on.

"We're going to come around lunchtime tomorrow so we can prep everything, OK?" Nancy immediately moved on to planning, as she tended to do. She was referring to the Easter dinner that Matt and Nancy had planned to cook at our house and bring to the hospital to celebrate together.

"That sounds good, but I'm going to come here in the morning to hang with Carrie, while you guys prep. If that's OK with you," I said.

"Sure, sure!" Nancy said in a high-pitched sincere go-ahead. "We don't need you for the cooking and we'd rather Carrie not be alone."

The next day, as Carrie and I sat around in the hospital room chatting and playing cards again, "Hello, hello," chirped along with a knock on the open door. Matt and Nancy walked into the room with two rolling coolers, a large cooler hung on Matt's shoulder, and a big shopping bag in Nancy's free hand.

"Oh my lord!" I said as I got up and jumped over to assist. "What did you do?" I said jokingly, looking at all of the bulk they'd brought with them.

"We cooked dinner!" a proud Nancy struck back. "We've got it all. Easter, delivered!"

"Aw, thank you guys so much," Carrie said as she peeked over at the items being opened. "Ooh, it smells *good!*" she shouted with widened eyes as the various scents wafted across the room.

Matt and Nancy unpacked the many dishes in what appeared to be a clown car of food. One dish after another, packaged into Styrofoam to-go boxes and in coolers to keep them *warm*, not cold. Everything was fresh out of the oven and ready for transport to the hospital. They used the hospital over-bed table, tops of coolers, and any other open surface as buffet tables. Nancy opened up the shopping bag and pulled out heavy-duty paper plates, plastic flatware, napkins, cups, serving spoons, and more.

"Bon appétit," Nancy said when the spread was complete. We all began making our meals. Carrie called out to me what else to put onto her plate and I filled it to capacity before handing it off to her.

"I just want to say thank you guys so much for coming and for doing all of this. I love you," Carrie said to her parents. They teared and placed down their plates to come in for hugs and kisses.

We all sat and chatted while we enjoyed an incredible home-cooked Easter meal. There were Cornish game hens, mashed potatoes, gravy, and corn. We all took our turns for seconds and then turned our attention to the fresh desserts. Warm chocolate pecan pie, cookies, ice cream, and whipped cream were all on hand. Why Cornish game hens? Matt and Nancy know I'm not a fan of ham, so they work around me, no matter how many times I tell them not to. I guess that's what parents do.

A rap at the door and the four of us looked up. For the second day in a row, Dr. Jain stood in the doorway with a smirk upon her face. I smiled back at her and shrugged my shoulders.

That evening, as we were getting ready to leave the hospital, Carrie shared a long and teary goodbye with her mom and dad. They were set to leave early the next morning and nobody knew what the next day, days, and weeks ahead held for us. Carrie and Nancy took turns wiping away each other's tears. I came in for the last kiss. "I love you, sweet. I'll see you tomorrow right after work, as usual."

# 61. SURPRISE!

As we moved through the days and past twenty-nine weeks, we approached Carrie's twenty-eighth birthday on Sunday. I had been planning and organizing for a special day as best I could given the circumstances. Carrie was growing marginally more depressed by the situation. Most of the time, she was alone in a hospital room. I was there as often as possible, but at work most of the day during the week. I usually stayed until after ten at night and then headed home for some rest before the train to work the next morning. The situation came with a massive loss of privacy as the door could open at any time with a nurse, doctor, or staff to take vitals, provide new information, or just clean the room. She hadn't been outside to enjoy the burgeoning spring weather or able to see her friends.

A birthday surprise could be just the thing to help lift her spirits.

Saturday morning, I turned the corner into Carrie's room to find the blinds again already raised and Carrie eating breakfast. "Good morning and Happy Birthday Weekend!" I called out. My hands were filled with flowers and a giant card.

"What is *that?*" Carrie asked with a smile, motioning to the giant envelope under my arm.

"It's for you, of course," I answered and handed it to her with a kiss. I reached over to place the fresh flowers into the vase, replacing older dying flowers. Carrie ripped open the three-foot-wide card to find a goofy cartoon wishing her a great birthday. Just a silly gesture but fun. I took it from her and taped it up onto her wall and handed her another normal-sized card. I had done it for years—multiple cards for her birthday that come all throughout the day. "And one more thing," I said a little loud for just the two of us in the room.

"What was that? Why did you just shout at me?" she asked and then looked up to see Matt and Nancy walking in. "What are you doing here?" Carrie asked in disbelief.

"We're here for your birthday!" Nancy responded and the two quickly embraced.

"But you were just here last weekend!" Carrie exclaimed, still confused.

"Sure, I know. And we're here again," Nancy easily responded.

We sat around, chatted, and caught up as I checked my watch regularly. Around eleven o'clock, I slithered out of my chair and into the hallway. Moments later I returned to the room with a wheelchair.

"What is that?" Carrie asked.

"It's a wheelchair," I said.

"I mean what's it for, dummy?"

"It's time for a trip outside," I said with a broad smile.

"W-What? What do you mean?" she asked, accusingly. "You can't just steal me out of the hospital."

"I know. I handled it. I spoke to the nurses. We can take a little stroll to the back entrance and get some air for a little while." It was late April and warming up. That day happened to be one of those perfect clear spring days, with the usual early spring nip in the air taking a break for the day.

"Really? You '*handled*' this?" she accused again.

"Just get your butt in the chair and let's go," I demanded playfully.

She sat. I released the locks and the four of us slowly sauntered down the hall. I wheeled to the right when we got out of the elevator.

"Where are you going?" Carrie asked.

"Tsst. Tsst," I demanded. "Just you relax and not worry about *stuff*."

I wound our way to the quieter back entrance to the hospital where the first set of automatic double doors opened. We pushed forward and the second set opened to let in a fresh whoosh of spring air. I looked down to see Carrie take in a sudden breath.

"Oh my God. It feels so good," she said quietly to herself and I smiled.

I pressed on and walked toward an area with some benches for the four of us to soak up the beautiful air.

"This is sooo nice," Carrie said to all of us and wiped a small tear. "Thank you guys for coming. And J," she turned to look at me, "thank you. I love you."

"I love you, too," I said and finished my stare into her eyes with a flick of my head and eyebrows back over her left shoulder.

"What?" she asked. I motioned again.

Carrie turned around and her good friend Erin was walking up the way with her boyfriend at the time. "Erin? What? What are you doing here?"

"It's your birthday, silly," Erin said from behind a large bouquet of flowers.

She jogged the last couple of steps to Carrie and leaned down for a tight embrace. Carrie's confusion continued as she worked to process the developments.

"Hi, Mom," I said as my mother came walking around the bend as well.

"Dor? What the heck is going on?" Carrie said, getting overwhelmed. "And where's Barry?" Carrie asked.

"He's parking," she said as she reached in for her hug.

"Ah, there he is," I said.

My dad was jogging up the pathway, arm held way out front, being pulled like a sled by Socks, ears flapping in the air. The two of them quickly ran up and we all parted like the Red Sea to let them through. Socks lifted up, front paws on Carrie's legs and panting with her tongue flapping to the side. Carrie's face was the most confused yet, almost as though she didn't recognize Socks.

"Socks? You guys brought Socks?" Carrie asked my parents, completely perplexed.

"She wanted to see you," my dad answered simply.

Carrie looked up at me. "You did all of this?" I just shrugged back as a few tears dripped down her face.

Smiles all around. Conversation flowed freely and splintered into several different lines of chatter. For the next hour, Carrie caught up with Erin, laughed with my parents and hers, and smiled at me several times. Socks got up onto Carrie's lap a few times and slathered her face with kisses. She may look like a lap dog, but she never sits still for very long and spent most of the time bouncing back and forth to each person, getting treats that my parents were handing out from a Ziplock baggie.

"She's *big,*" Carrie said to me after a while.

Socks was never a big dog, but she had gained her share of sympathy weight. "Yeah, I know. I think Jeannie gives her really big helpings for meals and gives her a lot of treats." With my being at the hospital so much, we had our dog walker coming sometimes two or three times a day.

My mom turned around away from the group and fidgeted with a bag she had brought along, while I diverted Carrie's attention, lifting up Socks again for kisses.

"Happy Birthday to you," my mom began to sing as she turned back holding a cake dotted with candles.

"Oh you did *not!*" Carrie exclaimed.

"Happy Birthday to you," everyone else joined in and laughed as we sung on. "Happy Birthday, dear Carrie. Happy Birthday to you!" we finished strong.

She leaned in, closed her eyes, and paused in silence. The whole group fell silent. The quiet held in what turned into a small and unintended prayer vigil. There was only one thing to wish for. We all knew what Carrie was thinking and we all took the moment to make our own version of the same wish.

When Carrie's eyes reopened, she inhaled and extinguished all with a single sweeping breath.

"Yay!" we all shouted and clapped for the woman of honor. Nancy walked over to help my mom with the cutting, plating, and passing of the slices.

I kneeled down next to the wheelchair and placed my forehead against Carrie's. "I love you and wish you a very happy birthday. You deserve it. We have great things to come."

She whimpered once and lifted her head slightly so her lips could meet mine. She kissed me once softly and said simply, "Thank you for today."

# 62. THE WATERS GET CHOPPY

We all tried to give Carrie as positive of a birthday weekend as we could, given the circumstances. From Carrie's reaction, we all nailed it. Fresh air, family, friends, and Socks was a perfect cocktail. In fact, a cocktail would have been the only thing to make it a step better, but that could wait a while. The beautiful day was giving way to darker clouds.

"Hi, Mom," I said, answering my cell phone.

"Hi, Jas. Do you have a minute?" Her voice was serious.

"Yes, sure. What's up?"

"Just needed to let you know that Grandpa just passed away." My dad's father's health had been going south for a little while, particularly since his wife, my Grandma Marion, passed.

"Oh no. I'm so sorry. How's Dad?" I asked. The end of having parents on the planet must be an intense feeling. Carrie and I were lucky not to know the feeling ourselves and still to this day.

"He's all right. We're just dealing with some of the arrangements," she said.

I paused for a moment to collect my thoughts. "Well, you know that Carrie isn't going to be able to…"

She cut me off. "Oh, of course. We know that. Don't even think about that."

In the coming days, we would gather to bury my grandfather with a small funeral service. I spent some time with my parents at their house as close family came to pay Shiva calls. The weight of so many life developments was at times raising the stress and pain levels for me and at others turning me somewhat numb. The news flow was coming so regularly that I was left with little time to process each item before something else interrupted. Sitting Shiva with my parents, I turned my mind to Carrie, sitting alone in the hospital. She had missed on coming back to be with my family for my father's heart surgery and now sat staring out into the hospital parking lot while we gathered to recall memories of my grandfather.

Days later I was back at work. Carrie would call me between the daily routine of NSTs and ultrasounds, but this one was more concerning.

"They said it's OK, but need to just continue to watch it closely," Carrie explained to me as I sat at my desk. She was relaying to the best of her ability the level of concern the doctor expressed to her upon seeing more frequent absent-end diastolic velocity. The flow was still technically "intermittent," meaning the blood velocity wasn't dropping to zero right before each new heartbeat, but it was happening more often. The AEDV was slowly starting to get worse. This also meant less oxygen and nutrients getting to Maddie and that could cause her growth to slow further. The growth retardation, the IUGR, could get worse.

"Should I come there now?" I asked.

"No, no. There's not anything to do. I'm back in my room and just hanging out. I have another scan later today. I'll give you the update after that one."

She called after that scan and after each of the two scans the next day, with the bad scans starting to outweigh the good ones. More and more absent-end flow was present.

"It's not reversing, so they're happy about that," Carrie told me.

"OK, we'll take what we can get," I accepted. "Hey, also. I spoke to Pinelawn a couple more times and I think we are good. At first they said they require a name and a date. I explained the circumstances and they told me they have to review it. They did and just came back to me that it was approved. So they're going to do it how we discussed it—'Our Three Angels' and 'Mandel' only."

"OK, good," Carrie answered. "I can't believe that we don't even have a *year* to give them, much less an exact date. It's just crazy."

Wednesday morning, I called early to catch Carrie before they might take her for the first scan of the day. "Good morning and happy thirty!" I said. We had hit thirty weeks of pregnancy, a major milestone in development. That said, we were both well aware that the AEDV had been causing IUGR, which was slowing Maddie's growth. The clock may say thirty weeks, but her body was well shy of that count.

Friday right before five o'clock, I grabbed my coat and headed straight for the elevator, subway, and Long Island Rail Road. I jogged from the train to my car, parked as usual at my friend's parents' house, and drove over to the hospital. The parking garage was across the way from the hospital, making it a long ten-minute walk from the car to the building, down the hall, up the elevator and to Carrie's room, so I jogged that. Also, as usual.

"Hey, babe. How are you?" I asked as I turned into the room.

Carrie's face was blotchy red, eyes bloodshot and tearing. "What's wrong?" I asked quickly and raced to the bed.

"It's OK. Nothing's happened. She's still OK," she whimpered to me. "I just finished another scan and there was some reverse flow. Not the whole time. But there is some now."

I touched my head to hers. "Oh, shit. I'm sorry, baby. Do we do anything?"

"No. Just like usual, they 'just have to watch it closely,'" she said somewhat mockingly.

"Oh no. So just more pins and needles for us? Are they being good to you?" I asked, concerned about her tone.

"Yes, yes. Sorry. I'm not mad at them. It's just all so frustrating. There isn't anything I can ever do. I'm just this big host. It doesn't matter what I do. I can't make it better. I feel like I'm doing something wrong," she said as more tears flowed.

I reached around to embrace her. "Not at all. You're doing great. You're taking care of yourself the best you can. You do everything the doctors tell you to do. You're doing great. It just is what it is. You can't take any blame," I told her.

She snapped her head up from the cry to look me in the eyes. "And these damn student nurses are so fucking annoying," she said, pointing to the doorway.

"What does that mean?"

"It's like student nurse season or something. They keep coming in along with my regular nurses for vitals and everything else. To shadow and learn. But they're always so chipper. It's nice, I guess, but everyone on this hallway is dealing with something and they're all like, 'you'll be fine,' or 'everything's going to be all right.' I mean, what the fuck do they know?" she said and flipped into a laugh with her cry.

"All right. I hear you. I know," I said, hugging her. "I know you know it's not their fault."

"I know. I'm just really emotional right now," she said, sniffling.

We sat in silence, hugging. Carrie's breath began to calm and slow and the tears ceased. I reached for some tissues and helped wipe her face dry.

I looked her straight in the eyes and wiggled my eyebrows up and down. "How about some Antonino's?" I smiled back as she broke into a smile. We had ordered incredible Italian food from there more than a dozen times already—fried zucchini, fresh, cheesy pasta, delicious chicken parmesan.

We were finishing up an incredible Italian meal when in walked Carrie's favorite vitals nurse for the regular checkup. Unfortunately, she was flanked by a student—younger and wearing a different color scrubs. "Hi, how are you?" said the student in a high pitch. "Oh, it smells so good in here. How are we feeling tonight?" she finished with a huge smile.

"Fine," Carrie answered, trying to head off any further questions or conversation. Our nurse smirked at Carrie, knowing why she'd bring such a response.

Vitals were taken and the two headed back out the door.

"See," Carrie said, turning her head to me with her eyebrows lifted.

"Yes," I giggled back. "I get it."

I stuck around later than usual that night, wanting to be sure Carrie was in a better place than when I found her hours earlier.

"You should go," Carrie said. "It's getting late and Socks has been alone a long time. And you need your sleep, too."

"Are you sure? You sure you'll be OK if I head out?" I was exhausted from another long week bouncing back and forth between work, the hospital, and home.

I got up to help prep the room for bed. I helped Carrie pull the shades shut, refilled her water pitcher, tossed out the garbage from dinner, and walked the leftovers out to the nurses' station. I came back into the room and with a sigh, suggested, "OK. I guess I'll head home." We hugged for a long time and I whispered calming thoughts in her ear. I finished it simply with, "...and I'll be back here in just a few hours. Bright and early." I kissed her and walked out.

I pulled into the driveway at home all alone. I keyed the door open and Socks came running to greet me. "Hey, Socksy-girl," I cheered and kissed and rubbed her all over. I turned off the alarm, angry from the front door being opened. I closed and locked the door behind me, took Socks out in the yard for a minute, and came back in. I flopped down onto the couch face-down and exhausted. The house was completely silent.

I held, stuck in position as I nearly fell asleep, until the phone rang.

"Ugh!" I shouted at nobody. I stood and grabbed at the receiver. "Hello."

"They're moving me!" Carrie shouted into the phone and finished with a sob.

"What? What? Moving you where?"

"They need the room, so they need me to move out right now," Carrie said, excitedly.

"Well..." I didn't know how to respond. "What the fuck? What for? I'll come back right now."

"No. Don't come. I'm handling it. The first nurse who came in I had never seen before. She just straight told me they need the room and 'we're moving you.'" Carrie tried to slow to catch her breath and continue. "She says to me 'Why do you have so much stuff?' in a snotty, mean voice."

"Maybe because you've been living there for weeks!" I shouted back, wishing the nurse could hear me.

"I know. She was so mean." Carrie tried to calm. "I have to go right now. I need to finish putting all of my stuff on my bed so we can wheel it over. I'm supposed to be on bed rest, but I guess that'll have to wait a few."

"I'll come back over to help you get settled in wherever they put you now," I suggested.

"No. I don't know exactly what the plan is. I'm just frustrated. And of course this has to happen right after you leave to go get some sleep yourself." She took a deep breath. "Let me go. I'm going to figure out what the plan is and call you back soon. I love you."

"Love you," I quickly said back and the line cut.

*Wonderful*, I thought. She's supposed to be just resting and now piling belongings onto her bed to rush to another room. I contemplated just grabbing the keys and heading back over there, but opted to wait for more news.

About ten minutes later, the phone rang again. "Hi, babe," I said after picking up a half ring in.

"Hey," Carrie said in a calm tone. "I'm settled now, I'm in a double."

"What happened?" I asked.

"They couldn't say, but my nurse-friend filled me in. There's a pregnant woman going in there that they think might have TB."

"Oh, well that sounds bad. I guess at least there's a good reason." It seemed like a reasonable rationale for uprooting Carrie right after I walked out.

"I'll be fine. I'm exhausted now and settled in. I'm going to just try to go to sleep. I love you," she said with her quickly tiring voice.

"I love you too. I'll see you early tomorrow morning."

The next morning, I had to stop at the nurses' station to find my wife. They directed me to a room that was just a few doors down from her old single. I cautiously approached and knocked lightly.

"Hey, I'm in here. Come over," Carrie said.

I walked in, straight ahead with a pulled curtain on my right. "Hey. I'm so sorry about what happened last night. Holy shit."

"Yeah, it's fine. I'll deal. I was just caught really off-guard by how sudden it was." She continued after recalling, "And how *mean* that nurse was about my stuff."

"I know. Bitch," I whispered to get a laugh. I kept the whisper. "So, what's the deal with this one?" I could hear some moans coming from behind the curtain.

"She's a fucking wimp," Carrie whispered back. "She had her baby yesterday and they keep trying to get her to get up and go to the nursery to see him, but she doesn't want to. She says she hurts too much and can't go. It's bullshit. I'm making it to go see Maddie when she's born."

"I know you are," I nodded and smiled, approvingly.

We ate breakfast together and waited around until the first call of the day to head for the NST and scan. Carrie was wheeled down the hallway while I walked right by her side. The NST was fairly boring as usual. Twenty to thirty minutes of monitoring Maddie's heartbeat and watching for contractions. Then we moved in for the scan.

"Good morning," Dr. Pine said.

We greeted her back and watched as the show began. She started with several measurements and indicated there was some, but still slow and limited growth. Then she switched to the blood flow view and I grabbed Carrie's hand.

*Wha wha*, the monitor repeatedly called out as lines dashed across and jumped with each beat. We all watched in silence. By this time, Carrie and I knew for the most part what we were looking for and we didn't like what we found. Most mid-beats, the tracing line was dropping into the red before bouncing back up. The room remained silent as Dr. Pine remained focused on the readings.

"It's reverse, right?" I eventually asked.

"Yes. Today it seems we're seeing a lot of reverse flow," she confirmed. "I don't love that for sure. I just want to look at a few other things, so be patient."

We remained quiet to let her do her work. She seemed to be twisting the probe around a lot, trying to get into position for something. She pressed for printouts repeatedly and the roll of images was starting to gather on the floor.

"All right," she finally said, dropping the device back into its holder. "I want to talk to some of the other doctors and we'll come up in a bit to discuss where we are now, OK?"

We agreed, and our doctor walked out of the small room. Carrie and I shrugged at each other and prepared ourselves for the escort back upstairs.

# 63. A HAMMER DROPS

Back in Carrie's new double, we sat waiting for any new word about Maddie's condition. We aired our concerns with each other that the reverse flow could be the thing that triggered the doctors to decide to take Maddie out.

A soft knock at the door led our eyes up to Dr. Jain and Dr. Pine. "Hi, guys," Dr. Jain said. Nothing to smirk at this time, she walked over with all business on her face. "Dr. Pine brought something to our attention and we've been looking at the scans. It is incredibly hard to diagnose certain things in-utero and this is one of them, but we felt the need to raise it to you."

Carrie grabbed my hand and we prepared for a hammer to the head.

"Maddie could have something called Hirschsprung's disease. It is a disease of the intestines where the normal digestive bodily functions are impaired. What we are seeing could be nothing. But it could be indicative of Hirschsprung's."

I cleared my throat. "So what does that mean? What happens or what do we do if she does have it?"

Dr. Jain continued, "It would very likely require surgery and depending on how serious, it's not clear if it could be fixed as normal. There is a chance she could need a colostomy in order to pass her stool."

The four of us sat silent for a minute.

With the doctors in the room with us now, I was searching for the practical. I was searching for what I needed to ask and what we needed to know. But the idea of what sounded like a lifelong disability struck hard and fast.

"So," I stumbled. "What do we do? I mean is there anything we do right now?"

"No," she answered plainly. "We can be prepared to take action if we confirm the diagnosis once she's born, but there's nothing we or you can do about it right now. It's something we need to make you aware of. An anomaly we are seeing that can be indicative of Hirschsprung's."

We thanked them for their frankness and just like that, the conversation was over. The two of them walked out and Carrie and I grabbed on together and wept.

"I don't even know what we do right now," I said. "We just sit here with a pit in our stomachs, waiting to find out if it's true when she's born? That's it?"

"I don't know," she snapped back at me, angry at the news, not at me.

"What can we do about another opinion? Or find someone who knows more about this?" I asked.

"I don't know. Maybe we ask your parents again. Maybe they know someone," Carrie responded, wiping her tears.

At that moment, our nurse walked in with the rolling tower of instruments for taking vitals, trailed by a cheery student nurse.

"Should I come back in a little bit?" our nurse asked, sensing the tension in the room.

"Yeah," I confirmed, "maybe just give us twenty minutes or so?"

They turned to walk out and Carrie grabbed my forearm. "Please don't make me deal with those student nurses today!" she begged.

I immediately stood up. "Absolutely. I'll be right back."

I walked into the hall and pulled our favorite nurse aside to make the request. She understood fully and promised we'd be free of them for the day.

Back in the room, I dialed. "Hey, Dad."

"Hey, Jas, what's wrong?" He could immediately hear the distress in my voice.

"We got another round of not-so-great news. The doctors told us Madelyn *might* have a digestive disease—something called Hirschsprung's." I tried to stress the uncertainty. "We don't really know much about it or whether she might really have it. If she does, it at least means surgery once she's born. But they're telling us there's nothing at all we can do about it now."

He exhaled hard. "Jas, I'm so sorry. How's Carrie?"

"Not great. We're just trying to figure out what we can at least learn about it or what more we can do." Expecting there was a chance, I asked, "Is there any chance you guys know someone who might know something about this?"

"Yes," he said quickly. "Our friend Michael is a pediatric surgeon. I can get him in touch with you right away."

"Oh wow. That would be really great if you could." I cupped the phone and whispered over to Carrie, "They have someone."

My dad gave me details but offered to reach out and have him call me as soon as possible.

Just an hour later, my phone rang and Michael was there, introducing himself and asking what he could do to help. I explained the situation and he was immediately dismissive. He wasn't putting down the other doctors, but suggesting such a diagnosis in-utero is extremely difficult. "I'm not telling you that they are wrong, I am just telling you that I've seen things like this over and over again and we often find out that the OBs are overly cautious and overly concerned about things that turn out simply to not be there or that correct themselves before birth."

He suggested that we would be far better off not stressing about it and helping Maddie to stay inside for as long as possible. "The reality is, even if they are right, surgery can be very successful. But since there's nothing to do now, it very honestly is *not* something you should be at all focused on."

His words were calming me, but I was the only one on the phone. I was trying to quickly whisper the key items over to Carrie while I listened.

"Can he help with a second opinion?" Carrie whispered back to me.

"Is there any way that you can help with a second opinion?" I relayed into the phone.

"Sure, no problem. Give your doctors my information and we'll connect. I can have them send over some of the scans and we'll discuss. No problem," he finished.

"I will do that," and I took a deep breath. "Michael, thank you so very much. We greatly appreciate your thoughts on this and your help."

"It's not a problem at all." He continued, "Anything for the Mandel family." We hung up.

I walked over to the bed, noticing just then that I'd been pacing the whole phone call. I sat down and we hugged. I leaned back and we discussed the call, trying to calm ourselves with the new viewpoint we were just given.

Later in the day, we were ushered downstairs for the second round of NSTs and scans for the day.

"Hi, guys," Dr. Pine greeted us solemnly.

"Hi, Dr. Pine," I said and sprung right into the request. "After we spoke this morning, I reached out to my dad who put us in touch with a family friend who is a pediatric surgeon. We were just looking to understand more about Hirschsprung's."

She nodded, waiting for the next part. I continued, "We talked about it a bit and he offered to take a look at the scans alongside you guys and confer about the concern. Would you mind connecting with him on this?" I wasn't sure how a doctor would take a request like this. We weren't trying to second-guess the potential diagnosis, especially since they made it clear it was a possibility, not a certainty. That said, we had also earned the right to second-guess any doctor's diagnosis or recommended course of action.

"Of course," she said, immediately accepting the coordination. "If you give me his info, I will call him right after the scan."

Carrie and I both breathed a small sigh of relief. This special group of doctors had given us no reason up to this point to question them. And thankfully, she wasn't taking it that way.

The scan started with the usual look-around inside and then measurements. Same day and day to day it was hard for the doctors to determine much growth, so it was more of a rolling change in measurements over a few days. No new news this scan on that front. Then we again turned to the blood flow. For whatever reason, this scan was somewhat better. Fewer drops below the line to reverse flow and more intermittent absent flow. I tried to understand how it could change so much from one time to another and at times I asked that question of the various doctors, mostly to find out sometimes it just 'is what it is." My mind lives more in the world of math, logic, and hard science, but when it comes to the human body, or bodies, there's much that can change on its own and much that we don't fully understand, especially in terms of causes.

Sunday morning, I woke early and gathered myself for the day. The early morning weekend trips to the hospital were typically the least stressful. No traffic, more parking at the hospital lot, and less activity in the lobby, halls, and elevators. "Hey, babe," I said, turning the corner. Carrie was missing.

"Do you guys know where Carrie is?" I asked at the nurses' station.

"Oh yes." I was greeted with a smile and a point down the hallway. "She got her room back."

A smile came across my face as well. "Oh, awesome. Thank you."

"Hey, babe," I tried again.

"Hi. They just helped move me. Turns out she didn't have TB," Carrie said. The sun was shining and some privacy had returned, but the smile wasn't all the way back. Even when not thinking about the latest news—the possible Hirschsprung's and the reverse blood flow—it was always there. It sat both in the back of my mind and in the bottom of my stomach.

We sat around, replacing some of the items on the windowsill, but it was suggested to Carrie that we start bringing things home. The more advanced things got, at some point Maddie would be born and we wouldn't want to deal with all of this stuff. It was an honest, appropriate, and fair point, so we selected item by item what would stay and what would go. Most of the picture frames were selected for the bag and most of the essentials were left for the room. It was nice to have the single back, but it didn't feel nearly as homey as it once did and the mood had shifted.

My phone rang and I called out, "It's Michael!" I quickly pressed to answer and lifted the phone to my ear. "Hello?"

"Hi, Jason, this is Michael. We were speaking yesterday about your baby?" the voice responded, trying to remind me of the conversation. I remembered.

"Yes, yes, of course. Good morning," I said, surprised to be speaking again so soon.

Michael continued in a calm, matter-of-fact tone. "Listen, I had a chance to talk to your doctor and review the images. It's not worth worrying about this. Diagnosing this with what they saw is really hard. I've seen this many times. They're trying to cover their bases and prepare you for anything that could happen. I see what they're talking about in the images and it honestly could be anything and is probably nothing."

I shook my head to Carrie and whispered, "He said it's nothing." I raised my voice for the phone. "Thank you for taking the time and helping us out so quickly. I'm sure you can understand how disturbing this news was—we were just looking for anything more we could learn. So, thank you."

"Absolutely," he said. "Feel free to call me directly again if you have any other questions at all. I'm glad to help."

We hung up and I sat next to Carrie for a hug and to fill her in. We remained skeptical of both sides, so the pit remained, but it was diluted.

For the next several days, we returned to routine. The scans were almost always showing absent flow and more often reverse. We continued along on pins and needles.

# 64. NEARING THE THIRTY-ONE WEEK MARK

"Good morning," I wished Carrie from my office. "Closing in on thirty-one weeks!"

"Yep. Thirty weeks, five days," she responded. Carrie always knew the count.

"You should be really proud of yourself. I'm serious. You've put yourself through anything. Whatever it takes to stay healthy and protective enough of Maddie. Not sure about you, but I didn't really think we'd make it this far. I don't think the doctors did either. So, congratulations. You truly deserve it."

"Thank you, Jas," she responded sincerely. "But we're still not out of the woods. She's so little and not growing much."

"I know," I whispered into the phone. "I know. But she's had a round of steroids and she's been in you for almost thirty-one weeks. Those are big deals."

## 65. THIRTY WEEKS, SIX DAYS

I woke, showered, shaved, dressed, and hopped in the car for my borrowed driveway parking spot. I dropped the car and made the walk to the train station, jumped on, and sat down. Exhausted yet again, I closed my eyes and drifted to sleep within minutes.

Suddenly, I jerked, startled awake by a buzzing in my pocket. Quickly, I pulled my phone out and accepted the call. "Hey," I whispered. "You OK?" Carrie calling me on the train in the morning was not at all normal. She knows the train etiquette—silence and no phone calls.

"Jas, hi. Listen, I haven't been feeling Maddie for a while," she said immediately. "They're going to take me down to Labor and Delivery. It could just be testing, I don't know."

"OK. I'm getting off at the next stop. I'll be there right away," I answered and tapped the gentleman next to me to allow me to get up and into the aisle.

"No. I don't know. I don't know what's happening. I don't know if you should come. But I am a little scared," she said.

"It's OK. I hear you. Let me hang up on you so I can deal with getting off and getting a cab. I'll be there fast and come find you. Labor and Delivery, right?" I asked. She confirmed.

Off the train, I grabbed the first cab I saw and directed the driver straight to the hospital, abandoning my car at the nearby driveway. Pulling around into the circle of the hospital's main entrance, I passed up front enough cash to cover the fare and tip and quickly jumped out. I jogged down the hallway toward Labor and Delivery, weaving in and out of those in my way.

"Hey!" I shouted as I passed through the open door to find Carrie in a hospital gown and with an IV in her arm. Her regular dress for the stay up to that point offered a small subconscious feeling of home. Now that was gone.

"Hi," she said. "Hear that? It's her heartbeat. I'm still not feeling her move around at all, but she's OK, I guess."

"Oh, thank God," I said and bent down to drape myself over her and give her a kiss. "So what's the deal? The plan?" I asked.

"I don't know exactly. I think they want me to be on this NST for a while. I'm guessing they'll do a scan soon," she said. "I'm sorry I made you come here."

"Oh, come on. Stop. You tell me you're scared and not feeling Maddie and I'm coming. Hopefully I came here for no reason," I finished, with a smile.

A while later, they came for Carrie for a scan. As usual, I walked alongside the wheelchair to the small ultrasound room. "Hi, Dr. Pine," I greeted. In short order, we were right into the scan.

"Well, there she is," the doc said. Maddie came into clear view and then kicked her legs. "And she's moving," Dr. Pine said in a positive tone.

"Oh yay," Carrie said. "I didn't feel her. But I do see that." I grabbed a hold of Carrie's hand.

With the morning's complaint about a lack of movement, the scan seemed to be more intensive than the typical one. There were multiple measurements, scan prints, and switching around to different views—regular, 3D, blood flow, and more.

As she finished up, she stopped to give us the update. "Maddie's biophysical is an eight out of ten, not bad." The biophysical score is a compilation of factors from both the NST and the scan.

"Can you tell us her measurement?" I asked.

She grabbed again for the device and rolled it back into position on Carrie's belly. Once in place, she took a few measurements with the mouse on screen and told us, "Two point five."

Carrie twisted her lips to the side and looked up at me. I tilted my head to the side. With no words, we shared the same concern that Maddie didn't seem to be growing much more, stuck at just over two pounds.

On the roll back upstairs and to her room, we discussed the day so far. Less movement, more regular reverse flow, and little to no growth. Our learned skill to advocate for ourselves and question the doctors—even the good ones—kicked in again.

"Hi, guys," Dr. Henderson said as we arrived back to Labor and Delivery for more testing. Dr. Henderson was the only male doctor of the high-risk practice. We had only met a couple of times but he was always entirely aware of our situation and any developments.

"Hi, how are you? Do you have a second?" I asked. The three of us huddled up to discuss the events of the day and the final size measurement we just had done. I finished by raising our primary concern. "It seems Maddie isn't really growing anymore. The flow and IUGR are keeping her the same size. Is that a problem?"

"Yes," he said definitively. "That is absolutely a problem and it's one of the many things we've been watching very closely as we make judgment calls on what we recommend as the right next steps."

He referred down to Carrie's chart and went on, "Her biophysical is pretty good. An eight out of ten." He kept reading and looking at printouts. "I think we should actually go back downstairs and take one more look. Get yet another measurement. OK by you?" he asked.

"Of course," Carrie answered.

With that, we wheeled around and headed right back to where we'd come from.

He called out from behind us, "I'll be right down," as he turned to finish up with someone else.

"Round and round we go," I said to Carrie.

"Yeah. But I'd rather ask and be sure. I have no place to go anyway," she quipped.

When we turned the corner and walked back toward the small scan rooms, our motion caught Dr. Pine's eye. "You're back? Why are you back?" she asked, clearly confused.

"We ran into Dr. Henderson upstairs and he suggested we take another look and some more measurements. He'll be right down," I said.

Dr. Pine retained her composure fully, but her brows were slightly furrowed and she reached back to scratch behind her ear. I interpreted the body language as discomfort from an effective overrule.

We waited in the small room, prepared for the scan redo. Dr. Pine stood by, unsure exactly what else Dr. Henderson was looking for.

"Hi, guys, sorry," he said as he appeared through the doorway. He immediately took the controls and started taking all of the same measurements as usual—fluid, Maddie's size, blood flow and more. "Fluid two to three. Size two point five," he said aloud as he scanned.

When he finished up, he turned his eyes to Dr. Pine. "Quick conference?" he asked and told us they'd be right back.

They stepped outside of the room not far away, but we couldn't hear the content of the conversation. Carrie and I waited in silence, unsure what to expect and uncomfortable with the situation. They were out there speaking for a couple of minutes, then they walked back in, Dr. Henderson first. He took the reins. "We had a chance to discuss the measurements and the situation and we are both in agreement." He was clear to emphasize that there was consensus between the two.

"It is time to take her," he said.

A chill ran down my spine and my breath left me.

Carrie caught her breath before me and asked, "Are we talking today or tomorrow or what?"

Quickly, he responded, "Oh, definitely today."

The decision had been made. It was Maddie's birthday.

Back in Labor and Delivery, the nurses began to prep Carrie for surgery, a C-section to take Maddie from her. Encouraged by her, I ran out to the hallway to call our parents. Both sets were not surprised, but at the same time in shock to hear the news. Carrie's parents quickly prepared themselves to hop in the car and begin the drive from Michigan to New York.

Back at Carrie's side in the room, I watched as they made adjustments to her IV, drew blood for pre-op tests, and dressed her more fully for the delivery room—puffy blue cap and all.

"Here you go, Dad," one of the nurses said to me, pushing a set of scrubs my way. I was directed to the dad room down the hall. It was a small closet with a wall of small lockers for personal valuables—jewelry, wallet, phones, and anything else.

I stepped into the adjacent bathroom to don my scrubs. I stood there for a moment, deciding how scrubs worked. *Do I take off my clothes? Do I put the scrubs on over my clothes? They're not soft, more disposable-like. Uh-oh.* I hemmed and hawed and tried to figure it out. *Do I go ask a nurse?* Eventually I just made a command decision. Pants off, but underwear stays. Button-down off but T-shirt stays.

Back at Carrie's side, I leaned down by her head. "Hey, babe. How are you feeling?"

"I'm doing fine. Just nervous and I can't stop shaking. I'm nervous and cold."

"Oh no, I'm sorry. Shitty feeling. Want me to ask the nurse…"

"No," she cut me off. "I'm fine. I'll be fine."

Trying to make her giggle, I shared my adventure. "Was I supposed to put the scrubs on over my clothes or take them off?"

"Oh my God, J. Did you just put them on over?" she accused.

"No," I said carefully, still not for sure knowing the right answer.

"Good. They're scrubs. People wear them as clothing," she said and started laughing at my stupidity.

"Well…" I trailed. "…I don't know. I mean, I still left my underwear on."

"Holy shit, I hope so!" she railed back and burst into a bigger laugh.

"Oh no." She diverted her attention to the NST machine, scrolling the test paper out onto the ground. We both looked closely and saw the bump in the reading from her laughter.

"You'd better settle down," I said in a false attack.

"All right, it's time," said one of the nurses, walking in with a wheelchair. "We're all ready and the room is all ready." She helped Carrie out of bed and into the chair, released the brake, and began to roll. We pulled out of the room and turned to face double doors at the end of a long hallway. The final walk.

Carrie and I were quiet as I held her hand and kept pace alongside. The butterflies in my stomach accelerated with each footstep and each moment the double doors grew larger in my view.

We busted through one set of double doors to reveal two more sets of double doors, side by side. Two operating and delivery rooms. "OK, you'll wait here while we get her spinal taken care of and all set up. We will come to get you when it's time," the nurse said politely but professionally. She pointed at a bench behind me.

I leaned down and kissed Carrie. "I'll see you in just a couple minutes."

I sat, completely alone with my thoughts. I thought of Maddie: *This is it. For better or for worse. Please be healthy. Please cry. Please breathe.* I thought of Carrie: *Please be safe. Please be careful with the spinal. Please be given a reason to smile.* I thought of our family. I recalled when my brother came out when his little girl was born at twenty-five weeks. He cried, *It's a girl* into my dad's arms, barely getting the words out, not knowing what the next days would bring. Is it a great day? Is it a terrible day?

Plunk. Another man dropped down heavily onto the bench beside me. He exhaled in relief, smiled, and slowly shook his head. He turned and looked up at me. "My third. All girls."

I offered the best smile I could conjure. "Congratulations." I hoped he wouldn't ask me and my wish was granted as he leaned back and rubbed his eyes.

"Mr. Mandel," a voice came from the slightly opened double doors. "You can come on in. Pull your mask up over your mouth."

I hopped up and complied. She pushed the door open further for me and I walked in.

"Go Blue!" shouted Dr. Henderson. I had completely forgotten we traded notes about the University of Michigan—his alma mater as well as Carrie's and mine.

"Go Blue," I offered back, a little quieter. He was comfortable in the situation, having been there many times before, while I was taking instant non-verbal from all over about how to speak and act and where exactly to stand. I was directed and took a seat on a stool right next to Carrie's head.

A curtain set up about Carrie's mid-torso blocked our view of the action down below. I could see the heads and occasionally faces of Dr. Henderson and the nurses as they worked together to prepare for the moment. Nurses were fluttering about in the room, prepping instruments and towels. One waited next to an empty incubator.

As they prepared, the OR door opened again and in came Julianne. Carrie and Julianne had spent so much time together at the hospital. She was there to give Carrie her almost daily and sometimes twice daily NSTs, often while I was at work. Carrie smiled broadly to see her in the room with us.

"It's almost time," I whispered to Carrie. "They're going to take such good care of you and Maddie."

"I hope so," she said, looking back up at me with nervous eyes. All I could see was her face, with her hair and ears hidden underneath the blue scrub cap and body covered up to the neck.

"OK, we're going to get started," Dr. Henderson said. "You're going to feel pushing and pulling, but nothing else. You're all numb down here."

With that, I leaned in closer to Carrie and put the side of my face on her head. The activity began, but we couldn't tell at all what was going on. We had no idea how long until they should be to Maddie.

Suddenly we heard a high-pitched whimper of a cry, followed by another and another.

"She's out and she's breathing. Congratulations," Dr. Henderson said, but kept his head down, working as he passed Maddie off to a nurse who brought her to a table for some immediate critical tests.

"You did great. Again. I love you," I said as I leaned in to kiss Carrie's forehead, but was interrupted.

"Here's Maddie," said the nurse, suddenly holding our daughter just in front of us.

Madelyn had stopped crying for the moment. She opened her eyes revealing a striking bright color of blue amid the drab hospital color scheme all around. I don't know if she made eye contact with us, but for sure that is how I remember it now. Her face was tiny, about the size of an apple. As quickly as she appeared before us, she was whisked back away, to the incubator for warmth, more tests and to get hooked up to monitors.

I turned my attention back to Carrie. "Did you see that? Did you see her eyes?" I asked.

Carrie nodded and tears flowed around the sides of her face toward her covered ears. I cuddled Carrie's head with mine, both of us filled with emotion.

"Two pounds, five ounces," we heard from somewhere over by the incubator.

The events over the next couple of hours are some of the blurriest for us given the drugs they pumped into Carrie for the pain and the emotion involved for both of us. I was the first to get to go see Madelyn, checking in on her while Carrie drifted in and out of consciousness. I recall walking into the NICU to see Madelyn lying on a small bed under a set of bright lights, not in an incubator. She had no mask over her face for oxygen, rather a CPAP tube running across her nose. Her eyes were covered with a large mask to block the brightness and her body was splayed out, arms and legs spread. Little twitches and movements proved her life. Bells and chimes in the room were ringing constantly and I looked up at Madelyn's monitor to understand none of it this first time.

She looked helpless. Alive and breathing with some labor, but helpless. I took some pictures and video with the camera in my pocket, wanting to show Carrie as soon as possible. A doctor came by to discuss with me the first thoughts. He said Madelyn was in very reasonable health given the situation. They saw no obvious outer signs of Hirschsprung's or anything else abnormal. The first twenty-four to forty-eight hours are often the most crucial for a preemie and we should be prepared for anything. That said— there was no obvious reason for concern.

I didn't overstay. I wanted to get back to Carrie and report Madelyn's status. I found out that Carrie was already back in her regular room and darted right there. Carrie was more awake already by this time and I filled her in on the quasi-good news and showed her the first photos of our daughter from the outside world.

"I want to go," Carrie said. "I want to go see my baby."

Not a bone in my body thought anything other than *yes*. I found our key nurse and a wheelchair and together we helped Carrie get into the seat. I wheeled Carrie myself this time, down the hall and around the corner to the NICU. We buzzed into the unit and scrubbed our hands. I pushed Carrie into NICU room G and settled her next to Madelyn.

The rest of the world stopped for Carrie. Her pain disappeared, her frustration with the rushing and the control and the noises ceased. Madelyn was the only one in the world at that moment.

# 66. MADELYN

From the time she was born, Madelyn was Madelyn to me. I've rarely ever called her Maddie again. I'm not sure why that is. It is a beautiful name so there's no good reason to shorten it, but that was never the reason. Perhaps it was the struggle inside and out. After fighting for survival for nearly thirty-one weeks inside, she would go on to spend the next six weeks again fighting every step of the way to stay healthy and grow. She beat the tentative Hirschsprung's diagnosis. She fed from a tube until she could learn to breathe, suck, and swallow, and could take a bottle with Carrie's milk. She had setbacks. She had to take the feeding tube back into her stomach through her mouth. She had trouble with pooping and we cheered at the sign of a dirty diaper. She occasionally opened her eyes. She gained and lost weight. Some days the machines' warnings rang more than others. There were good nurses and those who were too busy to remember these are families. There were long nights sleeping on the couch in the family room.

Then there were the great moments. The first time we got to hold Madelyn—kangarooing they call it. Skin to skin contact that some say is the best medicine for these very little ones. We both believe that to be true, but it was also pretty amazing medicine for the parents. I watched with so much joy and pride the first time Carrie protected Madelyn against her chest. I recall the intense nerves the first time Madelyn was placed by a nurse against my chest. The nerves fluttered away quickly, but I held stiff in position, not wanting to hurt, frighten, or bother Madelyn.

We spent almost two months with Madelyn in that NICU. We bore the discomfort of the alarm bells all day long and often would hear them in our sleep. We found the journal Carrie kept for that time in the hospital. Here's a brief excerpt.

"Well, today it's been one week since Maddie was born. It is a tough day for me because I feel like I am missing out on so many things while she is in the NICU. We have not been able to bond the way I would be able to if she were home. I wonder if she even knows that I'm her mommy. J and I are in love with her…. she's so beautiful and tiny. Today she is wearing a knit white hat with a purple flower in the front. She is wrapped in a receiving blanket, but it makes it harder to see and touch her. I want to look at her cute little arms, legs, belly, etc.… I can't believe I'm a mommy. I've wanted this for as long as I can remember. However, as with so many things in life, I didn't expect it to happen this way. I am going to get to kangaroo with her after her next feeding at 2:00."

Over time, Madelyn graduated to other NICU rooms where older and bigger babies, closer to going home, resided.

Eventually, on June 8, 2004, Madelyn came home. No warning bells, no poking, no IVs, no doctors and nurses coming and going. Just peace.

# AFTERWORD

Madelyn is fifteen years old now. She's an incredible dancer, student, friend, and daughter.

She is also a great sister. We had heard that pregnancy temporarily cures polycystic ovarian syndrome and we tested it. Carter was born at full term via C-section just seventeen months after Madelyn first opened her eyes for us. Carter is our second miracle and his pregnancy was quite the opposite of Madelyn's. It was still technically a high-risk pregnancy given Carrie's history, but most everything went well. I recall holding Carter for the first time thinking, "Holy crap. He's like a frigging tree trunk!" I was so used to handling delicate Madelyn that this boy's weight, core, and muscle tone were shocking.

Socks welcomed Madelyn into our home and joined Carrie and me in protecting her against all enemies, real or imagined.

Carrie's parents quickly became Nana and Papa and my parents retained their Gobbie and Poppie ordained upon them by my brother's daughter, Hanna. The grandparents all adored Madelyn and later, Carter.

We went through a lot—to get pregnant, to stay pregnant, to have Madelyn, and to get her home from the hospital. We left three babies to be met later on down the road when we pass. I'm not religious, but I find myself praying for them sometimes. I don't know where they are. I pray they are at peace. I beg for their forgiveness. Do I regret anything? That is a question I've struggled with. How could one not hold at least partial regret for some of the decisions we made? But I also sometimes wonder how things would be now for them, and for Madelyn and for Carrie and me, and if Carter would ever have been born if we had made other choices along the way.

JASON MANDEL

# PHOTOGRAPHS

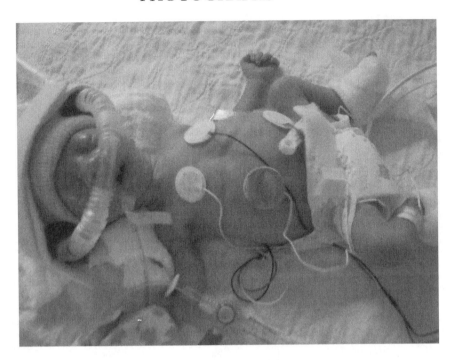

Madelyn on her birthday

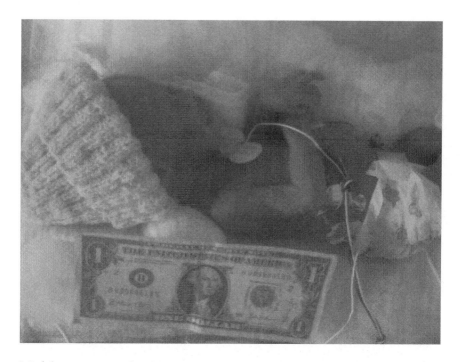

Madelyn at one week

Madelyn after coming home, with Socks

Madelyn with Socks

Madelyn at eight months

"Our Three Angels"